# SOCIAL WORK FIELD DIRECTORS

# SOCIAL WORK FIELD DIRECTORS

## FOUNDATIONS FOR EXCELLENCE

*Edited by*

### CINDY A. HUNTER
*James Madison University*

### JULIA K. MOEN
*Bethel University*

### MIRIAM S. RASKIN
*George Mason University*

LYCEUM
BOOKS, INC.

Chicago, IL 60637

© 2015 by Lyceum Books, Inc.

Published by

LYCEUM BOOKS, INC.
5758 S. Blackstone Avenue
Chicago, Illinois 60637
773-643-1903 fax
773-643-1902 phone
lyceum@lyceumbooks.com
www.lyceumbooks.com

6  5  4  3  2  1    14  15  16  17  18

ISBN 978-1-935871-47-7

Printed in the United States of America.

**Library of Congress Cataloging-in-Publication Data**

Social work field directors : foundations for excellence / edited by Cindy A. Hunter, James Madison University, Julia K. Moen, Bethel University, Miriam S. Raskin, George Mason University.
     pages cm
Includes bibliographical references and index.
ISBN 978-1-935871-47-7
 1.  Social work education—United States.  2.  Social service—Fieldwork—United States.
 3.  Fieldwork (Educational method)  I.  Hunter, Cindy A.  II.  Moen, Julia K.  III.  Raskin, Miriam S.
     HV11.7.S63   2014
     361.3071'55—dc23

                                                                                    2014001651

For additional information, materials, and updates or to schedule a consultation or training about *Social Work Field Directors: Foundations for Excellence*, visit our Web site at http://www.socialwork fielddirectors.com.

To the pioneers of social work field education who guided us through the early years with wisdom and critical inquiry, and to those field directors who will build on that foundation.

# Contents

# Preface

This book is written primarily for the field director. It highlights the many functions required to develop, execute, maintain, and evaluate a field program. The authors of the different chapters compile original insights on all aspects of these multifaceted tasks. The importance of the work of the field office cannot be underestimated, because it affects the student's competence, program assessment, renewal, and accreditation. The field director is a public face of the school of social work and identifies, trains, and supports social workers who serve as field instructors. Individuals who occupy this position play a central role in the practice community, orchestrating continuing education, setting standards for quality and competence, solving ethical dilemmas, and representing the program's mission and goals to field settings. It is of equal importance for field directors to invite and integrate the community's practice perspectives back to the school, to create a mutually interdependent relationship for advancing the social work profession.

Field practicum is a critical component of the foundation for educating social work professionals. Students find the practicum to be the most valuable part of their educational experience. The Council on Social Work Education (CSWE) has identified field as the signature pedagogy of social work education. What does this mean? Classroom interactions, lectures, and periodic exams are necessary for the development of the social work professional, but they are not sufficient. Field education allows students to apply theories to practice. Without field, social work practice would only be hypothetical challenges for students rather than real-time problem solving with client systems. The CSWE's current emphasis on student competencies and practice behaviors in the assessment of schools of social work increases the complexity of the administration of field education.

*Social Work Field Directors: Foundations for Excellence* will shorten the learning curve for new field directors by highlighting up-to-date information and research on technology, legal and ethical issues, safety, placing students, gatekeeping, professional development, evaluation of learning, and other contemporary topics. It describes and explains the accreditation standards relevant to field and proposes multiple ways to achieve compliance. For the seasoned field director, the book supplements calls to a colleague or posts to a Listserv when conundrums arise. It will assist the reader with problem solving, thinking through difficult issues, and identifying essential literature for practical and research purposes. Deans and directors, faculty, field instructors, and doctoral students will find the book useful in understanding the unique knowledge and skills required for field directors to competently administer the field program on a daily basis. Those who manage field programs in other countries can incorporate new thinking in social work field education that is relevant to their international context. The exchange of ideas can enhance the continuing dialogue with international colleagues.

After more than 100 years of social work education, implementation of the competency-based model mandated by the 2008 Educational Policy and Accreditation Standards (EPAS) requires more than business as usual. The authors of these chapters present new information to promote leadership, scholarship, and professional development for the field director. The intent is to educate and empower *all* field directors so deans, directors, faculty, and the research community look to field directors as innovators, researchers, developers of organizational partnerships, and leaders in curriculum change, assessment, and program renewal. This goes beyond the current practice of entrusting field to managers who are not recognized for their contributions to the pedagogical fabric of schools of social work.

The editors have been involved in field education in a variety of ways throughout their social work careers as students, field instructors, liaisons, scholars, directors, leaders of regional field consortia, and members of the national Council on Field Education and the Baccalaureate Program Directors' Field Committee. These involvements provided a perspective on the required components of a contemporary field program. The editors trained new field directors annually at the Baccalaureate Program Directors (BPD) conference and recognized that one day of training is not sufficient preparation. This recognition was the inspiration for this book.

The fourteen chapters were written by authors selected for their experience in field, recognition as accomplished researchers, and expertise in the chapter content. The authors are mindful of differences in programs such as baccalaureate and master level, program size, geographic regions (rural, suburban, and urban), and program delivery (face to face, hybrid, and online). Each chapter addresses everyday issues and provides a synthesis of relevant literature and three to five of the most essential readings. Throughout the book, additional contributing field scholars provide diverse and personal perspectives on the realities of field.

This book is not a recipe for a model field program or an encyclopedia that will cover everything under one subject heading. No resource can answer all the questions that directing a field program brings forth. Discussion with colleagues and systematic literature reviews are still required to capture the richness and variety of field delivery and to make adaptations in field.

Several themes emerged while reviewing the chapters. First, the field director position is multidimensional and radically different from what it was decades ago. The current skill set encompasses utilizing data management systems and communication technology, knowledge of the law, curriculum and policy development, teaching, and administration. It requires a balance of practice skills to support students who have academic and behavioral difficulties with administrative skills to apply gatekeeping procedures when necessary. Field directors must possess creativity in managing conflicts, understand ethics, apply the field education literature, and engage in research. They must be competent teachers, researchers, and practitioners as they direct a curricular space where competencies are demonstrated by students. These qualifications are also required of classroom faculty where assessment of competencies takes place. The position will continue to change, especially in the presence of technological advances and globalization. Deans, directors, and faculty must keep abreast of the field director's role in order to recruit highly qualified personnel who need adequate time, staff, and fiscal resources to manage successful field programs.

A second theme is the authors' call for more empirical study. Many common practices in field have not been supported by the literature as best practices. Even the field standards are lacking an empirical basis. The lack of research funding has limited the study of significant questions in field education. Institutional support for field directors to conduct research has been minimal. Future research needs to be related to how field policies and practices contribute to student outcomes. Field directors are in an excellent position to collaborate, conceptualize, and collect data for research purposes to improve social work practice and to use the research and data to influence either the continuance or the change of accreditation standards related to field.

The need to scrutinize and influence the revision of the next accreditation standards is another theme that appears in several chapters. The authors make recommendations such as the addition of safety training to the standards, the requirement for criminal background reports by the schools, and heightened accountability of social work programs to respond to the practice community in program renewal. The standards need to encourage the development, delivery, and assessment of new models of field education. In actuality, the standards can create barriers by requiring an extensive application for permission to operate outside the standards. This encourages the status quo and discourages field directors from thinking outside the box.

Finally, several authors present field education under ideal circumstances, but they acknowledge the reality of managing a field program. For example, in chapters 2 and 6 the authors recognize the difficulty of requiring field instructors to attend training, although training is mandated by accreditation standards. Sporadic attendance at training and high turnover of field instructors potentially affect the ability of the field instructor to teach and assess student learning. To stimulate thought and debate, the editors discuss other examples of the contrast between the ideal and the real in the introductions to each of the four parts of the book.

Only the major components of the field directors' roles and responsibilities are included in the book. The editors based the selection on our best collective judgment and experience. Our goal was to present the most critical tasks that would serve a new field director in the early career stage. Limitation of time and financial resources prevented us from an exhaustive search for innovations that are being executed in different parts of the country but are not published. The editors and chapter authors sought to find a balance between presenting practice wisdom and content that is supported by empirical research. We accomplished this, but readers may find that the scale is balanced more in one direction than the other.

Recognition is due by the social work education community to the field educators for the role they play in ensuring the competence and professionalism of future social workers. We hope this book helps to empower field directors through the practice wisdom, research, and personal experiences presented in the special features and in the fourteen chapters. It is imperative to continue to try new ways of doing business, evaluate those efforts, and use the results to launch field education into a new era of evidence-based field practices.

# Acknowledgments

The chapter authors are expert researchers, field directors, liaisons, and teachers. We owe them a great debt for their willingness to share their collective wisdom, honor our requests for rewrites, and wait long periods of time. Our gratitude is extended to those who wrote special features for the book: Shelagh J. Larkin, Xavier University; JoAnn McFall, Michigan State University; Lisa Richardson, St. Catherine University and University of St. Thomas; Lynda Sowbel, Hood College; Ruby M. Gourdine, Howard University; and, Kathy Cox, California State University-Chico. The collection builds on the hard work of other researchers and field directors who have made contributions prior to the publication of this book.

We thank the Baccalaureate Program Directors Field Committee and Council on Social Work Education Council on Field Education for their support and encouragement. Sonia Roschelli, graduate research assistant, George Mason University; and copy editor, Alison Hope, are appreciated for their assistance on this project. We are very grateful that Lyceum Books gave us the opportunity to spend time writing and reflecting about our passion, field education. Finally, we give a huge thanks to our families, especially Sam, Scott, and Ira, who made sacrifices during the preparation of the book.

# PART I
## Social Work Field Education
## Past, Present, and Future

The journey into the life of a field director begins with an orientation to the history and current context of the accreditation standards. With the designation of field education as the signature pedagogy of social work education in the Council on Social Work Education's (CSWE) 2008 Educational Policy and Accreditation Standards (EPAS), confusion about the implications for field education arose. Chapter 1, History, Standards, and Signature Pedagogy, by Dean Pierce, introduces Larry Shulman's conceptualization of this teaching/learning process. Pierce provides a clear definition of signature pedagogy. He supports his argument that class and field are of equal importance in social work education. At this time in the history of social work education, however, this idea seems more inspirational than real. Pierce recognizes that in order to become the signature pedagogy, field needs to be further refined and developed to completely meet all the criteria Shulman proposed.

Subsequent chapters rely on the first chapter's explication of the current standards and specifically those that affect the work of the field director. Learning how to read, interpret, and adhere to the standards is an ongoing process, one that is important for the management and leadership that a field director provides to students and the school of social work. Dean Pierce recommends areas of further research in field education and sets the tone for a strong message throughout this book: field directors must produce scholarly contributions to the social work literature and to the profession. Although scholarship/research may not appear in recruitment job descriptions for field director positions, this activity will propel the respect of field directors in such a way as to give meaning to the statement, "Class and field are equal."

In chapter 2, Roles and Responsibilities of the Field Director, Janet Bradley and Page Walker Buck give the reader a clear, broad-brush view of how the responsibilities of the field director are related to the EPAS 2008 introduced in the first chapter. They acknowledge that the expectations are at times overwhelming and demands are often competitive. This chapter will whet the reader's appetite for more in-depth information about responsibilities related to policy development, selecting field settings, employment-based placements, the placement process, student evaluation, and gatekeeping. These and other critical job requirements are introduced but explored in more detail in other chapters.

The strong take-away message from chapter 2 will be evident after a semester on the job: the professional life of the field director has many positive aspects, yet barriers to a wrinkle-free academic year are likely to arise when the field director manages a myriad of stakeholders including field liaisons, field instructors, students (sometimes in large numbers), faculty who have field responsibilities and who are tenured and of a higher rank than the field director, field advisory committees, administrators, and legal counsel. The role of the field director often resembles that of a magician: handling changing student demographics (need for flexible time, days of the week, and distance from students' homes) with the decreasing resources of human service organizations. Building strong relationships with community partners can reduce the impact of competing demands and provide satisfactory solutions.

Almost a decade ago, authors Julianne Wayne, Marion Bogo, and Miriam Raskin advocated for radical change in field education. In chapter 3, Nontraditional Field Models, they propose that selected longstanding field issues could be addressed by thinking about existing field models in a different and innovative way. They tackle the shortage of qualified master of social work (MSW) supervisors by proposing the expanded use of task supervisors combined with group supervision by an MSW. The lack of time for field instructors to supervise students and the need for sufficient field sites that provide generalist or advanced practice learning opportunities for students continue to be of concern. An approach to these problems that does not violate the requirements of the accreditation standards is to place MSW students in one practice site and allow them to remain in the same placement for the second year with new assignments and enhanced practice behaviors related to a specific concentration. This model may not be appropriate for all students, but even if 50 percent of the students remained in their practice settings, time could be saved for students and field directors to pursue other academic interests. A third innovation that social work programs utilize to a minimum extent is delaying entry to field for one semester. Field directors should consider the detailed description in this chapter of what students would do to prepare for practicum, so they enter field with some beginning skills; this could avoid re-placements and even terminations from field. This intense preparation involves highly developed simulations with extensive feedback that students must share with their field instructors when they begin field.

Whether field undergoes radical change or a more evolutionary process through innovations of existing models, the accreditation standards, including the designation of field as the signature pedagogy and the ever-increasing roles and responsibilities of the field director, point to the need for recognition that the field director's job has dramatically changed and the level of education, skills, and preparation for the job must keep pace with these changes. It is important for field directors to gain the support of administrators in order to empirically study and implement radical or innovative models of field education that affect student competence.

# 1

# History, Standards, and Signature Pedagogy

*Dean Pierce*

Learning to be a professional social worker has always included involving learners in practical experiences outside the academic classroom. The evolution of field education within social work education underscores the key role it has come to play in socializing learners to professional norms and behaviors, and in providing them with the opportunity to integrate theory and practice as well as to incorporate social work values and ethical behaviors into their emerging professional selves.

In Shulman's (2005b) conceptualization of professional learning, a profession's distinctive way of teaching and learning is considered its "signature pedagogy" (p. 52). This concept is based on his view of three dimensions of professional practice: thinking, or the intellectual aspect or knowledge base of a profession; performing, or the practical aspect or the profession's skills; and acting with integrity, or the moral aspect or the ethical base of a profession. Examples of signature pedagogies include the clinical rounds of medicine, the design studios of architecture and mechanical engineering, and the case dialogue of legal education (Pierce, 2008, p. 2).

Expanding on the notion that professional education involves learning ideas in order to practice, Shulman (2005a) notes that professional pedagogies not only aim to connect ideas and practice, but also must instill in learners a commitment to ethical service. The three interrelated elements of professional practice are frequently referred to as the mind, the hand, and the heart. In the integrated application of these three, a professional faces a great degree of uncertainty in practice situations and relies on professional judgment about the most likely course of action. Shulman (2005a) writes, "[P]rofessional education is about developing pedagogies to link ideas, practices, and values under conditions of inherent uncertainty that necessitate not only judgment in order to act, but also cognizance of the conse-quences of one's action. In the presence of uncertainty, one is obligated to learn from experience" (p. 19).

The Council on Social Work Education's (CSWE) 2008 Educational Policy and Accreditation Standards (EPAS), Educational Policy (EP) 2.3 states,

> Signature pedagogy represents the central form of instruction and learning in which a profession socializes its students to perform the role of practitioner. Professionals have pedagogical norms with which they connect and integrate theory and practice. In social work, the signature pedagogy is field education. The intent of field education is to connect the theoretical and conceptual contribution of the classroom with the prac-tical world of the practice setting. It is a basic precept of social work education that the two interrelated components of curriculum—classroom and field—are of equal importance within the curriculum, and each contributes to the development of the requisite competencies of professional practice. Field education is systematically designed, supervised, coordinated, and evaluated based on criteria by which students demonstrate the achievement of program competencies. (p. 8)

In discussing how professional education creates a practitioner, Shulman (2005c) identifies several elements that would characterize what is called a profession's sig-nature pedagogy. He identifies the three characteristics of a signature pedagogy as (1) distinctive to the profession, (2) pervasive within a curriculum, and (3) essen-tial to the more general pedagogy as part of instruction and socialization.

In many ways, social work's field education is distinctive to the profession. Students are placed in a service setting under the direct supervision of an agency employee. Their learning is guided by a learning agreement, based in a set of behavioral learn-ing outcomes common to all students. Field education is pervasive within the cur-riculum of social work programs because it is a requirement of accreditation and thereby offered by all programs. It also is essential to the general learning of stu-dents, constitutes a basic means of socializing students to the profession, and pro-vides the major means of integrating theory into practice.

Shulman (2005c) further argues that a signature pedagogy constitutes an identifi-able learning process. A signature pedagogy's process is habitual and routine, and is repeated over and over as students learn. The process makes the thoughts, ideas, and opinions of learners open and visible, and holds those learners accountable for speaking and thinking, which in turn leads to anxiety on their part. Dealing with this anxiety forms professional character through the transformation of self.

How do the elements of this process apply to social work's field education? In social work the process of field learning involves several features. The field placement setting includes assignments designed by a field instructor whose management and discussion of these assignments makes the ideas and thoughts of the learner visible and accountable. Programs that use integrative mechanisms, such as the field seminar and liaison visits by program representatives, also reinforce learner visibility and accountability. The emergence of the ten social work competencies and their forty-one related generalist or advanced practice behaviors as guides to student learning agreements and evaluation underscores the routine and habitual nature of learning and practice.

Of course, the question has been raised whether field education is a signature pedagogy, with cautious support (Lyter, 2012), critiques (Wayne, Bogo, & Raskin, 2010), and suggestions for improvement (Dedman & Palmer, 2011; Earls Larrison & Korr, 2013). As Shulman (2005a) points out, however, most signature pedagogies are flawed because they fail to incorporate completely the mind, the hand, and the heart. For example, the signature pedagogy of law emphasizes mind over hand and almost entirely excludes heart; medicine places greater emphasis on hand; and clerical training focuses on heart. Hyland and Kilcommins (2009) raise concerns about the case method of law as constituting a signature pedagogy. Typically, a signature pedagogy simply focuses on one of the three elements of professional practice or, at best, part of another one of them. This is not the case with social work's field education, which attempts to integrate the knowledge, values, and skills offered in the classroom into the practical world of the field setting. The broader scope of field education inherently makes for a more complex and, in some ways, less easily discernable process compared to the single focus of the signature pedagogies of other professions.

## The Development of Field Education as Reflected in the Council on Social Work Education's Accreditation Policy and Standards

The emergence of this complex pedagogy can be traced through an examination of the CSWE's curriculum and educational policies and accreditation standards that addressed field education in (1) 1969 (as revised and expanded in 1971a,

1971b, 1973, 1974, and 1976); (2) 1988 (revised in 1991); (3) 1994a; (4) 1994b; (5) 2001; and (6) 2008. Students move from field experiences carried out in a variety of ways to student field learning that is similarly administered, monitored, and implemented.

Accreditation of a professional program certifies to the public that it has met a set of curriculum and resource standards designed to produce a minimum or threshold level of competence in its graduates. Such accreditation incorporates the principle of quality assurance, leads to institutional or program improvements, and informs potential consumers of quality.

In the United States, accreditation of universities can be traced to the establishment in 1885 of an association of colleges in New England. By 1919 six regional organizations devoted to accrediting colleges and universities were in operation. In addition to the regional associations, several national associations accredit universities and colleges based on factors such as religious affiliation. There are also around seventy specialized accrediting bodies in the United States that accredit, among others, professional programs in universities and colleges.

Several key elements have come to define accreditation in the United States. American accreditation is under the control of the institutions or programs being accredited, as opposed to the European model of accreditation, which is typically managed by governmental agencies. Self-regulation extends to the development of accreditation standards by the peers of those being accredited. Universities or specialized programs write a self-study in relation to the standards. The program submits the self-study to the accrediting body, which uses a site visit to the institution or program to collect information in addition to that presented in the self-study. The volunteers and the staff of the accrediting body make the final decision regarding compliance with the standards.

Specialized accrediting bodies include the Commission on Accreditation of the CSWE. Prior to the emergence of the CSWE in 1952, antecedent organizations were responsible for accrediting social work programs. The Association of Training Schools for Professional Social Workers, which was established in 1919, evolved into the Association of Schools of Social Work (ASSW). ASSW came to focus on graduate social work education only and, in the mid-1930s, developed accreditation processes based on those used by the regional accrediting associations, replacing those that had been used earlier by organizations of social work practice specialties. The National Association of Schools of Social Administration emerged during the economic depression of the 1930s and championed undergraduate education and public social services. A conflict between it and ASSW led, in part, to the organization of the CSWE in 1952. The ASSW approach to accreditation included the use of a statement of curriculum policy as well as a set of accreditation standards. Until 1969 the CSWE used the last curriculum policy and accreditation standards developed by ASSW (Kendall, 2002).

## The Field as a Learning Experience (1969, revised and expanded in 1971, 1973, 1974, and 1976)

In 1969, under the first set of policy and standards developed entirely under the auspices of the CSWE, the practicum was discussed as part of the section on learning experiences in the curriculum policy for the master's degree program in graduate schools of social work. This work identified three areas of the curriculum, including social welfare policy and services, human behavior and the social environment, and practice. The discussion under the learning experiences section of the 1969 curriculum policy included classroom courses, laboratory experiences, tutorial conferences, research projects, and the practicum. The standards deemed the social work practicum to be an essential component of professional education. Its patterns could vary, but a critical element included experiences that provide students with direct engagement in service activities.

The practicum intended to enhance student learning in all areas of the curriculum. It provided for the development, integration, and reinforcement of competence through performance in actual service. In addition, the practicum's structure permitted students to acquire and test skills relevant to emerging conditions of social work practice. Students fostered the integration and reinforcement of knowledge, values, and skills acquired in the field as well as in courses and concentrations. Finally, programs offered students the opportunity to delineate and comprehend questions for research, which might arise in the course of practice.

Students could attain these objectives through diverse practicum designs and various instructional formats. All objectives were to be based in clearly stated educational purposes. Each school could determine the nature of its practicum as well as the degree of variation for groups of students and the timing, level, and character of the instructional experience. The Manual of Accrediting Standards outlined specific criteria to carry out the intent of the policy statement, including the use of field teachers and their qualifications and the clear use of the practicum as a learning experience (CSWE, 1971a).

On July 1, 1971, the CSWE board of directors adopted Standards for Approval of Undergraduate Programs in Social Work (CSWE, 1971b). These standards required a coherent educational program including broad liberal arts; courses with social work content; and appropriate, educationally directed field instruction with direct engagement in service activities according to stated educational objectives.

On February 12, 1973, the CSWE adopted Standard 1234A. This standard added the expectation to the existing standards that programs make continual efforts to enrich the program by providing racial, ethnic, and cultural diversity in its student body, at all levels of instructional and research personnel, and within corresponding educational supports. The planning guide to deliver on this requirement noted that the content of the educational program, in both class and field instruction, should reflect the intent of the standard. In 1976 the CSWE extended diversity to include attention to the role and status of women. Gender nondiscrimination was to be applied in the selection of students, staff, and class and field instructors.

Effective July 1, 1974, the CSWE's Standards for the Accreditation of Baccalaureate Degree Programs replaced the 1971 baccalaureate approval standards. The educational program was to build on and be integrated with a liberal arts base, including the humanities and the social, behavioral, and biological sciences. The program was to provide content in the areas of social work practice, social welfare policy and services, human behavior and the social environment, and social research. In addition, the standards required an educationally directed field experience with engagement in service activities for at least 300 clock hours, for which academic credit commensurate with the time invested was to be given.

## Toward Standardization of Field Learning (1988, revised in 1991)

The CSWE's 1988 curriculum policy statement (CPS) for the master's and baccalaureate degree programs in social work education reinforced and expanded on the earlier policy statements regarding the field practicum. The 1988 CPS noted that the field practicum must be an integral part of the curriculum. The practicum was to engage students in supervised direct service activities, providing practice experience. While the CPS allowed individual programs to organize their field experiences differently, it also reinforced the expectation that those experiences were educationally directed, coordinated, and monitored. Each program was to establish standards for field practicum settings, including the nature of service processes, professional practice, personnel assigned as field instructors, and student learning assignments.

The 1991 Bachelor of Social Work (BSW) and Master of Social Work (MSW) Evaluative Standards and Interpretive Guidelines, which offered clarification for each standard, called for clearly articulated standards for selecting agencies and field instructors (CSWE, 1991). Programs were to reflect nondiscrimination in field placements. The field practicum objectives were to reflect attention to racial, ethnic, and cultural diversity as well as the role and status of women. The Interpretive Guidelines required a minimum of 400 hours of practicum experience for the BSW and a minimum of 900 hours for the MSW.

## The Introduction of Learning Outcomes (1994)

The 1994 CPS for MSW and BSW degree programs again viewed the field practicum as an integral part of the curriculum (CSWE, 1994a, 1994b). The required hours remained the same: a minimum of 900 hours for the MSW and a minimum of 400 hours for the BSW. However, the requirements for these hours were moved from the interpretive guidelines to the policy itself. Requirements were added to articulate clear practice and evaluation goals for the field practicum and for each individual student, and to offer orientation and training programs for field instructors.

The policies that programs were to follow expanded beyond those related to the required curriculum content. A key role in this new approach to policy was the adoption of BSW- and MSW-level learning objectives. The objectives differed at the MSW and BSW educational levels, with the MSW level indicating greater autonomy and an increased degree of expertise. The 1994 CPS defined these objectives as what program graduates were expected to do in practice.

The interpretive guidelines for the 1994 field education standards required MSW programs to select field instructors with an MSW (CSWE, 1994c). These guidelines also called on programs to prepare a field manual, evaluate agency placements, develop a plan for students employed in the agency where they were placed, and, if the field instructor did not have an MSW, to develop a plan to provide the social work perspective in such placements.

### The First Educational Policy and Accreditation Standards (2001)

In 2001 the Commission on Accreditation replaced the earlier conception of using a social work CPS and related standards to guide the accreditation of programs by the idea of a broader EPAS (CSWE, 2001). The required content for the curriculum areas was continued and the learning objectives were retitled as program objectives, divided into foundation objectives for both programs and concentration objectives for MSW programs.

Field education was to be designed, supervised, coordinated, and evaluated such that students could demonstrate the achievement of the foundation and concentration program objectives. In addition, the accreditation standards had the expectation that field instructors for BSW students have an accredited BSW or MSW degree. The expectation that field instructors for master's students have an MSW degree was moved from the interpretive guidelines, which were no longer used, to the standard.

### Competencies and Practice Behaviors (2008)

In the CSWE's 2008 EPAS, the principal relevant section for field education is EP 2.3 Signature Pedagogy: Field Education; for field education the relevant sections are AS 2.1.1 through 2.1.8; for the field education director it is AS 3.4.5; for diversity it is AS 3.1; and for assessment it is AS 4.0. In addition to the sections of the 2008 EPAS that are directly relevant, field education is also connected to several other standards because of the requirement to use the social work competencies and related practice behaviors in the development of the classroom and field curriculum.

1. For BSW generalist practice, the relevant accreditation standards include the following:

   a. AS B2.0.1 (generalist practice)

   b. AS B2.0.2 (social work competencies)

   c. AS B2.0.3 (practice behaviors)

    d. AS B2.0.4 (rationale for class and field curriculum design)

    e. AS B2.0.5 (curriculum content that operationalizes program competencies and practice behaviors)

2. For MSW advanced practice, the relevant accreditation standards include the following:

    a. AS M2.0.2 (advanced practice)

    b. AS M2.0.3 (social work competencies)

    c. AS M2.0.4 (practice behaviors)

    d. AS M2.0.5 (rationale for class and field curriculum design)

    e. AS M2.0.6 (curriculum content that operationalizes program competencies and practice behaviors)

These standards, whether for the BSW or the MSW program, guide curriculum design from the identification of program competencies and their related practice behaviors, through selection of content for teaching those competencies and behaviors to students, and through the design of an assessment plan to measure graduates' attainment of those social work competencies.

This emphasis on competencies and related practice behaviors is carried over into the standards on field education. The traditional requirement of a systematic and educationally designed, supervised, coordinated, and evaluated field program shifted to a focus on one in which students demonstrate the attainment of the program's competencies and related practice behaviors. Programs also must select and train field instructors in accordance with the competencies and related practice behaviors.

The standards require that programs establish generalist practice opportunities for BSW students and advanced practice opportunities for MSW students. The ten core competencies (CSWE, 2008, EP 2.1) needed by generalist social work practitioners are:

1. Identify as a professional social worker and conduct oneself accordingly

2. Apply social work ethical principles to guide professional practice

3. Apply critical thinking to inform and communicate professional judgments

4. Engage diversity and difference in practice

5. Advance human rights and social and economic justice

6. Engage in research-informed practice and practice-informed research

7. Apply knowledge of human behavior and the social environment

8. Engage in policy practice to advance social and economic well-being and to deliver effective social work services

9. Respond to contexts that shape practice

10. Engage, assess, intervene, and evaluate with individuals, families, groups, organizations, and communities

In other words, student learning in the field, parallel to student learning in the classroom, will need to reflect all of the social work competencies that define generalist practice as they are carried out in practice through the practice behaviors that define them. Similarly, advanced practice field settings are to include opportunities to apply the advanced practice behaviors that define a program's concentration or specialization.

## The Emergence of a Signature Pedagogy

Viewed over time, changes to the accreditation requirements for field education reflect movement from a variety of experiences based in program and individual learner needs to a more highly uniform pedagogy. It is clear from the overview of the 1969 policy and standards that the standards permitted a variety of practicum experiences across programs and even among students within a program. Although it was connected to the three required curriculum content areas and based in direct involvement in service activities, any program could use a range of practicum designs and instructional formats.

The 1971 Standards for the Approval of Undergraduate Programs in Social Work (CSWE, 1971b) employed the idea of an educationally directed field experience. This concept differentiated field education from on-the-job-training. This idea was reinforced in 1988 and reframed in 2001 to focus on program objectives (CSWE, 1988, 2001). It was reframed again in 2008 to focus on competencies and their related practice behaviors (CSWE, 2008).

Racial, ethnic, cultural, and gender diversity was added to the standards in 1973 and 1976. Programs were to apply diversity to the content of field instruction settings and the selection of field instructors, serving as one basis in the establishment of guidelines for field instructor qualifications. The CSWE's 1974 Standards for the Accreditation of Baccalaureate Degree Programs in Social Work required a minimum of 300 clock hours in the field, for which the program was to give academic credit. This constituted another milestone in the standardization of field learning; this standardization was extended to graduate programs and was increased for BSW programs under the CSWE's 1988 curriculum policy and accreditation standards. The CSWE's 1988 social work accreditation requirements, however, still contained the possibility of variation in student learning. For example, programs could organize the field practicum in different ways, but the practicum was to be educationally directed, coordinated, and monitored, reinforcing the idea introduced in the CSWE's 1974 BSW standards.

The 1994 CPS and accreditation standards articulated learning objectives at both levels and added requirements regarding orientation and training for field instructors (CSWE, 1994a). It was the interpretive guidelines for the accreditation standards that added significant new features regarding the mechanics of field education. The 1994 CPS required that field instructors possess an MSW degree, and that all programs prepare a field manual, evaluate agency placements, and develop an employment-based plan for students employed in the agency where they were placed.

The CSWE's 2001 EPAS turned the substantive pedagogical requirement of learning objectives into foundation and concentration learning objectives, defined as what practitioners did in practice; these objectives were to serve as a major guide to student learning. The field director was to design and coordinate the field education program such that the same learning objectives were to be demonstrated by students in all programs, clearly moving away from any individual variations. In addition, the routine and habitual pedagogical elements received greater emphasis. This standardization of learning outcomes was furthered in the CSWE's 2008 EPAS with its adoption of ten social work competencies and related generalist and advanced practice behaviors that were to serve as the basis of class and field curriculum design and evaluation.

The changes that occurred between the CSWE's 1969 and 2008 in social work education's accreditation policy and standards for field learning laid the groundwork for greater uniformity in the mechanics or process of field education as well as in the substance of what students must learn. In 1969 both the mechanics and, in part, the substance were guided by the individual program. By 2008 the mechanics were to be more uniform across programs, as demonstrated by the requirements for the number of hours in placement, field instructor qualifications, the integration of the conceptual and theoretical learning of the classroom into field learning, and evaluation of student performance. The substance of the experience, as guided by the competencies and related practice behaviors, also was to be more uniform. Although field settings may vary, the context of these settings should not be as important as the application of the social work competencies and their related practice behaviors in student learning. For example, while the settings vary for other professionals such as nurses or surgeons, their professional competencies and behaviors do not.

## The Field Director and Accreditation

The mechanics or processes and the substance of field education, resulting from the evolution of social work's accreditation standards, not only indicate its emerging potential as social work's signature pedagogy, but also serve as an outline of the key responsibilities of the field director's role. The key aspects of a field director's role and responsibilities are reflected in the latest iteration of social work's accreditation policy and standards.

For example, field directors work with the program's faculty to conceptualize how classroom learning is connected to the field setting. Field directors carry out this responsibility by designing and providing oversight to integrative mechanisms such as field seminars and liaison visits by program representatives. In addition, directors develop and implement program and field instructor education and training on the relationship between the theoretical learning in the classroom and its application in the field setting.

The field director creates policies and procedures by which field settings are selected and evaluated in relation to the standards on diversity and program outcomes. Field directors will need to strengthen the field setting's understanding of the social work competencies and practice behaviors and develop means to determine the potential of the site to deliver them.

The director also develops and disseminates the policy and procedures by which the required number of field hours are set and monitored. These policies and procedures are typically found in the program's field manual. Along with program faculty, field directors develop admission criteria that reflect students' readiness to enter field and criteria for the completion or attainment of specific criteria determining admission to the field.

Additionally, the field director develops the criteria by which field instructors are selected, oriented, trained, and evaluated in line with accreditation requirements. In carrying out this responsibility, field directors identify the practice credentials and experiences of field instructors who select learning opportunities for students that allow them to demonstrate the program's competencies and practice behaviors. Field directors develop training for experienced and new field instructors regarding the program's field education policies and procedures, its curriculum, and its approaches to supervision. These responsibilities also include training field instructors to understand the social work competencies and practice behaviors, and how to supervise students in the development of learning agreements that are based on those competencies and behaviors.

Field directors must develop specific policies and procedures regarding the placement and evaluation of students. Moreover, the field director develops policies and procedures to guide the placement of students in agencies where they are employed so that the student and employee roles are separate in order to protect the student's role as learner.

Finally, the field director collaborates with program faculty in creating an assessment plan that incorporates the evaluation of student performance in the field setting. Because the field setting focuses on the integration of classroom and practical learning in relation to program competencies and practice behaviors, the field setting has a strong potential to serve as a measure of student learning outcomes. Field directors will want to create a field program that evaluates student performance in such a way that it can be used as a source of data about student attainment of program competencies and practice behaviors (Pierce, 2008).

In carrying out the aforementioned roles and responsibilities, field directors bring into and keep the field program in compliance with accreditation standards and also further its place as social work's signature pedagogy.

**Next Steps: Field Education's Future as Social Work's Signature Pedagogy**

Over the past several decades greater similarity has emerged as field directors have brought their field education programs into compliance with the expectations of social work education's curriculum, educational policies, and related standards. During this period, social work's field education has developed from a disparate learning experience into a singular, more-focused pedagogy. Given what currently exists, the framework for a universal signature pedagogy can be found in the nature of the student experience, the qualifications of the field instructors, the number of hours for student field learning, the emphasis on mechanisms to integrate class and field, orientation and training for field instructors, and the required competencies and related practice behaviors.

Social work education faces the opportunity to create a holistic signature pedagogy, one that engages the learner in all aspects of professional practice—the thinking, the doing, and the valuing. While other professions appear to be content with the use of single-focus signature pedagogies, social work should not be so easily satisfied. A signature pedagogy is of limited usefulness to the learner if it does not include all elements of a professional's practice. Of course, it is difficult to conceptualize and implement a signature pedagogy as complex as one that integrates the mind, the hand, and the heart. To do so will require pursuing additional research and thinking, refining field education requirements in accreditation policy and standards, and strengthening field education organizations.

Given the emerging similarity across field education programs, future research should focus on understanding how these common elements work best. For example, such research and thinking should uncover:

- how to develop the most competent field instructors through effective training programs such that they challenge students in the expression of their ideas and guide them in their transformation into professionals (see Dedman & Palmer, 2011);

- the required number of student hours that facilitate competency-based learning outcomes;

- the role and use of the competencies and related practice behaviors in making student learning routine and habitual;

- effective methods of integrating class and field learning and how they heighten the visibility and accountability of the expression of the ideas and opinions of learners (e.g., see Wayne et al., 2010); and

- the most effective role and nature of the field education director in furthering field education as a signature pedagogy (see Lyter, 2012).

Future research should give attention to accreditation policy and standards that require programs to use the same set of competencies and their related practice behaviors. Additionally, there should be a focus on clearly mandating that these competencies and practice behaviors serve as the basis of field setting and field instructor selection, field instructor orientation and training, student learning agreements and evaluation, and integrative seminars and liaison visits. Without the substance of common outcomes and their use in the creation of universal field related learning processes, there can be no holistic signature pedagogy.

The existing field education organizations can be strengthened as a resource in the refinement of field education as the profession's signature pedagogy. They constitute an underutilized communication, research, and educational resource. The creation of a network of the regional associations, the North American Network of Field Education Directors, the Field Education Committee of the Association of Baccalaureate Program Directors (BPD), and the Field Council of the CSWE could be used to uncover in greater detail how field education currently operates. This network could also be used to identify opportunities for research and to sponsor uniform training opportunities for field instructors.

Stronger research efforts, accreditation standards, and field education organizations would assist in understanding and refining field education as the profession's signature pedagogy. The Commission on Accreditation could revise accreditation standards to mandate universal processes or mechanisms as well as to reflect research about what works best. The network of field director groups could disseminate and train field directors and field instructors. As legal education—following the introduction of the case method of instruction in 1875 by Christopher Langdell, dean of the Harvard Law School—developed the case method as its signature pedagogy (Shulman, 2005a), so social work education has the opportunity to refine and further develop field education as a complex and comprehensive signature pedagogy.

## Essential Readings

Council on Social Work Education (CSWE). (2008). Educational policy and accreditation standards (rev. March 27, 2010/updated August 2012). Alexandria, VA: Author. Retrieved from http://www.cswe.org/Accreditation/41865.aspx.

Pierce, D. (2008). Field education in the 2008 EPAS: Implications for the field director's role. Retrieved from http://www.cswe.org/File.aspx?id=31580.

Shulman, L. S. (2005b). Signature pedagogies in the professions. *Daedalus, 134*(3), 52–59.

Wayne, J., Bogo, M., & Raskin, M. (2010). Field education as the signature pedagogy of social work education. *Journal of Social Work Education, 46*(3), 327–339.

## References

Council on Social Work Education (CSWE). (1969). Curriculum policy for the master's degree program in graduate schools of social work. New York: Author.

Council on Social Work Education (CSWE). (1971a). Manual of accrediting standards. New York: Author.

Council on Social Work Education (CSWE). (1971b). Standards for the approval of undergraduate programs in social work. New York: Author.

Council on Social Work Education (CSWE). (1973). Guidelines for implementation of accreditation standard 1234A. New York: Author.

Council on Social Work Education (CSWE). (1974). Standards for the accreditation of baccalaureate programs in social work. New York: Author.

Council on Social Work Education (CSWE). (1976). Guidelines for implementation of accreditation standards on non-discrimination. New York: Author.

Council on Social Work Education (CSWE). (1988). Curriculum policy statement for the master's degree and baccalaureate degree programs in social work education. Alexandria, VA: Author.

Council on Social Work Education (CSWE). (1991). Handbook of accreditation standards and procedures. Alexandria, VA: Author.

Council on Social Work Education (CSWE). (1994a). Curriculum policy statement for baccalaureate degree programs in social work education. Alexandria, VA: Author.

Council on Social Work Education (CSWE). (1994b). Curriculum policy statement for master's degree programs in social work education. Alexandria, VA: Author.

Council on Social Work Education (CSWE). (1994c). Handbook for accreditation standards and procedures. Alexandria, VA: Author.

Council on Social Work Education (CSWE). (2001). Educational policy and accreditation standards. Alexandria, VA: Author.

Council on Social Work Education (CSWE). (2008). Educational policy and accreditation standards (rev. March 27, 2010/updated August 2012). Alexandria, VA: Author. Retrieved from http://www.cswe.org/Accreditation/41865.aspx.

Dedman, D. E., & Palmer, L. B. (2011). Field instructors and online training: An exploratory survey. *Journal of Social Work Education, 47*(1), 151–161.

Earls Larrison, T., & Korr, W. S. (2013). Does social work have a signature pedagogy? *Journal of Social Work Education, 49*(2), 194–206.

Hyland, A., & Kilcommins, S. (2009). Signature pedagogies and legal education in universities: Epistemological and pedagogical concerns with Langdellian case method. *Teaching in Higher Education, 14*(1), 29–42.

Kendall, K. (2002). Council on Social Work Education: Its antecedents and first twenty years. Alexandria, VA: Council on Social Work Education.

Lyter, S. C. (2012). Potential of field education as signature pedagogy: The field director role. *Journal of Social Work Education, 48*(1), 179–188.

Pierce, D. (2008). Field education in the 2008 EPAS: Implications for the field director's role. Retrieved from http://www.cswe.org/File.aspx?id=31580.

Shulman, L. S. (2005a). Pedagogies of uncertainty. *Liberal Education, 91*(2), 18–25.

Shulman, L. S. (2005b). Signature pedagogies in the professions. *Daedalus,* *134*(3), 52–59.

Shulman, L, S. (2005c). The signature pedagogies of the professions of law, medicine, engineering, and the clergy: Potential lessons for the education of teachers. Irvine, CA: National Research Council Center for Education.

Wayne, J., Bogo, M., & Raskin, M. (2010). Field education as the signature pedagogy of social work education. *Journal of Social Work Education, 46*(3), 327–339.

# 2

# Roles and Responsibilities of the Field Director

*Janet Bradley and Page Walker Buck*

The management of a field education program is an exciting responsibility, one that field directors experience as both incredibly satisfying and occasionally overwhelming. The most satisfying moments come from seeing evidence of extraordinary professional growth in students when their hours of hard work, coordination, and negotiation skills pay off. The overwhelming moments come when the realization that rising expectations from students, university administrators, and accreditation standards confront diminishing resources in the field (Buck, Bradley, Robb, & Kirzner, 2012).

This chapter provides an overview of the roles and responsibilities of the field director in an environment of competing demands. It focuses on policy development and emphasizes the Council on Social Work Education's (CSWE) 2008 Educational Policy and Accreditation Standards (EPAS) related to field education.

## Position of Field Director

The field director is responsible for the field education program; while most are members of the faculty, some field directors are staff. This position can be permanent or rotating, the latter more common in smaller programs. In most cases field directors are not full-time faculty members. In the 2010 Annual Survey of Social Work Programs, only 8 percent of full-time faculty had the title of field director, while 1 percent reported being an assistant field director (CSWE, 2011). In larger programs the field director is often responsible for policy and curriculum, in collaboration with field coordinators who place students in the practice settings and perform the field liaison work. In very small programs the field director often does all of the administrative work, field curriculum development, placement of students, field liaison work, and teaching other courses in the program. Regardless of the size of the program, Educational Policy (EP) B3.4.5 (c) and EP M3.4.5(c)

(CSWE, 2008) specify that the field director must have at least 25 percent assigned field time in BSW programs and 50 percent assigned field time in MSW programs. These policies also state that the program must demonstrate that the field director has enough time to fulfill the roles and responsibilities of the position.

The field director's role is demanding, complex, and rewarding. Studies suggest that the complexity evolves, in part, when the demands that field directors face are in competition with each other (Buck et al., 2012). In a 2012 mixed-method study of 186 field directors, the most reported source of demand was a changing student demographic (Bradley, Laster, & Buck, 2012). Field directors report an increase in the types of requests that students make, including requests for specific types of field placements in terms of population, distance from home, and time of day. Students often make these requests because they are balancing multiple responsibilities at work and at home. The need for flexible field settings, however, comes at a time in the history of social work practice when agencies are facing tremendous budgetary retrenchment. Field sites are often not able to provide the type of learning environment that a student requests, especially in terms of field instruction and supervision. In their management of the field program, field directors must also consider the fact that faculty members are pulled away from pedagogy toward scholarship and funding sources. Administrators press for student satisfaction and retention, while social work colleagues in field sites ask field directors to be mindful of their commitment to gatekeeping. Key to the management of the field director role is active participation in policy development. Following an introduction to policy development is an overview of key policy areas including administration of admission to field (CSWE, 2008, Accreditation Standard [AS] 2.1.4), selection of practice settings (AS 2.1.5), negotiating employment-based practica (AS 2.1.8), selecting field instructors (AS 2.1.6), and provision of orientation and training (AS 2.1.7). Careful crafting of these policies will prepare the program for the CSWE accreditation self-study.

## Policy Development

The development of field education policy is both influenced by and must be responsive to the mission of the university and social work program and the specific needs of the university, its students, and the community. The interests of these stakeholders might be at odds. For example, policies and procedures of the field program must reflect state licensure standards for social workers, particularly with regard to any criminal background. In states that will not issue a social work license to someone who has a felony conviction, the social work program needs to consider the ethics of accepting into the program students who will not be able to practice as licensed social workers in that state. Another example of how university and agency policies may differ is illustrated in the case of sexual harassment in Feature 2.1. Although the field director may take the lead in developing and implementing policies related to field, the policies are not created in a vacuum. Depending on the policy, others must be consulted: university and agency administrators, deans and directors, faculty, students, field instructors, and field advisory committees. The university's legal counsel should review policies related to student admission, progression, and termination.

### Feature 2.1. Sexual Harassment: Policies at Odds

Student safety is of utmost importance to field directors. Although most students in field are safe and will not experience violence or harassment, there are experiences for which the field director must be prepared. In particular, sexual harassment does occur in field settings. An incident of sexual harassment is more complex when policies of the agency and the university conflict.

In an agency practice setting, a student was approached by a worker on several occasions; this worker asked the student to go out to a bar in the evening. The worker also made inappropriate comments that were sexual in nature. The student was very uncomfortable and began to dread going to practicum. When reporting the incident to the liaison and field director, the student had to deal with the situation, which was equally stressful as the situation itself. The sexual harassment policies of the university and the agency were different. Since the student was at the practicum when the sexual harassment took place, the agency's strict reporting policy took precedence over the more victim-friendly policy of the university in which students can decide if they want to report. The student had no choice in the agency setting but to report the incident, which left her feeling disempowered. The student's status in the agency further complicated the situation and the student blamed herself. She was more concerned about what was going to happen to the worker than she was about what she had been through. In order to assist the student, the field director, liaison, and field instructor explained the rationale with regard to the reporting requirements and reassured the student that she would be supported throughout the investigation. The student was given the option of going to a new placement or continuing at the agency, since the perpetrator had been placed on leave. A way to empower the student was to provide her with the option to decide about the next placement. It was important for the student to discuss what happened with the field instructor in order for the student to see that, according to the National Association of Social Workers' *Code of Ethics*, the worker had violated boundaries. A professional with a higher status is responsible for maintaining clear boundaries, and therefore the incident was not the student's fault.

To prepare for such issues, field directors should have (1) a sexual harassment policy in the field manual that is in concert with university policies, (2) a required module during student field orientation on appropriate boundaries and relationships in the agency, and (3) an expectation that students familiarize themselves with the sexual harassment policy of the practice setting. Incidents of sexual harassment occur and field directors should be prepared to address the trauma and emotional impact of experiencing sexual harassment, noting there could be past trauma in the student's life. Field directors must give attention to an affected student's need for referral and counseling and the impact of the incident on the student's academic performance. If the student has disclosed the incident to others, it is important to assess the potential impact on other students and to create a safe and supportive learning environment for all.

Shelagh J. Larkin, MSW, LISW
Clinical Faculty
Director for Field Education
Xavier University

The field director must consider the relationship of program policies to federal and state laws, state professional regulations, and other university policies, including policies concerning academic and student affairs. University policies can be an important source of support and validation for bolstering specific program policies. In some programs, for example, a violation of the discipline's *Code of Ethics* (National Association of Social Workers, 2008) constitutes a violation of academic integrity. There may be times, however, when university policy is in conflict with program policy and/or social work values. If the university has a semester break, the social work program and practice settings might require students to return to their placements early in order to maintain the ethical obligation for integrity and continuity of the relationship with client systems. Asking students to return to field before the official start of the semester requires proactive consideration from the field director, especially with regard to liability and faculty support. If the university maintains insurance coverage for all students, the field director should ensure that coverage is in place before the semester begins.

University policies can compete with the needs of the field education program. Field directors who are in a program whose mission is to prepare social work professionals to work in rural areas need to consider transportation challenges when developing a client transportation policy. The university may have a blanket policy that students cannot transport others while in internship/service learning settings. In a social work program, however, driving clients might be a student function for some field settings. The field director must be aware of university policies and take steps to address competing demands when they arise. One potential source of support in a situation such as this would be to use feedback from a field advisory committee that could provide current, practical data on the reality of social services in the local area. If relationships with the local community agencies are key to university administrators, a field director may be able to negotiate a policy exception. Such an exception could be to allow social work students to transport clients when they use an agency vehicle, after the field instructor has thoroughly considered safety issues.

Field policies must be published, distributed, and made available to all faculty members, students, and field instructors. Field directors develop a field manual for this purpose that includes all the information necessary for students and field instructors to understand the field program and its connection to the entire social work program and university. This manual outlines the responsibilities of the university and practice setting, including the responsibilities of the field director, field liaison, field instructor, and student. It also includes field policies and procedures, grievance procedures, evaluation forms, syllabi, and assignments.

Because the social work environment is constantly evolving, the field manual and field policies and procedures should be reviewed and updated annually. Similar to a university catalog, the field manual is often an agreement with the student. Some programs ask students to sign a form indicating he or she has read the field manual. Keeping up with the changes in field is time consuming. The field director needs current information about the changes in practice settings and changes in academia. Being appointed to the program's curriculum committee, having social workers from the practice community on the field advisory committee, and being connected to other local field directors either through a field consortium or other professional relationships can assist the field director in remaining current.

### Administration of Admission to Field

The field director is typically responsible for ensuring that students have met the program's criteria for field prior to starting at a practice setting (CSWE, 2008, AS 2.1.4). Field education has an important stake in the program's admissions process given that all admitted students are required to participate in field practicum and that most admitted students are retained and graduate. High retention and graduation rates are a function of the ambiguity that social work educators feel about terminating or counseling out students who they deem as inappropriate (Sowbel, 2012). As a result of this ambiguity, even students who might be questionably suitable for the profession have a right to a field placement while enrolled.

When gatekeeping ambiguity is combined with enrollment pressures to increase cohort sizes, the field education program is directly affected. Increased enrollment requires additional field sites with qualified field instructors, resources that are scarce in some locales (Buck et al., 2012). Pressure to increase enrollment can also raise the possibility that applicant screening will be less rigorous. The burden of admitting a student to field who is ill-suited for social work falls on the field program where professionalism, emotional stability, and ethical practice are core expectations. Some students who are able to manage or even excel in a classroom setting are not able to meet expectations in the field setting, requiring substantial time and energy from the field director, field liaison, and field instructor. Other consequences of increased enrollment can include the use of subpar placements where the experience and/or supervision in field is not ideal. Navigating and supporting these settings requires significant resources from the field education office.

A proactive stance in field admissions can be taken by advocating for both effective gatekeeping in program admissions and a cap on the number of students who can realistically be placed in suitable placements. This may require educating those responsible for admissions and university administration on the realities of the local social service environment. While some areas continue to have access to high-quality placement opportunities, others are experiencing a significant decrease in the number of available field sites as a result of budget cuts and competition from other social work and related professional programs (Bradley et al., 2012).

## Selection of Practice Settings

Field directors are responsible for determining the policies, criteria, and procedures by which field practice settings will be selected, pursuant to AS 2.1.5 (CSWE, 2008). These criteria are developed by the field director with input from program director or chair and faculty. As indicated in AS B2.1.2 and M2.1.2 (CSWE, 2008), practice settings for BSW and foundation-year MSW students need to provide generalist practice experiences that offer students the opportunity to demonstrate the core competencies. The settings need to provide advanced practice experiences that allow advanced practice MSW students the opportunity to build on the core competencies and demonstrate advanced practice behaviors. The specificity and number of criteria set by the program for advanced practice settings can create a challenge for the field director. A program offering a concentration in social work practice with immigrant populations would require concentration students to have advanced practice field experiences in these settings. These placements, however, may not be readily available in the practice community.

In addition to providing appropriate generalist and advanced practice opportunities, practice settings must also be willing to provide an identified field instructor with time and expertise to offer field instruction. The CSWE's 2008 EPAS does not specify a minimum amount or a required format for field instruction of social work students, although many programs require supervision hours that are consistent with the state licensing boards. Supervision expectations are typically sixty minutes per week, with a range of guidelines about the proportion spent in individual and group sessions. Because practice settings are under increasing pressure to manage with limited resources, time available for field instruction is diminishing in some cases. Field directors report losing field sites that can no longer afford to have their paid staff providing unbillable supervision (Bradley et al., 2012). These issues have been addressed through creative means, including arrangements for field instruction to be provided off site by degreed social workers. The arrangements for compensation and workload credit for such responsibilities vary.

The criteria necessary for the setting to be and remain a practice setting, as well as responsibilities of the practice setting, the university or college, the social work program, and the student, should be spelled out in an affiliation agreement or memorandum of understanding signed by the university and practice setting administrators. Research has shown that this type of formal agreement benefits the learning environment through increased collaboration (Bogo & Globerman, 1999).

### Negotiating Employment-Based Practica

Since the 1980s the number of students requesting to use their place of employment as a field placement has increased significantly (Newman, Dannenfelser, Clemmons, & Webster, 2007). Not unlike their peers in other fields, social work students are struggling with increases in tuition as public funding for higher education decreases (Valentine, 2004). The CSWE's (2008) EPAS AS 2.1.8 requires that programs develop policies for employment-based practica so that the field education experience is different from the work experience.

The key in employment-based field practica is to keep the integrity of the learning experience. Dilemmas specific to employment-based practica can arise when there is a lack of understanding among all parties about the arrangements. In some cases students can carve out time from their paid work for their field experience. Some programs require students to complete their field education hours in addition to their regular work hours. This can reduce commuting and orientation time for students. The reality of completing a placement in addition to a full-time job and coursework is often a struggle for students, even those with solid organizational skills. It is the responsibility of the field director to set policy, as well as to negotiate and monitor these arrangements.

### Selecting Field Instructors

Field directors are responsible for ensuring that field instructors meet minimum criteria as outlined in EPAS AS 2.1.6 (CSWE, 2008). For bachelor-level students, field instructors are required to have a bachelor of social work (BSW) or a master of social work (MSW); for master's-level students, field instructors are required to have an MSW. Since the current EPAS does not specify the number of years of postgraduate experience that a field instructor needs prior to providing field education, a program might be willing to have a recent MSW graduate who has many years of experience as a BSW social worker provide field education for foundation-level students. Field directors should develop criteria and procedures to assess field instructors' social work knowledge, practice skills, and values as a way to evaluate their ability to assist the student in achieving the core competencies. The more stringent the criteria, the more difficult it is for a field director to secure qualified field instructors. Regardless of the expectations for selecting potential field instructors, this process should be consistent and documented.

In some cases an appropriate practice setting will not have a social work–degreed supervisor on staff; this is common in grassroots and community-based organizations, including community mental health, domestic violence settings, outreach to homeless, and refugee services. These settings can be used if the field director can demonstrate that the social work program has assumed responsibility for reinforcing the social work perspective (CSWE, 2008, AS 2.1.6).

One of the common experiences of field directors who are charged with recruiting qualified field instructors is the prevalence of turnover in social work settings. The U.S. Government Accountability Office estimates the turnover of child welfare workers, in public or private agencies, to be between 30 and 40 percent per year, with the average stay in child welfare work being less than two years (2003, p. 5). This happens not only from year to year but also mid-semester, often leaving students and field directors to scramble with a re-placement strategy. When a new placement is needed, field directors often resort to using their "back-pocket" practice settings and field instructors with whom the field director has developed a good relationship to support the accommodation of last-minute or mid-semester placements. These relationships are invaluable to field directors.

### Provision of Orientation and Training

Accreditation standards require that programs provide an orientation and field instructor training as well as continued open communication (CSWE, 2008, AS 2.1.7). Orientation for field instructors typically covers all elements of field instruction, including policies, procedures, and techniques for supporting student learning. Field instructors are not always able to attend orientation meetings, given time and travel constraints. Studies by Dalton, Stevens, and Maas-Brady (2009, 2011) showed that a large majority of BSW and MSW programs offer orientation for field instructors but that only 72 and 60 percent, respectively, require it. Furthermore, only 26 percent of those who require it reported consequences if field instructors did not attend (Dalton et al., 2009, 2011). Many programs cannot afford to lose field instructors because of failure to attend an orientation. In addition to orientation, many field programs offer a series of seminars that help field instructors enhance supervisory skills and incorporate new research and changes in social work education. Dalton et al. (2009, 2011) also found that 89 percent of BSW programs and 96 percent of MSW programs offer training separate from orientations. Some programs require these seminars, although field directors have found it difficult to enforce this requirement. One way to remedy this situation is to provide online training. Dedman and Palmer (2011) explored perceptions of online training, finding that approximately 80 percent of field instructors indicated that they "might" or would "definitely" participate in an online training if offered.

### Managing Field Liaisons

It is important to clearly articulate the responsibilities of the field liaison that can vary within the department or program, including tenure-track faculty members, clinical faculty members, adjunct faculty, and staff. Job descriptions for liaisons consist of expectations for student and field liaison contact, including the frequency and mode of communication. Tenure-track faculty are expected to carry out the same responsibilities as other liaisons. There is some evidence that tenure-track faculty are less likely to be field liaisons and less likely to give full attention to the role, given increasing institutional recognition to scholarship and grant development (J. Wayne, Bogo, & Raskin, 2006). This is a missed opportunity for faculty to utilize knowledge from the field to inform teaching, research, and the program's curriculum.

Quandaries can arise in the management of field liaisons when issues of rank, tenure, and seniority are at play. It can be difficult for a field director with a staff or junior faculty position to manage the activities of a senior faculty member who either does not carry out the job functions or does so in an unsatisfactory manner. For example, when field liaisons do not complete required field visits or if those visits are perfunctory, the relationship with the field instructor that the field director has cultivated can be at risk. Field instructors appreciate the support of the field liaison. Sparse communication from the liaison risks sending a message to field instructors that their time is not valued.

Field directors are responsible for ensuring that liaisons maintain contact with the placement sites (CSWE, 2008, AS 2.1.5). Programs use a variety of mechanisms to keep track of liaisons' field visits. Some require monthly reports, including travel reimbursement forms, while others rely on liaisons to carry out the visits with limited oversight. This element of the field director's role can be challenging without a clear articulation of responsibility around performance evaluation. Specifically, field directors and liaisons must be clear about expectations of performance; the program director is often involved in aspects of the evaluation of the liaison.

## Placing Students

One of the major administrative roles of the field director is to place students in field practica (CSWE, 2008, AS 2.1.5). The process varies from one end of the spectrum (programs that expect students to identify and arrange their own field placements from an approved list of organizations) to the other (programs that manage the process almost entirely, without substantial input from students). In some cases students are instructed not to contact agencies until a preliminary placement has been made.

The field director is ultimately responsible for ensuring equity in the process for both students and practice settings. Disputes can arise between students with placements that offer stipends or are in desirable settings. For these placements, sometimes the practice setting establishes the student requirements, such as level of academic attainment (e.g., second-year MSW student), proficiency in a second language, and/or previous work experience. At other times the social work program sets the criteria, such as maintaining a minimum GPA or completing a child welfare course prior to placement in a child welfare agency. The manner in which students are placed should be delineated in the field manual to ensure transparency.

Predicaments involving the placement of students can involve student expectations for certain work conditions. Students often expect that they will be able to choose the population, the work climate, and the location of their field site. This is difficult for field directors who are working in locations with limited field sites due to either the locale or competition from other schools and programs. Depending on the model for placement, students and the field director may perceive the students' readiness for certain types of work differently. These perceptions may be tempered by policies that link placement to the assessment of the student's learning needs and a field site's ability to provide corresponding learning experiences.

Other dilemmas related to placement arise when the field director has sensitive and undisclosed information about a student from personal interactions or from faculty members, including issues relating to mental health, addiction, and trauma. In some cases a student's best chances for success are supported when a field director can communicate honestly and openly about the student's strengths and concerns with a field instructor. The point at which this communication violates students' rights to confidentiality, however, is debated. A review of the Family Educational Rights and Privacy Act by The Jed Foundation suggests that the Act allows communication about a specific student among Institution of Higher Education staff, faculty, and administrators who are concerned about the welfare of the student or community (The Jed Foundation, 2008). Whether field instructors would be considered members of the Institution of Higher Education in a court of law is unknown. What is clear is that disclosure of a student's disability status without consent would violate the Americans with Disabilities Act of 1990.

### Overseeing Clearances, Background Checks, and Liability Insurance

Although not mandated by the 2008 EPAS, field directors must make decisions about whether to require criminal, child abuse, and FBI clearances as prerequisites to the field placement process. In some cases programs defer to the requirements of specific field agencies, and in other cases programs require all students to obtain clearances. In a study of BSW and MSW programs by Daehn Zellmer and Knothe (2011), the main issues that programs considered before adopting these policies were (1) the safety and welfare of future clients, (2) student privacy, and (3) legal issues that could arise if checks were not conducted. In some programs self-reported information about criminal background is gathered during the admissions process in order for students to be aware of the issues that felony convictions can pose (Haski-Leventhal, Gelles, & Cnaan, 2010).

The use of clearances presents several organizational issues: how clearances will be collected, who will review them, what will be done if there is an incident on the clearance, how the information will be stored, and what will happen in case of student noncompliance. For example, if a student refuses to provide clearances for personal reasons, is that grounds for dismissal from the program? In addition to requiring clearances, some agencies require students to pass drug screenings, have physical examinations, and have certain vaccinations. It is important for field directors to consider the financial burden of these tests. If students are unable to pay the additional fees related to the placement process, the program can help students identify available funding.

Field directors often oversee students' liability insurance. Some programs require students to purchase liability insurance, while others provide this coverage for all

*[handwritten: consult w/ contracts regarding background]*

students through an umbrella policy purchased by the university. The field director should be actively involved in this process to be sure that liability issues are satisfactorily covered and that policies do not create situations that systematically deny some students field opportunities. Given the legal nature of this area, field directors should consult with members of their local consortium and their legal counsel at the university.

## Monitoring Required Hours

The field director is responsible for ensuring that students meet the minimum required hours in field education: 400 hours for BSW students and 900 hours for MSW students, as outlined in AS 2.1.3 (CSWE, 2008). The number of field hours necessary for a student to demonstrate competency has never been empirically tested (Raskin, Wayne, & Bogo, 2008). Some programs require more than the minimum number of hours. Students who must also work full time and/or care for family members struggle to meet the demands for field hours. Because more students have increasingly complex work and family lives, field directors will be tasked with developing formal policies and procedures to ensure the integrity of the educational program and fairness to all students.

Questions that commonly arise around issues of illness, family emergencies, weather, and travel time can complicate the monitoring of required field hours. Field policies should outline expectations for accruing field hours that count or do not count. Policies should also address the expectations for students if they need to be absent from field. Whom do they notify? Do they contact their field instructor or their faculty field liaison, or both?

## Supporting the Practice-Theory Connection

Key to the role of managing a field education program is participation in curriculum design. Field directors assume a leadership role related to the curriculum that purports to "connect the theoretical and conceptual contribution of the classroom with the practical world of the practice setting, fostering the implementation of evidence-informed practice" (CSWE, 2008, AS 2.1.1, p. 9). According to Pierce (2008), "Field directors, along with other program faculty need to conceptualize how what is learned in the classroom is connected to the field setting. Field education directors do so by participating in the design of the explicit curriculum, assisting in the development and monitoring of integrative seminars and the field liaison activities of faculty, and creating and carrying out field instructor and classroom faculty training and education on the relationship between class and field" (p. 9).

Field liaisons and practice faculty take the lead in assisting the student to apply theory to social work practice. Ideally, this application of theory occurs when faculty and liaisons help students use field experiences as examples in the classroom and relate concepts and theories to the field setting. Field seminars and field visits are specifically designed to facilitate the integration of theory and practice. This integration can happen as a result of field discussions, case presentations, written and oral assignments, and role plays. Practice faculty who are also the students' field liaison find that they are particularly able to facilitate this connection, given their knowledge of the practice setting. The field liaison then links the field experience back to the practice faculty and the classroom curriculum back to the field instructor. This full circle provides the optimum learning environment. Given the program structure and institutional culture of faculty roles, however, it is not uncommon for the field liaison and practice faculty to not be in communication. The field director should establish a strong culture of routine communication as a way to help support student learning (Homonoff, 2008).

### Evaluation and Gatekeeping

Field directors are responsible for evaluating and monitoring the field education program in terms of both student learning and the effectiveness of the practice setting (CSWE, 2008, AS 2.1.5). Field instructors evaluate student performance by observing the demonstration of practice behaviors aligned to the ten competencies specified in the EPAS (CSWE, 2008). It is the field director's responsibility to ensure that students, field instructors, field liaisons, and practice faculty are clear about the role of competency assessment in the evaluation of student performance. The CSWE (2008, AS 4.0.4) requires that the program post its program outcomes of achievements on competencies and practice behaviors on the social work program's Web page.

Evaluation of student performance necessarily demands intervention when issues of poor performance arise. The field director is involved when a student's behavior or skills in field do not meet competency expectations. Clear policies about student performance, specifically practice behaviors, are essential, including policies for evaluation of professional behaviors such as suitable dress, appropriate use of technology and social media regarding client information, and adherence to privacy and confidentiality laws. When students are not demonstrating professional behaviors in the field, certain personal characteristics might be identified: some students lack empathy, or are defensive, shy, needy, demanding, or judgmental (Bogo et al., 2006). Working with students who demonstrate these behaviors and who are not performing well in the field can be time consuming and challenging for the field director. The field director is involved in developing a remediation plan and manages the decision making on student re-placement, placement disruptions, and/or dismissal from field. In collaboration with the program director and/or faculty, the field director needs to develop policies on how many times students can be re-placed before they are terminated from the program. If students are not re-placed, but instead are dismissed, the program needs to adhere to due process and provide an appeals process (R. Wayne, 2004). Orienting students to clear expectations and policies of the field program will assure students that due process will be involved if a student is asked to leave a placement and/or if a student requests a medical leave.

In addition to monitoring student performance, the field director continuously monitors the field settings, field instructors, and liaisons. Routine formal and informal communication with liaisons, practice faculty, and field instructors is crucial. It is in this context that the field liaison assesses the ability and willingness of the practice setting and the field instructor to continue to provide the student with the learning opportunities necessary to demonstrate the knowledge, skills, and values of the ten competencies. Many field directors require that field liaisons complete forms that evaluate each practice setting.

Field education staff obtains feedback from students about the practice setting. This feedback is essential for the field director to determine whether to continue to place students at the site or whether more work is needed to improve the experience for students. Settings often provide feedback to the field director in verbal conversations; AS 2.1.5, however, requires that programs evaluate the effectiveness of the practice settings through a formalized process such as online surveys (CSWE, 2008).

## Managing It All

Many of the demands faced by field directors are in competition with each other. For example, what students need and want can be at odds with what the field setting can provide, and what administrators want from admissions can be at odds with what is realistic in terms of placement opportunities. These conflicts present opportunities for collaboration, creativity, and advocacy.

The roles and responsibilities outlined in this chapter require significant time, energy, and management expertise. From policy development to evaluation and monitoring, the key is attention to relationships. When field directors maintain productive relationships with the many different constituent groups—including their faculty, administrators, students, field instructors, site administrators, and other field directors in the region—the competing demands of the position are far more manageable. In some cases these relationships require advocating for administrative support and additional release time. Other supports include an active field advisory committee that can assist with policy development, participation in regional field directors' consortia and Listserv discussions, and access to workshops at the annual Baccalaureate Program Directors conference and Annual Program Meeting of the CSWE. The job of field director is one of balance, requiring the discipline of programming and policy planning, organization, communication skills, wisdom, and insight.

## Essential Readings

Bogo, M., & Globerman, J. (1999). Interorganizational relationships between schools of social work and field agencies: Testing a framework for analysis. *Journal of Social Work Education, 35*(2), 265–274.

Buck, P. W., Bradley, J., Robb, L., & Kirzner, R. S. (2012). Complex & competing demands in field education: A qualitative study of field directors' experiences. *Field Educator, 2*(2). Retrieved from http://fieldeducator.simmons.edu/article/complex-and-competing-demands-in-field-education/.

Homonoff, E. (2008). The heart of social work: Best practitioners rise to challenges in field instruction. *Clinical Supervisor, 27*(2), 135–169.

Newman, B. S., Dannenfelser, P. L., Clemmons, V., & Webster, S. (2007). Working to learn: Internships for today's social work students. *Journal of Social Work Education, 43*(3), 513–528.

Sowbel, L. (2012). Gatekeeping: Why shouldn't we be ambivalent? *Journal of Social Work Education, 48*(1), 27–44.

Wayne, J., Bogo, M., & Raskin, M. (2006). The need for radical change in field education. *Journal of Social Work Education, 42*(1), 161–169.

## References

Americans with Disabilities Act of 1990, PL 101–336, 42d Cong., § 1201.

Bogo, M., & Globerman, J. (1999). Interorganizational relationships between schools of social work and field agencies: Testing a framework for analysis. *Journal of Social Work Education, 35*(2), 265–274.

Bogo, M., Regehr, G., Regehr, C., Woodford, M., Hughes, J., & Power, R. (2006). Beyond competencies: Field instructors' descriptions of student performance. *Journal of Social Work Education, 42*(3), 579–593.

Bradley, J., Laster, R., & Buck, P. W. (2012). *The new social service environment, through a field director lens.* Washington, DC: Council on Social Work Education.

Buck, P. W., Bradley, J., Robb, L., & Kirzner, R. S. (2012). Complex & competing demands in field education: A qualitative study of field directors' experiences. *Field Educator, 2*(2). Retrieved from http://fieldeducator.simmons.edu/article/complex-and-competing-demands-in-field-education/.

Council on Social Work Education (CSWE). (2008). *Educational policy and accreditation standards* (rev. March 27, 2010/updated August 2012). Alexandria, VA: Author. Retrieved from http://www.cswe.org/Accreditation/41865.aspx.

Council on Social Work Education (CSWE). (2011). *2010 statistics on social work education in the United States: A summary.* Retrieved from http://www.cswe.org/File.aspx?id=52269.

Daehn Zellmer, D. A., & Knothe, T. E. (2011). The use of criminal background checks in social work education. *Journal of Baccalaureate Social Work, 16*(2), 17–33.

Dalton, B., Stevens, L., & Maas-Brady, J. (2009). Surveying the BSW field director. *Journal of Baccalaureate Social Work, 14*(2), 17–29.

Dalton, B., Stevens, L., & Maas-Brady, J (2011). "How do you do it?" MSW field director survey. *Advances in Social Work, 12*(2), 276–288.

Dedman, D. E., & Palmer, L. B. (2011). Field instructors and online training: An exploratory survey. *Journal of Social Work Education, 47*(1), 151–161.

Haski-Leventhal, D., Gelles, R. J., & Cnaan, R. A. (2010). Admitting convicted felons to social work programs: Conceptual dilemmas and practices. *International Social Work, 53*(1), 87–100.

Homonoff, E. (2008). The heart of social work: Best practitioners rise to challenges in field instruction. *Clinical Supervisor, 27*(2), 135–169.

The Jed Foundation. (2008). *Student mental health and the law: A resource for institutions of higher education*. New York: Author.

National Association of Social Workers (NASW). (2008). *Code of ethics of the National Association of Social Workers*. Washington, DC: NASW Press.

Newman, B. S., Dannenfelser, P. L., Clemmons, V., & Webster, S. (2007). Working to learn: Internships for today's social work students. *Journal of Social Work Education, 43*(3), 513–528.

Pierce, D. (2008). *Field education in the 2008 EPAS: Implications for the field director's role*. Retrieved from http://www.cswe.org/File.aspx?id=31580.

Raskin, M., Wayne, J., & Bogo, M. (2008). Revisiting field education standards. *Journal of Social Work Education, 44*(2), 173–188.

Sowbel, L. (2012). Gatekeeping: Why shouldn't we be ambivalent? *Journal of Social Work Education, 48*(1), 27–44.

U.S. Government Accountability Office (GAO). (2003, March 31). Child welfare: HHS could play a greater role in helping child welfare agencies recruit and retain staff (GAO-03-357). Retrieved from http://www.gao.gov/assets/240/237373.pdf.

Valentine, D. (2004). Access to higher education: A challenge to social work educators. *Journal of Social Work Education, 40*(2), 179–184.

Wayne, J., Bogo, M., & Raskin, M. (2006). The need for radical change in field education. *Journal of Social Work Education, 42*(1), 161–169.

Wayne, R. (2004). Legal guidelines for dismissing students because of poor performance in the field. *Journal of Social Work Education, 40*(3), 403–414.

# 3

# Nontraditional Field Models

*Julianne Wayne, Marion Bogo, and Miriam Raskin*

A profession develops out of a past and into a future; it has a history and a destiny. Action is responsible when the challenges of the here and now are illuminated by a historical perspective and responded to with a sense of destiny. (Huebner, 1964, p. v)

This chapter will present three examples of nontraditional field models that can be executed by any social work program that requires master of social work (MSW) field instructors for its students. Utilizing MSW field instructors is required for all MSW programs and for bachelor of social work (BSW) programs that have elected to maintain this standard of teaching in field, but is not required at the BSW level. The models address field issues that many schools are facing: a shrinking number of qualified field instructors and agencies willing to participate in the education of social work students, intrinsic rewards that once motivated skilled practitioners to supervise students, rewards that are now outweighed by external pressures, and the transition of social work education to a framework of competencies and practice behaviors that presents a new challenge to many experienced field instructors. The models discussed are (1) a shared field instruction model (i.e., a greater use of task supervisors through the division of supervisory functions and group supervision); (2) a single-placement model (i.e., ability to complete mandated field hours in one placement rather than two); and (3) a delayed entry into field model (i.e., field begins following a semester-long simulation-based teaching at the school).

It is important that field directors understand the historical roots of the predominant field model and its limitations. The most widely used field instruction structure, of one agency-based MSW field instructor supervising one student, has its roots in the European tradition of training apprentices who were involved in philanthropic activities (Kendall, 2000). As social work education developed from the

1930s to the 1960s, psychodynamic theory supported the significance of the relationship of a single student and a single supervisor as the predominant field model. That theoretical formulation emphasized the importance of the interpersonal dynamics in the client–therapist relationship, and the parallels between that dyad and what transpires between field instructors and students.

The quasi-therapeutic approach to supervision emphasized the need to include discussion of the students' own personality traits as critical components of their becoming skilled practitioners. This early educational structure influenced the builders and leaders of the profession, as well as of social work field education. In subsequent years variations in the delivery of field education have occurred in response to new knowledge, theories, and changes in academia and in social and economic realities. From the 1960s to the 1980s the number of social work programs mushroomed and social service agencies expanded. Caseloads were manageable, most students were not employed while attending school, and employment-based placements were not yet on the horizon. Under these conditions a field instructor was able to accommodate several students (sometimes from different schools) and provide individual and/or group supervision.

At the same time, economic and societal unrest spawned many grassroots agencies that had community leaders assume positions in social service agencies even though many of the staff did not hold credentials from institutions of higher education. In the early 1970s the Council on Social Work Education (CSWE) accredited the first baccalaureate programs. The CSWE did not require undergraduate students to be supervised by an MSW, and graduate programs recognized the potential of exceptional educational placement opportunities in the newly developed advocacy, substance abuse, and mental health agencies. Without an MSW on the staff, field directors eager to utilize these new agency partners again varied the predominant field model but remained within the approved standards. In this model students had a non-MSW task supervisor who assigned cases, guided students through agency policy, and helped students with service provision. The standards required, however, that an MSW provide students with the social work perspective, supervise practice, and facilitate integration of theory and practice. The responsibility of MSW supervision was delegated to the schools of social work, and several methods were developed to make this model viable.

With the establishment of the CSWE in 1952 (Kendall, 2002), accreditation standards began to guide classroom content and field education requirements and structures. Programs were mindful to stay within approved standards. Based on factors such as location, size, resources, and student demographics, schools began to experiment with how they offered the field component. Some variations of the traditional model included utilization of both concurrent and block placements, enrollment in coursework during the academic year with the practicum component of the curriculum offered in a block during the summer, and a delay entering field while students learned skills in a skills lab (the delay ranged from a few weeks to an entire semester). Students working full-time and attending school full-time had become common at the end of the twentieth century and the beginning of the twenty-first century. This led to the introduction of evening and weekend placements. Periodic recessions, an influx of new immigrants, returning veterans, and single parents attending college made it necessary for students to remain employed while in school. Agencies were interested in social work students that spoke the languages and understood the cultures of new population groups. The profession also wanted to reach out to minority students who had special contributions to make to agencies and clients. Schools worked hard to make social work education accessible to those with fewer resources. To respond to many societal changes, the accreditation standards introduced an option that would permit students to use an employment site as a field placement, providing that the site met specific criteria.

The first decade of the twenty-first century has passed and a variety of conditions again challenge the prevalent field model. Issues related to agencies include unmanageable caseloads, supervisors unable or unwilling to take on yet another responsibility, reduction of funding sources from the local to the federal level, and the complexity of client problems and challenges. Students struggle with available time to read, study, complete the required number of field hours, and support themselves and their families by working full time (Wayne, Bogo, & Raskin, 2006). In 2014 the country still faces significant adverse economic conditions. Because of the risk of becoming unemployed for long periods of time, students do not leave their jobs. The economic crisis in the first decade of the twenty-first century produced large numbers of evictions of families who could not pay their mortgages, a rise in the homeless population, and educational programs trying to adapt to changes in agencies, student populations, technology, and environmental factors. Field programs have adapted in the past by implementing nontraditional and innovative field models. In this millennium, schools are reexamining their long-standing policies and structures of their field programs.

In many parts of the country, field education has to deal with students who request to be placed in agencies that do not impose on their very limited free time; supervisors who are willing to supervise a student due to budget cuts that require taking on more cases; and field directors who place students twelve months per year due to a perceived accreditation mandate that students must have two different placements and cannot remain in the same agency for the two years of an MSW program. Wayne et al. (2006) advocate the need for radical change in field education and believe that the challenge of "accommodating students often leads to educationally compromised field arrangements" (p. 164). Field directors must look at their field programs and consider changes that allow for implementation of nontraditional field models that can bring field education closer to a better fit with signature pedagogy.

## Shared Field Instruction Model

Most social work programs adhere to the objective requirements of eligibility for instructors to serve as a field instructor for MSW students (i.e., an MSW and often two years of post-MSW experience). Because of the current difficulty in finding volunteer field educators who meet these criteria, and limited field office resources to carry out a more selective process (e.g., letters of reference and personal interviews), social work programs add few other formal requirements. Yet the objective criteria alone do not guarantee that all field instructors are master practitioners/educators. In spite of field education being designated as the signature pedagogy of social work education, not all students have excellent field instructors. The challenge remains to find ways to enable those identified as skilled field educators to work with more than one (or two) students in any given period.

The shared field instruction model of field education reduces the ratio of MSW field instructors to students and potentially contributes to higher-quality field instruction than results from the arrangement of a single field instructor per student. It will elaborate and add specific guidelines for the implementation of shared responsibilities between task supervisors and MSW field instructors. Additionally, it includes the value of group supervision as an educational structure that could further expand the use of skilled MSW practitioners/educators.

### Division of Supervisory Functions

Supervision has long been conceptualized as comprising three separate major functions: administrative, supportive, and educational (Kadushin & Harkness,

2002). The traditional model of field instruction holds each student's field instructor responsible for all these functions. In actuality, there is considerable overlap of these functions that would make it difficult to clearly separate the responsibilities that are part of each function. For example, evaluation is considered an administrative function but is also an integral and critical component of the educational process. Helping students engage in critical thinking and an ongoing problem-solving process is an educational function that is also supportive of students facing the challenges of practice.

However, while it may be limiting to view these functions as if they were displayed in a spotlight without the possibility of seeing anything beyond the lit area, the separate functions and their components can also be viewed as if displayed by a floodlight, which highlights certain aspects but also allows one to see the peripheral, related components. This view of the three functions permits the development of supervisory partnerships that allow the task supervisor and the field instructor to each have both primary and overlapping focuses in their work with a student.

## The Task Supervisor

There are many valuable educational opportunities in settings that are unavailable to social work students, either because the MSWs on staff cannot take the number of students that could take advantage of them, or because they do not employ MSWs. In these instances, many programs have arranged to have the day-to-day supervision carried out by non-MSW task supervisors with undergraduate or graduate degrees in fields and disciplines that prepare them for work in that particular setting. "In cases in which a field instructor does not hold a CSWE accredited social work degree, the program assumes responsibility for reinforcing a social work perspective" (CSWE, 2008, Accreditation Standard [AS] 2.1.6, p. 10). The required MSW perspective can be provided by others with an MSW who then do not have to attend to many aspects of the students' educational and agency-required activities. They would need to provide less time and attention than if they had full responsibility for all aspects of the student's experience.

## Task Supervisors with Graduate Degrees

The literature that defines professions and professionalism describes a shared foundation of values, practice skills, and, in some instances, a shared knowledge base. The shared criteria of a profession include self-awareness and professional use of self, focused interaction with client systems that are aimed at meeting professionally established goals and objectives, belief in the worth and dignity of each individual, and the need for a nonjudgmental stance toward those being served. All professionals are expected to demonstrate administrative responsibility related to agency expectations (e.g., agency documentation, time management, and general professional demeanor). It is reasonable to assume that a task supervisor with a graduate degree in a related profession (e.g., marriage and family therapy or a master's in counseling) would be able to promote these aspects of professional development. Each student would still need reinforcement of the social work competencies and practice behaviors.

### The Social Work Perspective

There is value in identifying the special contribution the MSW field instructor would provide. The social work perspective includes a commitment to competencies and practice behaviors that go beyond the aspects of work with individuals, groups, and families that are emphasized in many related professions. No matter what social work students choose as their specialization within the profession (i.e., micro or macro practice), they are required to gain skills that advance human rights and social and economic justice, apply social work ethical principles to guide professional practice according to standards of the National Association of Social Workers' *Code of Ethics* (National Association of Social Workers, 2008), engage in policy practice to advance social and economic well-being, and respond to contexts that shape practice. Field instructors need to provide opportunities for students to integrate these aforementioned areas into field instruction.

### Respective Responsibilities of the Task and MSW Instructors

Following are guidelines for the areas to be addressed by each party in its collaborative educational efforts. The exact balance of the responsibilities described could shift when the task supervisor and the MSW field instructor take the special skills of each person into account. For example, the macro principles described above could also be taught by task supervisors whose professional preparation includes attention to these factors as part of their profession's mission.

### Shared Responsibilities of the Task Supervisor and the Field Instructor

- Develop the educational contract with the student: identify the educational objectives, the planned assignments, and the respective roles and responsibilities of the student, the supervisor, and the field instructor.

- Maintain ongoing communication to share perceptions of the student's progress and to update and refine educational objectives as the year progresses.

- Discuss the student's progress and future educational objectives when preparing the formal end-of-semester field evaluations. The MSW has final responsibility for the evaluation.

### Responsibilities of the Task Supervisor

- Meet with the student every week and provide general supervision of service delivery.

- Oversee the administrative aspects of the student's performance (e.g., orientation to the agency, attendance, time management, required agency record keeping, and usual reports for supervision required by the agency).

- Select specific assignments (cases, groups, community, and policy projects) throughout the year.

- Help the student develop a focused agenda for the meeting with the MSW field instructor. This agenda could include a review of materials produced especially for educational purposes and a focus on social work competencies and practice behaviors that the student needs to strengthen.

### Responsibilities of the MSW Field Instructor

- Approve the educational contract.

- Be aware of the student's assignments and consult with the task supervisor on the appropriateness of those assignments.

- Review materials the student writes for educational purposes (e.g., process recording, logs).

- Focus on social work competencies and practice behaviors that the student needs to strengthen.

- Help the student link social work values, research, and theory to practice.

- Evaluate the student's work at the end of the semester.

Once the option of a division of supervisory functions and tasks is accepted it becomes easier to develop a range of field instruction models that permit non-MSW field teachers to assume responsibility for various aspects of field instruction, freeing up the MSW field instructor to provide more-focused supervision in less time per student than is currently required. The greater use of group supervision would further expand MSW teaching resources. Unlike field seminars, group supervision focuses on actual practice behaviors between students and their clients. It focuses on student self-awareness, effective application of appropriate practice behaviors to meet the agreed-on goals, and use of process and/or digital recordings as the basis for the supervisory process. Group supervision, unlike many field seminars, does not include activities such as résumé writing, content such as nonpractice-related general issues discussed with task supervisors, and interpersonal problems with other staff.

### Greater Use of Group Supervision

Individual supervision remains the dominant structure in social work field education. There are special contributions, however, that students can make to each other and to the instructor that are not available in exclusive teacher–student relationships (Wayne & Cohen, 2001). In recognition of this, Shulman's (2005) concept of signature pedagogy includes student-to-student accountability in his criteria of any profession's signature pedagogy. He also stresses the importance of avoiding educational experiences that permit learning-teaching processes to occur under a "cloak of invisibility" (p. 22). He defines signature pedagogy as eschewing dependence on learning–teaching situations that are mostly carried out in the privacy of the teacher–student interactions. Finally, accountability to peers has been defined as a criterion of a profession. The very structure of group supervision fosters this dimension.

Following are additional contributions of group supervision (Wayne & Cohen, 2001).

**All of Us are Smarter Than Any of Us.** Any discussion of the value of group supervision would do well to begin with the adage that all of us are smarter than any of us. Many classroom teachers have had the experience in which the results of joint problem-solving efforts were superior to the solution the teacher alone was prepared to offer. The different perspectives and thoughts that each participant brings often create a synergism that enhances the educational process.

**Creating New Behavioral Norms.** Some behaviors are taught through education and others through socialization. Social work programs rely on both approaches. It is one thing for a field instructor to repeatedly remind a student that he or she needs to complete preparations for supervisory sessions, such as process recordings and videos, in a timely manner. There is another dynamic involved when one is a member of a group whose members are dependent on using such materials as the basis for that week's group supervision session. In such instances preparing the necessary materials may well become the norm of the group. The mutual interdependence of group members is a strong motivator for incorporating these professional behaviors.

**Learning through Modeling.** In addition to the field instructor teaching through modeling professional behavior, students can serve as models to each other. There is no such thing as responding to a single group member. Every other member learns from each exchange, as well. As students receive positive reinforcement from the field instructor and from peers, those skills that further their professional competence influence the other students.

### Implementing the Shared Supervision Model

The major criterion of any MSW field instructor is that he or she is recognized as a highly skilled practitioner and educator. Once the ideas of split supervision and group field instruction have been accepted, master practitioners/educators could teach effectively while spending less time with each student than is traditionally expected. With this in mind, several students could be placed in a field setting that can be developed as a training center (Bogo & Globerman, 1995). They would each be assigned to a task supervisor and a single MSW field instructor. The MSW field instructor could be a staff person with a special interest and talent in field teaching and who could be excused from other responsibilities. The agency stands to benefit from such an arrangement because of the contributions made by students and the potential for collaborative activities with the social work program involved (Bogo & Globerman, 1999). MSW field instructors could also be drawn from volunteers who serve on the boards of directors of agencies, faculty members, alumni, and retired social workers. Private practitioners sometimes volunteer as field instructors for students in an agency placement because of their commitment to education and the intrinsic rewards of the role. Some programs hire MSW field instructors to provide the social work perspective and curriculum to students placed in agencies that have no MSWs but that could provide valuable micro and macro field assignments. Finally, in instances where a grant is secured (e.g., Title IV-E Child Welfare Grants), financial support for an MSW supervisor may be included in the budget.

Following is an example of how the above arrangement could be structured. Five students could be placed in a single agency (a training center), with each assigned to his or her own task supervisor. The students could share the same MSW field instructor. The task supervisors could attend to the aspects identified earlier in this chapter. The field instructor could hold group supervision sessions every other week and meet individually with each student for one hour on alternate weeks. This hour-long session would be used to review a focused agenda.

This model would permit a master practitioner/educator to serve as field instructor for five students in fewer hours per month than would be required in the one-to-one single field instructor structure. The specific number of hours could be determined according to the situations and requirements of particular social work programs and agencies. A staff or faculty member from the students' social work program could serve as an agency liaison and would be available to participate in dealing with educational problems that might arise.

## Single-Placement Model

Many programs on both levels require more hours than the minimum stated in accreditation standards (400 hours for BSW and 900 hours for MSW). Although most programs commonly expect students to divide this time between two different placements, the accreditation standards permit them to spend all their hours in one placement. Major advantages of placing students in two different settings include providing students with the opportunity to better appreciate the breadth of the profession, and adding depth to their social work skills by applying competencies and practice behaviors to different populations and problems. The difficulty in finding suitable settings has led some field education directors to reexamine this practice and to identify the gains of permitting students to remain in a placement that offers a high-quality education that provides a range of different educational experiences. Such an arrangement could especially be considered for students who enter their educational program with prior work experience in one or more social service settings.

While the impetus for considering this placement option may come from the challenges of finding suitable settings, there are educational benefits as well. Remaining in a single placement reduces the time students spend in becoming oriented to new settings. The reassignment within the same setting to a different field instructor and area of agency practice permits students to more quickly lose the self-consciousness that usually accompanies entering into a new learning arena. The reduced self-consciousness frees students to focus more directly on matters that contribute to their professional development (Reynolds, 1985).

Continuing in a placement also permits students to be given long-term assignments and to remain with clients who require ongoing care. These clients are usually assigned different professionals throughout their months or years in social service systems. This phenomenon is notable in many fields, including child welfare, substance abuse, and mental health. Students who work on macro level assignments often finish their part of a project before the entire project has been completed. There is much new learning that can take place as the student participates in different phases of a single person's care or a project's trajectory. There are also administrative advantages to a single placement model. The social work program is assured of maintaining and possibly strengthening its relationship with a desirable agency, and it reduces the time and energy that goes into finding an additional, suitable placement.

The above discussion has offered possible options for field placement arrangements. There are other field arrangements that can be created that meet the Educational Policy and Accreditation Standards (EPAS) standards (Bronstein & Kelly, 1998; Coulton & Krimmer, 2005; CSWE 2008; Ivry, Lawrence, Domron-Rodriguez, & Robbins, 2005; Muskat, Bogo, & Perlman, 2011; Poulin, Silver, & Kauffman, 2006). Programs do not need to look the same or offer only one single arrangement of their own. Aside from the value of the suggested specific approaches, the discussed arrangements also demonstrate that nontraditional models can be created to meet the educational and administrative needs that programs face today.

## Delayed Entry into Field Model

Some schools use a delayed entry model for field education. In this arrangement, students do not enter the field for the first few weeks or even for an entire first semester. While many undergraduate programs offer practice skills laboratories, the aim of these laboratories is largely to teach interviewing skills, relying on role-play scenarios between students. This use of delayed entry can be enhanced by using systematic simulated experiences in practice courses to provide a strong foundation to prepare students to engage productively in practice and learning when they enter the field. When field directors negotiate with agencies and field instructors who are reluctant to offer practicum to inexperienced students, they can point out that students have already been taught some foundation skills.

It may be possible in a delayed entry model to provide educational experiences that provide a firm foundation of beginning competence for students by using simulation in teaching. Such experiences would respond in part to field instructors' critique of educational programs' delegation of the "primary responsibility to the field practicum for developing and evaluating students' self-awareness, professional use of self, ability to self-assess, and level of practice competence" (Bogo, Regehr, Power, & Regehr, 2007, p. 109). When commencing their field practicum, students would still need assistance from their field instructors to transfer their practice knowledge and skills to the real-life situations they encounter in practice. Field instructors, however, have observed that students who have had these educational experiences are more able to engage with clients.

## Using Simulation in Practice Courses

Simulation refers to situations that are designed to imitate or represent real-life professional experiences that students are likely to find in their field of study. Simulation in social work generally involves actors (or drama students) who are trained by simulation educators or by social work instructors to enact the role of a particular client in a scenario. These scenarios are designed by social work instructors to reflect the type of social work situations students are likely to encounter in the field. The scenarios present information and agency context, relevant background information, emotional state of the client, and some orientation of the simulator to what the teacher is attempting to accomplish. Human simulators can also be trained to provide feedback to students from the perspective of the client being portrayed.

Simulation-based experiences differ from traditional courses where the emphasis is on knowledge acquisition, theoretical content, and critical analysis. In simulations, the focus can include socializing students to think and perform as competent social workers; to integrate values and ethics; and to learn theory, research evidence, and practice skills. The EPAS competency-based framework emphasizes education that results in students who are able to demonstrate their knowledge, values, and skills in complex practice behaviors (CSWE, 2008). Accordingly, the use of human simulation in teaching and in assessment of learning can provide supplemental and valued learning that bridges the program offerings in the school and field education in community settings. This simulation can be expanded to systematically integrate generic and specialized knowledge about practice, populations, and diversity in a wide range of courses.

In the design of structured simulations, instructors can focus on specific concepts and related performance behaviors they are trying to teach along with underlying values, knowledge frameworks, and empirical findings. Where students have the opportunity to work with trained simulators, they can practice the specific way in which these concepts are enacted through helping processes and skills in a deliberate, intentional, and focused manner. Additionally, they may be able to practice many times, without adverse effects on clients. Repetitive practice has been shown to lead to a mastery level in a range of learning activities when combined with external constructive feedback (Ericsson, Krampe, & Tesch-Römer, 1993; LeBlanc et al., 2011).

In classroom courses using simulation, instructors can structure content and address concepts and skills in a systematic manner. This can facilitate students' learning foundation competencies but is always one step removed from the real world of practice, where learning is stimulated by the unique circumstances of assigned clients in the particular setting. Field instructors aim to select assignments so that students can learn the expected competencies and focus their teaching not only on the circumstances presented in unique client situations, but also on the learning objectives required by the university program. Having some mastery of foundation competencies at the beginning of field can help students make better use of the learning provided when meeting the distinctive complexities presented by assigned clients.

A critical review of studies found that students in simulation-based social work courses achieve learning outcomes and are enthusiastic about the educational experience, as are instructors (Logie, Bogo, Regehr, & Regehr, 2013). Recent studies using simulation in social work have shown its effectiveness in teaching cultural competence (Lu et al., 2011), developing direct practice skill in undergraduate students (Rawlings, 2012), and teaching and assessment of performance of complex practice behaviors and integration of theory and practice in graduate students (Bogo et al., 2011; Bogo et al., 2012).

One approach to using simulation to teach elements of social work practice is to locate a simulation-based set of courses in a delayed-entry field model. In the academic term prior to field, students enroll in two companion courses. (For administrative reasons, these courses are designated and graded separately, but they are provided in an integrated manner, on the same day, and are taught by the same instructor to the same group of students.) The courses introduce key concepts in direct social work practice and demonstrate how these concepts are employed in practice through systematic use of video recordings and the conducting of interviews by the instructor with simulated clients. Instructors also construct case scenarios that are authentic and provide illustrations of the course material and related competencies to be mastered. They engage trained actors (or drama students) to portray these client situations and structure opportunities for students to practice, receive feedback, and develop their ability to use concepts and skills in these simulated practice scenarios. Learning activities and assignments involve students systematically analyzing their interviews, linking theory and practice. For example, regardless of the length of the simulation, students videorecord their interviews and select a ten-minute segment to transcribe verbatim. Based on the key concepts taught in the course, students are expected to label and discuss examples in the interview where they intentionally tried to use particular concepts in practice. Students also discuss and evaluate their efforts noting where they were successful, using the data in the interview to support their conclusions. Furthermore, students are instructed to discuss and develop alternative, more-effective approaches to respond to the client. Students are expected to comment on their efforts to explain to the client the nature of collaboration, as well as to identify how they used interviewing skills in this regard. Instructors can structure teaching and vary simulations to consider issues in relationship building when clients are mandated or voluntary; when there is significant diversity between the client and the student (by virtue of age, sexual orientation, ethnicity, race, religion, immigrant status, and ability); when the agency context affects their work (e.g., short-term service, risk assessment, referral service, or intake for a longer service); or when clients are not agreeable and forthcoming in the interview, and instead present with great sadness, anger, or hostility.

### Simulation as Bridge to the Field

A study was conducted that used both simulation to examine assessment of student learning, and an Objective Structured Clinical Examination (OSCE) adapted for social work (Bogo et al., 2012). To account for bias in grading produced by the relationship between the instructor and the student, an instructor on the teaching team other than the student's instructor rated the student performance on the

OSCE. The rater subsequently forwarded the rating scales and a brief narrative to the course instructor for inclusion in the student's final evaluation in the course.

Bogo et alia (2012) found a wide range of student performance scores on the OSCE, indicating that the OSCE captured differences in student competencies, in contrast to the grade inflation seen in field evaluation scores. Correlation analysis revealed an association between OSCE scales and field final evaluations. All students who did poorly in the field also did poorly on the OSCE, although there were a number of students who performed poorly on the OSCE but did well in the field. Students reported feeling more confident in their abilities and skills to work with clients after being tested on the OSCE.

Since these courses focus on preparing students for field learning, the course coordinator, the teaching team, the field director, and the director of the master's program created a structured link to the field. At the end of the courses, the student's instructor reviews all of the student's work in simulations, including performance on the OSCE. The course instructor completes a written evaluation that consists of specific details about areas of mastery, areas for future growth and development, and any suggestions for learning (e.g., the need to take more initiative or more opportunity to observe and debrief).

Students and field instructors are informed that students will bring these evaluations to the practicum for use in developing the learning plan and contract. Faculty field liaisons review the learning contract in relation to these evaluations to ensure that the field practicum will address key areas identified for attention. The intention is to build on the knowledge gained in the school about the student's learning and performance. In summary, these simulation-based learning courses provide students with a foundation for engaging with clients in the field and also provide an educational assessment and some direction for field instructors.

## Implementation

Field directors are in the unique position to advocate on behalf of field instructors who would welcome increased preparation of students for practice. They can also link the importance of more opportunities for students to learn practice competence in the educational program to the available quality of field practicum, as presented at the beginning of this chapter. These efforts will be strengthened if teaching faculty are part of this analysis and change effort.

The field director might work with a classroom instructor to pilot an innovative course similar to that described in this chapter and attempt to involve a number of classroom faculty in considering the use of a delayed-entry model to provide opportunities for students to develop practice competence. Use of the time afforded in a delayed-entry model to provide a firm foundation of practice knowledge and skill through simulation in practice courses appears highly consistent with the competency-based educational framework in EPAS 2008.

## Conclusion

Examples of nontraditional field models can be gleaned from the history of social work education and the literature. The traditional model does not have to be abandoned to incorporate new ideas and still remain within standards. Generations of skilled social work professionals have been educated through the use of a field instructor supervising one student in a field site and repeating the model as the (MSW) student moves to a second field site for concentration year. Field directors, however, need to be alert to the changing times and encouraged to think and implement innovative, nontraditional ways to meet the challenges faced by schools of social work and by the practice community.

## Essential Readings

Bogo, M., Regehr, C., Logie, C., Katz, E., Mylopoulos, M., & Regehr, G. (2011). Adapting objective structured clinical examinations to assess social work students' performance and reflections. *Journal of Social Work Education, 47*(1), 5–18.

Ivry, J., Lawrance, F. P., Domron-Rodriguez, J., & Robbins, V. C. (2005). Fieldwork rotation: A model for educating social work students for geriatric social work practice. *Journal of Social Work Education, 41*(3), 407–425.

Wayne, J., Bogo, M., & Raskin, M. (2006). The need for radical change in field education. *Journal of Social Work Education, 42*(1), 161–169.

Wayne, J., & Cohen, C. (2001). *Group work education in the field*. Alexandria, VA: Council on Social Work Education.

# References

Bogo, M., & Globerman, J. (1995). Creating effective university-field partnerships: An analysis of two inter-organization models for field education. *Journal of Teaching in Social Work, 11*(1/2), 177–192.

Bogo, M., & Globerman, J. (1999). Interorganizational relationships between schools of social work and field agencies: Testing a framework for analysis. *Journal of Social Work Education, 35*(2), 265–274.

Bogo, M., Regehr, C., Katz, E., Logie, C., Tufford, L., & Litvack, A. (2012). Evaluating an objective structured clinical examination (OSCE) adapted for social work. *Research on Social Work Practice, 22*(4), 428–436.

Bogo, M., Regehr, C., Logie, C., Katz, E., Mylopoulos, M., & Regehr, G. (2011). Adapting objective structured clinical examinations to assess social work students' performance and reflections. *Journal of Social Work Education, 47*(1), 5–18.

Bogo, M., Regehr, C., Power, R., & Regehr, G. (2007). When values collide: Field instructors' experiences of providing feedback and evaluating competence. *Clinical Supervisor, 26*(1/2), 99–117.

Bronstein, L. R., & Kelly, T. B. (1998). Field education units: Fostering mutual aid in multicultural settings. *Arete, 22*(2), 54–62.

Coulton, P., & Krimmer, L. (2005). Co-supervision of social work students: A model for meeting the future needs of the profession. *Australian Social Work, 58*(2), 154–166.

Council on Social Work Education (CSWE). (2008). *Educational policy and accreditation standards* (rev. March 27, 2010/updated August 2012). Alexandria, VA: Author. Retrieved from http://www.cswe.org/Accreditation/41865.aspx.

Ericsson, K. A., Krampe, R. T., & Tesch-Römer, C. (1993). The role of deliberate practice in the acquisition of expert performance. *Psychological Review, 100*(3), 363–406.

Huebner, D. (1964). *A reassessment of the curriculum.* New York: Teachers College, Columbia University Press.

Ivry, J., Lawrance, F. P., Domron-Rodriguez, J., & Robbins, V. C. (2005). Fieldwork rotation: A model for educating social work students for geriatric social work practice. *Journal of Social Work Education, 41*(3), 407–425.

Kadushin, A., & Harkness, D. (2002). *Supervision in social work* (4th ed.). New York: Columbia University Press.

Kendall, K. A. (2000). *Social work education: Its origins in Europe.* Alexandria, VA: Council on Social Work Education.

Kendall, K. A. (2002). *Council on Social Work Education: Its antecedents and first twenty years.* Alexandria, VA: Council on Social Work Education.

LeBlanc, V. R., Bould, M. D., McNaughton, N., Brydges, R., Piquette, D., & Sharma, B. (2011). *Simulation in postgraduate medical education.* Retrieved from http://www.afmc.ca/pdf/fmec/18_LeBlanc_Simulation%20and%20 Technology.pdf.

Logie, C., Bogo, M., Regehr, C., & Regehr, G. (2013). A critical appraisal of the use of standardized client simulations in social work education. *Journal of Social Work Education, 49*(1), 66–80.

Lu, Y. E., Ain, E., Chamorro, C., Chang, C., Feng, J. Y., Fong, R., & Yu, M. (2011). A new methodology for assessing social work practice: The adaptation of the objective structured clinical evaluation (SW-OSCE). *Social Work Education, 30*(2), 170–185.

Muskat, B., Bogo, M., & Perlman, I. (2011). Making rotational field placements work: Review of a successful pilot of rotational field placements in hospital settings. *Journal of Practice Teaching and Learning, 11*(1), 5–18. doi:10.1921/ 175951511X651922.

National Association of Social Workers (NASW). (2008). *Code of ethics of the National Association of Social Workers.* Washington, DC: Author.

Poulin, J., Silver, P., & Kauffman, S. (2006). Serving the community and training social workers: Service outputs and student outcomes. *Journal of Social Work Education, 42*(1), 171–184.

Rawlings, M. (2012). Assessing BSW student direct practice skill using standardized clients and self-efficacy theory. *Journal of Social Work Education, 48*(3), 553–576.

Reynolds, B. (1985). *Learning and teaching in the practice of social work.* Silver Spring, MD: National Association of Social Workers.

Shulman, L. S. (2005). Pedagogies of uncertainty. *Liberal Education, 91*(2), 18–25.

Wayne, J., Bogo, M., & Raskin, M. (2006). The need for radical change in field education. *Journal of Social Work Education, 42*(1), 161–169.

Wayne, J., & Cohen, C. (2001). *Group work education in the field.* Alexandria, VA: Council on Social Work Education.

# PART II
## The Nuts and Bolts of Field Education

Chapters 4 through 8 focus on the practical aspects of directing a field program. The authors give comprehensive coverage to the fundamental processes, policies, and major considerations in decision making based on the current literature and best practices. The order of the chapters represents the flow of the administrative activities: developing and maintaining partnerships with practice settings, placing students, training and supporting field instructors, facilitating student learning between classroom and field, and, finally, evaluating student learning. The various roles and activities that a field director performs overlap and interact. While some students are being placed, another cohort is being monitored and evaluated. Simultaneously, new instructors are being recruited. If a placement is disrupted and a student is re-placed, all three processes overlap more intensively. Although there are differences between programs, the basic processes are adaptable.

Chapter 4, Developing and Maintaining Partnerships with Practice Settings, guides field directors in the tasks of recruiting, selecting, and evaluating setting; and the importance of crafting formal agreements with practice settings. The authors emphasize the value of marketing schools of social work to constituents and offer strategies for expanding the pool of educational opportunities for students. The authors, Cindy A. Hunter and Nancy Trantham Poe, promote the development of interorganizational partnerships that offer a more stable field structure where teaching, scholarship, and program renewal is a collaborative endeavor for all partners in the institutional arrangement. This ideal partnership contrasts with a unidirectional flow of knowledge and contributions from the university to the practice community that too often exists.

In chapter 5, Placing Students, Riva Zeff, Lynn Kaersvang, and Miriam Raskin address program policies on student admission to field, the placement process, and factors in decision making when placing students. The authors describe orientation, applications, and interviews as common practices that underpin an array of placement models. The authors recognize that field directors lack empirically tested processes and procedures for this time-consuming task. They discuss inherent challenges of placement disruptions and working with students who are experiencing academic difficulties. Finally, the authors argue that programs require criminal background checks, and argue that these need to become part of the next accreditation standards.

Field directors play an integral part in making the transition from class to field seamless. Chapter 6, Training and Supporting Field Instructors by Carolyn Knight, observes that a successful field placement is predicated on a working relationship between a student and a field instructor who is well trained in teaching the knowledge, values, and skills of the social work profession. Readers are presented with an in-depth analysis of the developmental nature of the field instructor–student relationship and associated tasks and skills of instruction as the students progress through their placement. The author's emphasis on the field instructor as educator assumes there is organizational support (e.g., adequate time and resources) to teach the elements of social work practice in their settings and to facilitate students' integration of the program's curriculum, competencies, and practice behaviors with their field experiences.

Julia K. Moen, Denice Goodrich Liley, and Sheila R. Dennis prepare field directors for their role in chapter 7, Facilitating Student Learning between Classroom and Field, by introducing learning theories that are integral to student growth toward competence. These theories underpin the teaching and learning process in field education and provide a framework for integrating theory and practice. Student reflection about their practice in systematic ways is an important learning process in field.

The ideal field delivery model, highlighted in both chapter 4 and chapter 7, is a collaborative partnership involving a synergistic learning exchange among students, field educators, faculty liaison, and university faculty. In this collaboration, failure to make a meaningful commitment by any partner can negate the work of the others. The authors envision the faculty liaison as a master teacher, related to student learning in both the university and the agency domain. Liaisons are encouraged to contribute to curriculum decisions, maintain communication with all partners, and collaborate on field education research and scholarship. In reality, liaison functions are carried out in numerous ways, often by adjunct part-time faculty; no standards exist for realizing this vision. The field director's leadership in working with liaisons and developing effective integrative seminars including the role of seminar in preparing reflective, competent social work practitioners concludes this chapter.

In chapter 8, Evaluation of Student Learning, Marion Bogo discusses the importance of understanding competence as a concept and the issues related to its assessment in the field. Evaluation of student performance is crucial for providing feedback that promotes learning and assessment of student competence for practice. Aggregate data from field evaluations can be used as outcome data indicating the degree to which students meet competencies and how the program is meeting its mission and goals. Bogo expands the notion of a collaborative partnership by involving experienced field instructors, students, liaisons, and practice faculty in building a school's competency model. Field directors are charged with training field instructors in understanding how generic competencies and practice behaviors fit with their practice settings, and then understanding how to assess what students are able to do.

In preparing field instructors to provide feedback and summative evaluation to students, field directors must attend to the meaning of each competency and the process of evaluation. The author describes and provides examples of challenges related to student evaluation. Marion Bogo's ground-breaking contribution to articulating and assessing competence in social work students is reflected in this chapter.

# 4

# Developing and Maintaining Partnerships with Practice Settings

*Cindy A. Hunter and Nancy Trantham Poe*

Field practicum is not "just another course" in social work education. Each program designates a field director with release time who is responsible for providing educational and administrative leadership for the field program (Council on Social Work Education [CSWE], 2008, Accreditation Standard [AS] 3.4.5). Other curricular areas are not mandated to identify policy coordinators or directors of practice. A significant responsibility of the field director is to design and implement strategies to recruit, engage, equip, support, and evaluate field instructors as partners in the education of the next generation of social workers. This partnership opens an opportunity for field instructors to influence the social work program by keeping faculty current on emerging practice issues.

Establishment of teaching relationships with outside entities is governed by accreditation standards and university regulations. As per accreditation, the field education program "Specifies policies, criteria, and procedures for selecting field settings; placing and monitoring students; maintaining field liaison contacts with field education settings; and evaluating student learning and field setting effectiveness congruent with the program's competencies" (CSWE, 2008, AS 2.1.5, p. 9). University policies govern matters of formal affiliation agreements, student insurance coverage, and requirements regarding enrollment status, handling of educational records, and endorsement of academic credit for the field practicum. Accreditation and university requirements compose the context in which the field director operates when involving new educational partners. This context necessitates that field directors manage interorganizational relationships and that they are sensitive to the stressors and strengths of practicum partners in order to maintain a corps of qualified field instructors and available placement sites.

"Field setting," "practice setting," and "practicum sites" are terms used interchangeably to refer to the agencies or organizations where field assignments take place. Developing initial and lasting relationships with practice settings that offer generalist and/or advanced practice experiences requires field directors to manage communication on multiple levels, depending on whether the site has: (1) a social worker instructing a student, (2) multiple social workers offering their time at the same setting, or (3) a more structured program that incorporates field-based students into the fabric of the agency. Workers volunteer their time in the first two situations, and they are likely to have teaching as part of their job description in the third situation (Bogo & Globerman, 1999). In every case there is a designated contact person on site who is authorized to coordinate practicum opportunities with whom field directors communicate. This person may also be the designated field instructor, the agency director, or an individual with the title of educational or volunteer coordinator.

Communication between the field director and the setting occurs at three levels. The first level of communication with a contact person on an organizational level involves field directors making contact for recruiting and vetting the site, sharing of practicum expectations, managing the memorandum of understanding (MOU), screening and approving the field instructor's credentials, and assessing the appropriateness of the learning environment. A second level of communication occurs between the field director and field instructors during orientation and training, and throughout the university–practice setting relationship. A third level occurs at the time of placement when the liaison steps in to develop a relationship with the student and field instructor; the liaison, in some cases, is a task supervisor.

The field director maintains oversight of the quality of the setting to provide opportunities for students to demonstrate required competencies and, ultimately, the final evaluation of the field instructor and setting, thus providing oversight of supervision. In large programs that span a wide geographical region for placements, the field director may manage a team of field staff who serve in territories to reach out to potential field settings, conduct interviews, and develop contracts with agencies in students' respective geographic areas. This chapter acknowledges the variations of field programs and setting configurations, and outlines overarching processes associated with developing and maintaining positive and productive educational affiliations among social work programs, practitioners, and agency settings.

## Recruiting Practice Settings and Field Instructors

It is ironic that field education, as a highly structured area of the social work curriculum, is also where programs necessarily abdicate significant instructional responsibility to community practitioners. As students move into field placement, primary guidance for their applied professional development transfers from academic personnel to volunteers who serve the vital role of field instructors. As such, an essential aim for field education is securing and maintaining a cadre of experienced and committed field educators in a variety of settings who possess a strong command for social work practice and knowledge of the curriculum, are capable of directing students in day-to-day service delivery, and want to teach and mentor students on an ongoing basis.

There is great variability in the manner by which settings and their instructors are brought into partnership with social work programs. Some programs allow or require students to locate and contact settings on their own and submit information to the field director for screening and final approval. Others designate agency identification and selection as an exclusive responsibility of field directors or field staff who manage this process in-house. There is a lack of literature that examines the merits of these divergent models. Commonly, field directors struggle with lack of quality field placements due to geography, competition, or saturation. Field directors can borrow from the field of marketing, tap nontraditional placements, or examine the structure of their field programs to overcome such placement barriers. Language from the field of marketing may sound foreign to social workers' ears, yet it offers innovative strategies for the recruiting challenges that field directors face.

Through a marketing lens, the social work program could be viewed as a product to be pitched to potential field settings whereby field directors share information on the school's unique qualities. Communication with settings should articulate what students bring to the table: hundreds of hours of service and a fresh perspective and energy. In addition, these students are potentially prescreened and trained candidates for employment following completion of the practicum or graduation from the program. Student presence also contributes to professional culture and professional development of the instructor (Globerman & Bogo, 2003). Incentives such as making university resources available to instructors, ongoing training with continuing education credit, library access, and consultation with faculty and liaisons may be attractive to settings as resources for staff development diminish. Individual professional growth and an obligation to contribute to the growth of the profession are factors encouraging social workers to supervise students (Globerman & Bogo, 2003). Field directors ought to consider these factors in any messages crafted to recruit field settings.

Field directors use these methods for reaching and communicating with potential field instructors in a formalized plan of action. Approaches for recruitment among different constituencies such as alumni, professional organizations, and social workers in agencies not yet related to the university include university publications, school Web sites, networking media, word of mouth, and cold calls to agencies. Any combination of these, such as cold calls to alumni or network media posts to professional organizations, should be carefully tailored: the message to alumni who have a sense of commitment to the institution is likely to look different from the message sent to a new agency or phone calls to social workers who may be unfamiliar with the school. Since accreditation standards allow for students to perform their field practicum in organizations where they are employed, these work places are another source for agency recruitment (CSWE, 2008, AS 2.1.8). The field director can also conduct periodic surveys of full- and part-time faculty for settings where they are consulting, working, or serving on boards. An additional way to expand the pool of practicum sites is to use nontraditional field models that allow a higher number of students per field instructor or use of an outside field instructor in settings that otherwise meet the criteria to work with students.

Routine environmental scans help to update field directors' understanding of the context of social work in their geographical catchment area and keep up with new and changing agencies through reports from sources such as United Way and the Council of Non-Profits. Honoring the definition of generalist practice, field directors can expand the pool of potential placements by considering macro opportunities for bachelor of social work (BSW) and first-year master of social work (MSW) students. Either a macro setting or a macro placement within an agency offers an experience that is predominantly indirect practice (political work, community organizing, administration, program and policy development and implementation, and networking). These activities are consistent with the preamble to the National Association of Social Workers' *Code of Ethics* (2008) and the Baccalaureate Program Directors' definition of generalist practice. Although the setting may or may not provide regular contact with vulnerable individuals, it is understood that engagement, assessment, intervention, and evaluation occur in larger client systems and that students must possess and demonstrate good relationship skills to effect desired change (Hunter & Ford, 2010). In their national study of BSW field directors (n=181), Hunter and Ford (2010) revealed that although there is widespread discomfort with these types of placements among field directors, more than half of the field directors are placing selected students in macro-oriented placements. Still, the proportion of students placed in indirect practice settings remains minimal, leaving room for growth in the pool of possible field settings.

Recruitment for international settings often occurs through a combination of personal or professional faculty contacts, formal university affiliation with international agencies, and occasionally through the students themselves (Pettys, Panos, Cox, & Oosthuysen, 2005). A guidebook on international field placements by Lager, Mathiesen, Rodgers, and Cox (2010) contributes substantial information regarding this process. Sample forms adapted to the unique needs of international institutional relationships can be accessed through this resource.

A consideration in recruitment is that practice settings and instructors must fully understand the investment they are being asked to make, including attentiveness to the educational process, regular time for supervision and communication with university personnel, space for students to work, and other specifications of the program. Instructors are concerned about the quality and ethical aspects of practice and will calculate the effort they are willing and able to expend. Where and how potential field instructors can find information about a school's field program is a strategic consideration. If the process is complicated or unknown, the prospective instructor might opt for another school of social work or other departments in the same university offering practicum students. An easily located online application and a swift, attentive response to applications from field staff are warranted. A word of caution regarding overrecruitment: a surplus of new settings that the program is not likely to use within two semesters risks wasting everyone's time because of turnover.

Evaluating the success of marketing the program extends beyond the initial number of placements gained. A survey about marketing efforts, targeting the recently recruited settings as well as those who did not sign on, will yield information for future recruitment efforts. Improvements will be based on feedback such as these: Did the field staff serve the needs of the field instructor? Did the field staff address concerns in a timely manner? How can students' readiness for field be improved? What facets of the communication exchange need revision? Answers to these questions would help to address field instructor concerns and improve the likelihood of future placements. Recruitment takes a great deal of a field director's effort and needs to be carried out in a cost- and time-effective manner.

Each of these recruiting efforts to develop field partnerships needs to be customized according to social work program context. Feature 4.1 illustrates what one field director learned about building relationships in a distance education program.

---

**Feature 4.1. Partnering from a Distance**

The Michigan State University School of Social Work has had an evolving distance education program since 1979. From an early car-net program where faculty drove to distant sites for classes and field visits, to our current statewide blended model composed of small learning communities connected through the Internet, interactive TV, and local relationships, the main campus has been solely responsible for quality field learning experiences at all sites. A few things we have learned:

- Acquire available resources. A quality distance field program can flourish with university and department support for the concept. Required program financing, a technology infrastructure on which to depend, and investment in the new community are essential to its success.

- Put relationships first. Invest energy into developing the important community connections and assess the buy-in potential of practice community leadership, early and often. Is there currently cohesion within the practice community? Will there be competition with other social work field programs that might feel threatened? What are the special cultural features of the community? How can the program be sensitive to the differences between campus and distance locations? Is there sufficient local social work expertise and supervision? By investing in relationships and gaining support for the program before the placement process begins, the program may address and likely avert potential barriers.

- Establish comparable programs. This is a key component for field program success as well as reaffirmation of accreditation. It is important that field policies established for the campus program apply equally to distance sites. Placement requirements and procedures, orientation and training, site visits and oversight, and evaluation and grading are all important considerations with regard to creating comparability among programs. Evaluative data can be helpful in assessing comparability. This feedback is important because openness to external and self-assessment with acceptance of change is a necessary component for any field education effort.

- View distance education as a community intervention. Any practice community will be affected in ideally positive and unpredictable ways by a university program's offering. Beyond the obvious increase in BSW and MSW practitioners and services in underserved communities, there is potential for new knowledge, interventions, and professionalism within agencies. University involvement may assist in bringing the practice community together through networking at orientation and continuing education events as well as offering part-time employment for local practitioners as coordinators and liaison field faculty.

Some final thoughts:

- Confidentiality and respect for proprietary information must be ensured; this best happens in the context of relationships.

- Lessons learned from distance sites are likely to lead to fine-tuning and improvement of policies, procedures, and curriculum for all programs.

- Adequate lead time and planning are essential because everything is more difficult and takes longer from a distance.

Jo Ann P. McFall, LMSW, RN
Associate Director for Field Education and Community Programs
School of Social Work
Michigan State University

## Screening Field Settings and Instructors

The search for quality field settings and instructors is an ongoing process. It runs simultaneously with a streamlined system of screening for suitability, formalizing the affiliation, and maintaining a relationship. Programs need a policy stating the criteria and process by which settings will be vetted prior to placing students. As part of the screening, field directors ensure that field instructors meet the minimum qualifications and criteria established by standards (CSWE, 2008, AS 2.1.6). Minimum criteria for practice settings are found in the Educational Policy and Accreditation Standards (EPAS), and programs are free to add additional requirements based on program goals and the learning needs of students (full time, part time, nontraditional, and online). MSW programs must explicate how a practice setting provides appropriate opportunities for students to demonstrate practice behaviors specific to competencies for advanced practice (CSWE, 2008, AS M2.1.2). The CSWE has developed curriculum resource guides offering examples of competencies for advanced practice in the areas of trauma, prevention of substance abuse disorders, clinical practice, gerontology, and military social work. Field directors can use these guides to identify criteria for selecting agencies for practica in these specializations (CSWE, 2013). BSW programs must screen field settings for opportunities that allow students to demonstrate core competencies and practice behaviors (CSWE, 2008, AS B2.1.2).

Programs must address the implicit curriculum by creating learning environments that help students understand and respect diversity (CSWE, 2008, AS 3.1). Field directors should seek practice settings that expose students to diversity in its many forms, demonstrate respect for the impact of difference on service delivery, and have field instructors who model cultural competence.

The process for screening field settings typically includes an application form to solicit information such as agency and program descriptions; how the agency welcomes diverse populations; names, credentials, and résumés of potential field instructors; and descriptions of learning opportunities available for students. Field staff review the application against program criteria and generally visit the site. Despite the understandable eagerness of signing up a new agency interested in serving as a field setting, careful screening for goodness of fit is advised. Placing a student in an environment that is not ready or adequately prepared to take on educational responsibilities can create a myriad of issues, such as having to remove and re-place a student or diplomatically discontinuing a setting that is interested in student placements. In screening a potential site, caution should be exercised in relation to:

- strict policies restricting student access to direct client contact or client records;

- understaffed agencies that need help but cannot provide adequate supervision; and

- agencies with high worker turnover. This may indicate a work culture that could significantly inhibit the student's learning and heighten the possibility of practicum disruption with a change of field instructor.

An additional criterion for a BSW program might state that field instructors with a BSW must have two years of postdegree social work experience before supervising a bachelor-level student. MSW programs develop criteria whereby the instructors demonstrate experience in the program's concentration areas. (See figure 4.1.)

### Figure 4.1. Agency Recruitment and Selection Checklist

Listed below are criteria for field directors to consider in screening settings. An acceptable site need not meet all these criteria. Social work programs may add to these based on program structure and competencies.

Field directors should screen possible settings for the following (James Madison University, 2013):

- A mission consistent with social work values and ethical principles
- The ability to provide generalist and/or advanced learning opportunities
- Institutional support for agency staff serving as field instructors to dedicate time to students
- Nondiscriminatory policies and practices regarding student eligibility for field placement
- Handicap accessibility
- Ability to provide learning experiences on micro, mezzo, and macro levels (as opposed to narrow training for one role)
- Opportunities for students to work directly with client systems
- Commitment to facilitate student demonstration of competencies
- Policies and plans for worker and student safety
- Experience with practicum students
- A commitment to diverse and vulnerable populations
- Sufficient space for students with adequate and appropriate privacy for carrying out work activities; adequate supplies; computer and agency online system access; and access to client and agency records appropriate to the learning experience
- Willingness to allow use of agency materials in classroom discussions and assignments, with an understanding that students will never remove records from the setting and that they will protect the confidentiality of those involved
- Qualified field instructors per accreditation standards with adequate time to:
  - Meet the educational needs of students, including orientation to the setting and its services; development of learning opportunities that include depth and variety; and regularly scheduling individual and/or group conferences
  - Communicate with the faculty liaison at periodic intervals to discuss student learning and performance
  - Attend appropriate social work program-sponsored field instructor training
- Willingness to prepare reports and evaluations as required by the social work program and described in a program's field practicum manual

Variation of state licensure regulations imposes other considerations for field site selection. In some states field instructors and even faculty must be licensed. It is important for field directors to identify the definition of practice in any given student's jurisdiction. For example, the licensing regulations in some states have had an impact on the kind of license a field instructor has—clinical or generalist. Field directors in schools situated close to the state line, who routinely place students in more than one state, are likely to have to negotiate different regulations. Licensed social workers who have been grandfathered in but who have no social work education would also pose a problem for programs in ensuring that field instructors hold a social work degree from an accredited program. Bibus and Boutté-Queen (2011) developed a systematic framework of analysis to guide students and faculty in learning about the role of regulation for practice.

## Formalizing the Relationship between the School and the Setting

The field manual and the MOU (also known as a letter of confirmation or memorandum of agreement) are two documents essential in the formal agreement process and ensure that all pertinent expectations and policies are expressly articulated. The MOU is the official contract between the university and field setting and outlines the basic provisions and expectations for the practicum experience. It is intended to capture and protect the interests of the school, student, site, designated field instructor, and client system. The signed MOU indicates that the university has approved the agency as a field site and the agency has accepted the school's policies.

Schools and regions handle the agreements differently. Some are made between the school and the field instructor rather than with the school and the field agency. The following are broad parameters for developing a useful agreement, adapted from Gelman (1990). Agreements should not be simply replicated between one school and another as a means of streamlining the process; the program must recognize and incorporate into the document the particular needs of each program. The language and provisions in the agreements should be straightforward; pertinent school administrators such as legal counsel, risk manager, and/or the contracts officer should review them. The agreements should define responsibilities of each party in such a way as to support and encourage quality education and quality service provision. Such agreements can serve to legitimize field liaison activities and allocation of faculty and agency staff time. The language used in agreements should be consistent with the provisions contained in the field manual, self-study materials, and requirements of accreditation standards. The field director should be sure that specific statements relating to safety and nondiscrimination are included in agreements between the school and settings.

## Maintenance of Relationships with Practice Settings

The goal in maintaining the collaboration with field instructors is to support their willingness to serve and to bring them into full partnership as coeducators. Field instructors need to be: (1) aware of the curriculum with an avenue to contribute to its design and renewal; (2) equipped to align field-based experiences with the program's mission, goals, and competencies; (3) knowledgeable of their role in providing learning opportunities for students to demonstrate practice behaviors; and (4) able to evaluate students on the social work competencies. Field instructors want and deserve information and input about enacting their teaching and mentoring role. By establishing a culture of collaboration between program faculty and community-based partners, field directors can enhance the academy–agency partnership.

Several scholars have investigated the issue of satisfaction and effectiveness of field instructors (Adler, McKinley, & Kuskowski, 2003; Bennett & Coe, 1998; Inkster & Ross, 1995). Drawing from these studies, field directors are advised to develop the role of field instructors beyond that of on-site task masters into positions regarded as instructors with university colleagues in social work education. Academy–agency linkages can reinforce such status by systematically supporting field instructors to embrace their role as educators and to participate as valued and essential contributors to the mission and goals of the social work program with which they are associated.

Practical avenues to strengthen the linkages include offering collaboration on research, inviting field instructors to the classroom as expert presenters and paying them an honorarium, creating student group projects that meet setting needs, consulting with field instructors for their significant input to curriculum changes, and inviting field instructors to serve on a field advisory committee. This level of inclusion goes beyond incentives currently used to attract field instructors such as library and fitness center privileges, free continuing education units, tuition waivers, letters of recognition, appreciation luncheons, appointments as non-stipend clinical faculty, and awards for field instructor or setting of the year.

From a macro perspective, field directors must keep up with the changing context of practice. Constant interaction with agencies and rotating field instructors on the field advisory committee keeps the field director's perspective fresh. Globerman and Bogo (2003) encourage universities to collaborate with agencies and professional organizations to create more resources for field education. These authors note that schools must find ways to collaborate with and support field settings. A focus on the organization's needs and an emphasis on reciprocity with the schools may enhance teaching programs, organizational commitment, and the quality of social workers' professional lives. In addition, the authors state this collaboration may provide the practice setting with educated and trained students as potential employees.

The challenges of advancing these relationships with field instructors are labor intensive. Fiscal reductions and the inevitability of tighter budgets for agencies and universities challenge conventional on-site visits and thick field manuals. It is imperative that the field director develop new and cost-effective means of communicating with field site personnel. Some social work programs have attached fees for students enrolled in the practicum to cover additional expenses such as criminal background checks, mileage reimbursement for faculty visits to the sites, and hiring liaisons. Fees are charged to student accounts much like lab fees are charged in the hard sciences. Not all universities support the fee-based approach; nonetheless, economic constraints imposed by tight budgets behoove field directors to explore the utility of different technologies for cost-effective ways to augment the face-to-face support necessary for field instructors' sense of satisfaction (Inkster & Ross, 1995).

A major factor in retaining dedicated field instructors and advancing their professional role is the support offered by the field liaison. Field instructor satisfaction is positively correlated with three aspects of the relationship with the faculty liaison: perceived availability, amount of contact, and provision of specific feedback to field instructors regarding their work with students (Bennett & Coe, 1998). Inkster and Ross (1995) found that field instructors desire a sense of "shared responsibility, clear expectations, and collaborative communication" (p. 12) between the academic unit and the practicum site. Responsibility for establishing these structures and dynamics belongs to the field director and field liaisons. A well-trained liaison team maximizes long-term relationships with practicum sites.

Although social work is a relationship-based profession, preserving the commitment of field instructors, especially in large and online programs, cannot depend solely on relationships between field staff and field instructors because of the sheer quantity of settings and instructors. Even in smaller schools the turnover of personnel in the academy and community calls into question the efficacy and sustainability of only relationship-based retention. One retention strategy is to provide stipends for field instructors; stipends would not replace the value of accrued social capital or other incentives, but would recognize the investment in student field education. This strategy could attract master teachers willing to educate students. In some programs field education credits are revenue generating, considering the faculty resources dedicated to field practicum. These funds would be used in financially supporting field instructors. Use of stipends for recruitment and retention of exceptional practitioners and teachers is an established practice in schools of education and nursing.

## Evaluation of Field Settings and Instructors

In a study of field education, Inkster and Ross (1995) identified collaborative communication as essential for positive student and supervisor outcomes. Field directors are responsible for developing and utilizing assessment tools that elicit feedback from students, field instructors, and faculty liaisons. The feedback reflects the expectations laid out in the MOU, field manual, and student experiences. Analysis of these data leads to improvement and change. Results of field data is critical when preparing the accreditation self-study and are often the impetus for curriculum change (CSWE, 2008, AS 4.03). Examples of field assessment tools include the following:

- Students' self-assessment of demonstration of the competencies

- Students' evaluation of the liaison

- Students' evaluation of the learning experience (setting and field instructor)

- Field instructors' final field evaluation of student demonstration of competencies

- Field instructors' evaluation of the interaction with the field program and liaison

- Liaisons' evaluation of each setting and field instructor

*we need to add this back in*

In addition, the stakeholders regularly provide informal feedback to the field director.

### Evaluation of Field Instructors

Evaluation of field instructors can be a sensitive area and points out the importance of preliminary groundwork to ensure that qualifications and expectations for instructors are clear. The field director reviews feedback about the setting and instructor from students and field liaisons, and shares the content, in some manner, with instructors. Within this communication channel, field directors walk a fine line between supporting field instructors, honoring student input, and maintaining the integrity of the academic experience.

Practice wisdom advises that one student's complaint of unmet expectations is usually not cause for alarm. However, a series of grievances or similar complaints from multiple sources should alert the field director to thoroughly evaluate the effectiveness of the setting or instructor. There are many reasons a field instructor or task supervisor may be ineffective. An instructor may not realize the academic expectations or may need further training. Field liaisons should be prepared to coach struggling field instructors and determine if shortfalls can be addressed through further training. Sometimes they cannot, and the field director has to be equipped to discontinue placing students with that field instructor.

Some instructors may be burned out and need a sabbatical from taking students; other long-term instructors who have become ineffective may need to retire from instruction. Given restructuring in agencies based on economic climate, the increased workload may overwhelm some field instructors and affect the time and attention available to instruct a student. Whether it is the field instructor, field liaison, field staff, or director initiating the parting of ways, field instructors should be given the respect they deserve so they can leave the service with dignity (McCurley, 2006). Some issues, such as total neglect of a student or boundary violations, should be documented and addressed with the appropriate administrator in the setting. Depending on the severity, a violation of this type might need to go to the state licensing board or the National Association of Social Workers. When possible, the field director, in collaboration with the liaison, should distinguish the problem with a field instructor from the problem with the setting itself by requesting the contact person not to place students under supervision of that particular social worker. Finally, in small agencies where there is only one field instructor and that person is ineffective, the field director should not continue to place students at that site.

## Maximizing Partnerships for Program Renewal

Located at the intersection of practice and the academy, field education is positioned to influence program renewal and curriculum change. Data garnered through field assessment tools inform faculty about the program's strengths and limitations. Field directors should be directly involved with program assessment, since field is one place where competencies and practice behaviors are measured. Data from assessment are used to "continuously inform and promote change in the explicit and implicit curriculum" (CSWE, 2008, Educational Policy [EP] 4.0).

Field directors enlist the assistance of experienced practitioners and master teachers to systematically improve the program. Field agencies adopt new interventions and policies as a response to mandates from federal and state governments, and from boards of directors, whereas the implications for practice of those mandates may take much longer to reach the classroom. Likewise, the academy is historically ahead of the practice community on research and theoretical models. Both class and field have roles to play in educating social work students. The communication and exchange of research and current practice realities acknowledge the context of practice and must systematically flow in both directions. For the purposes of program renewal, this entails more than community partners being asked to be a member of the field advisory committee that meets once or twice a year. Schools of social work need to devise concrete plans on how they will incorporate current practice knowledge with program renewal activities at the universities. Planned, ongoing, working groups of faculty, community partners, and administrators create a field–classroom partnership that is mutually accountable.

To recognize the importance of the practice community in the education of social work students, the authors propose that the next revision of EPAS EP 4.0 Assessment could be changed as shown in italics: "Data from assessment, *including feedback from regular planned communication with practice settings*, continuously inform and promote change in the explicit and implicit curriculum to enhance attainment of program competencies."

The program–faculty connection to field settings provides an avenue to continuous discovery, appraisal, and attention to the changing context. There are numerous examples of such partnerships in the literature. Carten and Finch (2010) illustrate an exemplary community partnership initiated by faculty who are committed to teaching, quality field learning, and contributing to the knowledge base in field and culturally competent practice with new immigrants. Their empirical study of a specialized community-based field unit, located in a New York City resettlement area, used surveys, content analysis of parent seminars, student learning contracts, and portfolios to provide rich data on community needs and the educational preparation of students for culturally competent practice. The field model bridged the learning of students in field and renewal of curriculum in the university, reflecting a commitment to evidence-based policies, practices, and service. Schools of social work can refer to successful models for building stronger partnerships.

## Conclusion

Conceptualizing field instructors as coeducators and full partners in social work education is not only appropriate but also essential. The onus is on field directors to create conditions by which field instructors are well versed in the curriculum as a whole, understand accreditation standards for social work field education, and are equipped to translate those mandates into meaningful experiences of service delivery for students. Field directors administer these conditions in their work with liaisons, field setting contacts, students, and the ever-changing cadre of field instructors. Creative collaboration with available field instructors, intentional marketing of programs, and multiple methods of monitoring effectiveness of field settings facilitate the work of developing and maintaining partnerships with practice settings and field instructors.

## Essential Readings

Bogo, M., & Globerman, J. (1999). Inter-organizational relationships between schools of social work and field agencies: Testing a framework for analysis. *Journal of Social Work Education. 35*(2), 265–274.

Globerman, J., & Bogo, M. (2003). Changing times: Understanding social workers' motivation to become field instructors. *Social Work, 48*(1), 65–73.

## References

Adler, G., McKinley, K., & Kuskowski, M. (2003). Field instructor perceptions of roles, rewards, and responsibilities. *Arete, 27*(1), 42–50.

Bennett, L., & Coe, S. (1998). Social work field instructor satisfaction with faculty field liaisons. *Journal of Social Work Education, 34*(3), 345–352.

Bibus, A. A., & Boutté-Queen, N. (2011). *Regulating social work: A primer on licensing practice.* Chicago: Lyceum Books.

Bogo, M., & Globerman, J. (1999). Inter-organizational relationships between schools of social work and field agencies: Testing a framework for analysis. *Journal of Social Work Education, 35*(2), 265–274.

Carten, A. J., & Finch, J. B. (2010). An empirically based field-education model: Preparing students for culturally competent practice with new immigrants. *Journal of Public Child Welfare, 4*(3), 365–385.

Council on Social Work Education (CSWE). (2008). *Educational policy and accreditation standards* (rev. March 27, 2010/updated August 2012). Alexandria, VA: Author. Retrieved from http://www.cswe.org/Accreditation/41865.aspx.

Council on Social Work Education (CSWE). (2013). *Accreditation.* Alexandria, VA: Author. Retrieved from http://www.cswe.org/Accreditation/EPAS Implementation.aspx.

Gelman, S. R. (1990). The crafting of fieldwork training agreements. *Journal of Social Work Education, 26*(1), 65–75.

Globerman, J., & Bogo, M. (2003). Changing times: Understanding social workers' motivation to become field instructors. *Social Work, 48*(1), 65–73.

Hunter, C. A., & Ford, K. A. (2010). Discomfort with a false dichotomy: The field director's dilemma with micro-macro placements. *Journal of Baccalaureate Social Work, 15*(1), 15–29.

Inkster, R. P., & Ross, R. G. (1995). *The internship as partnership: A handbook for campus-based coordinators and advisors.* Raleigh, NC: National Society for Experiential Education.

James Madison University. (2013). Memorandum of agreement, Field Practicum Manual. Retrieved from http://www.jmu.edu/socwork/practicum.html.

Lager, P. B., Mathiesen, S. G., Rodgers, M. E., & Cox, S. E. (2010). *Guidebook for international field placements and student exchanges: Planning, implementation, and sustainability.* Alexandria, VA: Council on Social Work Education.

McCurley, S. (2006). *How to fire a volunteer and live to tell about it.* Retrieved from http://www.worldvolunteerweb.org/resources/how-to-guides/manage-volunteers/how-do-i-manage-volunteers-additional-reading/doc/how-to-fire-a.html.

National Association of Social Workers (NASW). (2008). *Code of ethics of the National Association of Social Workers.* Washington, DC: Author.

Pettys, G. L., Panos, P. T., Cox, S. E., & Oosthuysen, K. (2005). Four models of international field placement. *International Social Work, 48*(3), 277–288. doi:10.1177/0020872805051705.

# Placing Students

*Riva Zeff, Lynn Kaersvang, and Miriam Raskin*

Placing students is a cornerstone of a school of social work. An effectively run, professional, organized, and fully resourced operation can have an immense impact on student satisfaction, course completion, community relations, and program accreditation. The placement of students is an intricate dance—the steps must meet the Council on Social Work Education's (CSWE) 2008 Educational Policy and Accreditation Standards (EPAS), as well as the mission and goals of the social work program, practice settings, and students. The success of the field placement process depends, in part, on the field directors' ability to obtain the commitment of an extensive array of qualified field sites and field instructors to accept students whose ages, life and educational experiences, and practice skills vary extensively.

There are many steps to complete before a student placement is considered accomplished. An information management system to organize data and to use in assessment is becoming a necessary tool for the field director to use, particularly in medium and large programs. A field director would be foolhardy to think there is a magic wand somewhere in the field office that creates perfect placements. Since the wand has yet to be found, experience, field literature, research, and mentors can help guide the field director. There is an inevitable balancing act between the ideal placement and the realities.

The social work literature has reported the factors that contribute to a satisfactory placement. Success has been defined as the grade received, the relationship between student and field instructor, or the skills and knowledge accrued by the student in the professional setting (Bogo, 2010). The relationship between the student and the field instructor influences the student's professional identity and affects the student's desire to remain in the social work profession (Barretti, 2007; Fortune, McCarthy, & Abramson, 2001; Knight, 1996). Suanna Wilson (1981) described an effective placement as a fit of students' personalities, desires, experiences, and

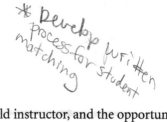

*Develop
process for written
matching for student*

learning styles with the teaching style of the field instructor, and the opportunities available in the practice setting. The growth of online programs has made it less feasible to incorporate some of these elements in placement decisions.

This chapter describes examples of and the challenges that accompany placement policies, procedures, and processes. These examples apply to bachelor of social work (BSW) and master of social work (MSW) programs of various sizes, geographic locations, student populations with a variety of needs, and types of programs (e.g., online). A discussion of gatekeeping and its relationship to the placement process concludes the chapter.

Almost thirty years ago an empirical study to determine whether placing students was an art, a science, or guesswork was conducted (Raskin, 1985). In the intervening years, accreditation standards have undergone several iterations, technology was introduced to assist with managing data and placements, and models have developed that allow students to seek and secure their own placements. Social work education still lacks best practices for placing students. What the reader will encounter in the following pages are some common practices, but no empirically tested model of processes or procedures for placing students. "Are variables (or factors) . . . being employed in field placement decisions, which are not significantly related to field work outcomes"? (Raskin, 1985, p. 56). It remains unclear if and which placement variables are significantly related to student outcomes. The move to competency-based social work education necessitates that the above question be empirically answered and that field placement, re-placement, and termination of students from field move toward a more scientifically based model. Achieving such a model can support the CSWE's aspirational goal of field education as the signature pedagogy of social work education (Wayne, Bogo, & Raskin, 2010).

## Admission to Field Education

Programs are required by the CSWE to develop and implement criteria for admission to field (CSWE, 2008, Accreditation Standard [AS] 2.1.4), but these criteria do not have to be consistent from program to program. Both new and experienced field directors should examine the existing criteria of their program and determine if changes, additions, or deletions are necessary. Policies and procedures for selecting field settings, selecting field instructors, and placing students are also mandated (CSWE, 2008, AS 2.1.5), but each school is responsible for development and the unique implementation of its guidelines. Policies provide the conceptual framework in which procedures can evolve to guide the placement and monitoring of students in the field.

Common admission criteria utilized by BSW field programs consist of, but are not limited to, (1) a completed field application including a résumé; (2) a required minimum overall GPA, and minimum grades in required social work courses; (3) submission of professional references; (4) an interview; (5) National Association of Social Workers (NASW) membership; (6) acquisition of malpractice insurance; (7) submission of a criminal background report; and (8) satisfactory performance in a junior-level placement or service-learning experience (Gibbs & Blakely, 2000). Additional academic criteria may address students' ability to be self-reflective, engage in effective working relationships, benefit from supervision, cope with stress, appreciate diversity, hold a value system congruent with the NASW *Code of Ethics* (2008), and exhibit adequate ability to express themselves orally and in writing. The academic criteria can be more difficult to ascertain for online programs. Mechanisms such as mandatory online interviews with field office personnel, personal essays, and detailed reference letters that address professional behavior can be used in these programs as criteria for admission to field.

Admission to field in MSW programs is generally automatic if a student has been admitted to the school of social work. Many of the BSW criteria are used by MSW programs. More emphasis may be given to work and volunteer experience and less to past GPA. Requiring the BSW field evaluation has become a common practice for advanced-standing applicants. Where feasible, it is important for the field director to be on the school's MSW admission committee or to maintain a relationship with its members. The field director apprises the committee about available accommodations in the community, new opportunities with diverse populations, limitations of the local practice community, licensing regulations that may affect applicants, and the type and number of practice sites available for the incoming cohort of students. In some circumstances, the field office is separated from the admissions process; valuable information and time can be lost with such a model. If students are admitted with special needs (e.g., students who need accommodations), with a criminal background, or on probation, the field director can begin the placement exploration in a timely fashion since it is more difficult to recruit, screen, and secure practice sites that accept students with unique requirements, and that process can take longer.

## The Placement Process

For the field director, the field placement cycle is not linear and has no beginning or end. Recruitment and (re)assessment of field sites and field instructors are ongoing activities. The great majority of students pass through and successfully complete the placement cycle of orientation, application, interview with field program, selection process including interview with potential field instructors, and, finally, securing the placement. Some students who require re-placement travel through the process twice (possibly more), and a small number who are not successful in securing a placement exit through termination prior to completing the cycle. While one cohort is placed, another is being oriented and placed, with re-placements or terminations occurring at any time.

Field directors are cognizant that students experience stress prior to and during the time they are in the agency seeking and interview phase of the process. Dettlaff (2005) found that nearly half of the student respondents in his study (N=117) felt stressed prior to entering placement. A high level of stress can affect student success in finding or being accepted by a practice site in a timely manner.

A field orientation early in the placement process helps reduce student anxiety by introducing students to field education, roles, responsibilities, expectations, and program requirements. Orientation can be conducted face to face, through a series of workshops, by a panel of current field students, or in an online format. Common topics for orientation are safety, self-care, ethics, required hours, field policies, professional behavior and dress, dual relationships, use of supervision, harassment, placement disruption, and termination from field. Meeting with the students' liaison and seminar peers (if a seminar is required) begins to establish group cohesion. Information and clear expectations generally help reduce anxiety. Additional strategies to assist students with high stress related to entering field include a meeting to role-play interview scenarios, identify student strengths, and communicate with the potential field instructor to introduce the student.

To address gatekeeping responsibilities, field programs establish written policies that stipulate the number of times (generally two or three) that a student can be turned down by field sites before the field director will not place the student. It is critical that the potential field instructor (or the person responsible for the interview at the practice site) provide the student and field director written feedback indicating why the student was not accepted for a placement. In BSW programs this means helping a student find a new academic major or delaying a placement until the student has satisfactorily addressed the identified concerns. The student could reapply to field if reapplication is stipulated in program policies. The decision not to place an MSW student can mean that student is terminated from the program; alternatively, the field director could ask that student to address concerns and then reapply to field in the future if it is permitted and specified in written policies.

At any point of the placement process, a field director needs to be prepared to be challenged by students, their parents/spouses/partners, or legal counsel. Field directors receive calls/emails/texts from well-meaning relatives about concerns they have related to field (e.g., the placement is too far, the neighborhood is not safe, the student does not like the agency, field instructor, or "those people"). Since most students are over age eighteen, the field office should not discuss or share information about the student, placement, content of their application, or concerns with anyone who inquires unless the student has provided a written consent for the field director to speak to a specific person about a specific question in keeping with the Family Educational Rights and Privacy Act (FERPA) of 1974. If the field office releases information without written permission, no matter how insignificant it may seem, it brings the field director, program director, social work department, school, dean, and president into murky waters. Ways to stay ashore and not be swept into the rushing tide include these:

1. If you are contacted by a relative/employer/friend of the student, tell that person that written permission from the student is required for you to talk to anyone other than the student. This generally stops the process if the student is upset that someone has called the school, and will not provide permission.

2. If the student provides permission, it is strongly recommended that you meet with the student face to face and document the salient points of the meeting.

3. If you are contacted by a non-university attorney, provide the phone number of the university legal office and do not discuss anything with that lawyer.

4. Seek the assistance of university legal counsel and be prepared to provide a professional rationale for decisions made.

The placement of students appears to be a straightforward activity to an outsider, but as seen in the points above, it can present many legal and ethical challenges for a field director. There is always a new twist to an old problem that leads to learning and improving policies, procedures, and the placement process.

## Field Applications

Managing placements requires deciding what information to collect, how to use it, and with whom to share it. Requiring a field application is common to both BSW and MSW programs (Dalton, Stevens, & Maas-Brady, 2009, 2011). Common elements found in field applications are

Field Application Information

- Name and contact information
- Demographics
- GPA (BSW)
- Prior volunteer/work experience
- Prior field placements
- Language proficiency
- Courses completed
- Concentration (MSW)
- Desired geographical location
- Populations of interest
- Transportation (availability/ limitations)
- Special considerations
- Résumé
- Letters of reference

Additional Information

- Official documentation of criminal history or felony convictions, and/or pending court involvement
- Employment disciplinary actions
- Driving record (DUI/DWI)
- Violation of academic honesty
- Familial or work constraints
- Personal issues or trauma *for place court involvements*
- F-1 or J-1 Visa (international students)

*Signature of student doc. can be included* *that resume*

Information in the left column can be shared with potential field instructors. The application should contain a section that requires students to review and sign the application; the student's signature attests that all the information provided is accurate. The signature can also serve as informed consent in which the student gives the field director permission to share any necessary information with potential field sites and field instructors (i.e., additional information in the above list). The application can notify students that past or current mental health challenges or a criminal history does not automatically preclude them from a field placement. It may, however, require additional information and more-selective placement options. In states where licensure restricts employment of social workers with a history of felony convictions, programs should document that students have been made aware of state licensing laws.

### Student Interviews

The placement process generally requires student interviews by the field office, potential field instructor, task supervisor, or designated contact person. In 2007, 127 MSW programs responded to a survey by Dalton et alia (2011). Seventy-nine percent of respondents (N=100) utilized interviews with the placement office to assist with placement decisions. Interviews of students by field instructors were found to be the most common placement procedure; field directors reported that their interviews of student cohorts were their most time-consuming activity. Prior to the interview phase of field placement, field directors should remind students to review their cell phone greetings for appropriateness, activate social media privacy settings, and write post-interview thank-you emails or notes to the professionals who interviewed them.

Students are responsible for arranging interviews at one or more sites depending on the placement model. Interviews can occur before the placement has been made, as part of the decision-making process, or after the practice site has been assigned. The field director must be notified of the status and outcome of interviews. When a placement is agreed on, the field office must have a way to ensure that all three parties are officially informed.

## Placement Decisions

What can a new field director rely on to make those first-time placement decisions? What should he or she base the decisions on? Should the focus be on student preference for placement? Strong agencies that can provide generalist or specialized experiences for students? The strengths, education, and practice experience of the field instructor? Or the agency location? Raskin (1985) studied eighty-one factors utilized in making placement decisions that were ranked by field directors. The most important factors in the decision-making process were (1) the quality of the agencies and field instructors, (2) field instructor interest in supervising a student, (3) the professional support system available, (4) availability of social work supervision, and (5) student placement preference. With all the available data about students, agencies, field instructors, and the community, which information should be used for field placement success? The answer to this question is not completely known. Schools adopt different placement structures that incorporate technology, school and community resources, geographic location, and program philosophy to achieve successful placements, where students can master and demonstrate program competencies and related practice behaviors.

How to take into consideration these factors depends on the size of the program. In small programs, the field director more easily considers multiple factors for each student. As the program size increases, placement committees may be assembled to assist the field director with placement decisions. The members can be faculty, liaisons, field staff, or a combination, depending on how many students require placements. The committee can review field applications, conduct interviews, and assign students to specific sites. Mission, goals, the placement model, and requirements of the field program must be familiar to committee members. This model retains decision making about placements within the field office but allows the workload to be distributed among several field-related staff.

In large programs and in urban areas where multiple schools of social work account for the annual placement of thousands of students, it can be overwhelming to keep agencies and student placements organized. A range of technology-based strategies to manage and coordinate placements is essential. Field directors may consider models that collaborate with neighboring field directors through a consortium and/or placement committees. Feature 5.1 describes a placement collaboration model among three schools. Where competition for placements is high, the field director needs to be able to distinguish the school's curriculum and strengths of the students in order for practice sites to want to take students for placement. A practice site will continue to request students if those students are well prepared.

### Feature 5.1. A Collaborative Field Placement Process

The field placement process for MSW students in Minneapolis–Saint Paul, Minnesota, follows a hybrid model, blending choice, assignment, competition, and collaboration. Students and agencies have a defined period for interviews, after which they identify their preferences. The schools then make final placement decisions. What makes the model unique is that the three local MSW programs (Augsburg College, St. Catherine University and the University of St. Thomas, and the University of Minnesota) follow agreed-on terms for the process, and collaborate on the results.

The collaboration begins with an agreement on the schedule for the field search. The three programs agree to a specific day when students and agencies can begin to make contact, and start and end dates for a five-week interview period. The programs also agree to the process, which includes students and agencies completing postinterview choice forms, ranking their preferred placements. The field directors then work together to assign students to placements.

The collaborative process includes contingencies. When students from more than one program are vying for a single position, agency preference guides the decision-making process. When students cannot be successfully matched with one of their preferences, agencies guide them to a second-round interview process, which is again coordinated and aligned across all three programs. Agencies can choose to consider candidates from any or all of the programs, but all agencies adhere to the timelines and process established by the collaborative.

This collaborative began in the early 1990s, when St. Catherine University and the University of St. Thomas, and Augsburg College, joined the University of Minnesota in offering MSW programs in the Twin Cities. The collaborative was created in response to feedback from field instructors who asked that the schools align their processes as much as possible. Some twenty years later the process continues to ensure fairness for students and agency partners across all three schools. It creates predictability and reliability. Field instructors and agency practicum coordinators can anticipate when they will hear from students. Students know that their search process will begin and end at the same time as students from other schools. With more than 500 students currently seeking placements in the Twin Cities, this collaboration supports managed competition, offering choice and parity, for students and agency partners.

Lisa Richardson, MSS, LICSW
Assistant Professor and Director of MSW Field Education
School of Social Work
St. Catherine University and the University of St. Thomas

A philosophy of learning underpins the placement models used in social work education. In the model where the field director selects the practice site for each student, he or she takes all the data collected into consideration before selecting a site. When students request a specific site or population, field directors discover that students often want to stay in their comfort zones and continue doing what they already have mastered either through work or volunteer experience. In making the placement selection, the field director can steer students into practice sites where they will be challenged by new populations, practice theories, and experiences.

Placement decisions in some programs shift to the student although the field director does not abdicate that position's role, responsibilities, and authority. In a student-initiated placement process, students select from among a list of approved settings. They interview in two or three practice sites before they indicate their preference either through a ranking of the sites or by mutual agreement with the field instructor. If a student is interested in a site that is not on the approved list, the field director conducts the initial screening to determine if it meets CSWE standards. These programs see students as capable adults who know their interests and can discern which agency and field instructor is most compatible with their learning needs. The field director is not a silent partner in this model and can assist students in exploring new populations, informing them about sites that request special characteristics such as language proficiency, and familiarize out-of-state students with the community. This student-initiated model needs specific guidelines for how the process works, what the student's responsibilities are, and when the field director is expected to step into the process as problems arise. Communication among students, practice sites, and the field office must be very strong for this model to work well. The intent of this model is to empower students in the decision-making process.

A student needs to take the initiative in the agency interview process. A delay in initiating the interview process for a large cohort can lead to delays even beyond the beginning of classes. A set deadline that confirms the placement is essential. Students compete with their peers and students from other schools for the best placements, and inevitably some students will be disappointed. When changes occur in a practice site (e.g., a supervisor leaves) in a confirmed placement, a re-placement may be necessary. The student will need to identify new sites and begin the interview process again. This might require more input from the field director since other students will have taken available slots. Self-determination and student opportunity for selection diminish over time.

### Employment-Based Placements

Students who are employed in social work settings may request their place of employment as the practicum site. These placements are less common in BSW programs. Students initiate the process and identify their employment site as their placement. In order to keep the educational integrity of the placement, the CSWE permits such placements with the provision that students must have a different supervisor and different experiences from those of their paid employment (CSWE, 2008, AS 2.1.6).

The field office generally uses a separate request form for employment-based placements. This form outlines the agreement made among the school, student, and place of employment. The form identifies the educational field instructor (who must not be the same person as the work site supervisor). The responsibilities that the student will be assigned are recorded; these responsibilities must be different from those the student provides as a paid employee. The days and time that will be devoted to the placement, and the educational goals and expectations of field education, are also delineated on the program form. It is critical not to move forward on an employment-based placement without the written agreement and signatures of the field instructor, work supervisor, agency director, field director, and student.

There are advantages and disadvantages when an employment-based site is used. One advantage to the student is that the placement may be the only way to complete a degree in social work, given the student's financial situation. The student gains experience with new populations and services and an in-depth perspective and understanding of clients served, policies, budget, community agencies, and alternative styles of supervision.

The decision to place students in the practice site where they work, however, can result in potential difficulties. Dual roles and relationships should be avoided in an employment-based placement—that is, when a student is paid a salary for work performed as a professional employee and is performing tasks at the same time as a student in a learning role. It is difficult to establish and maintain an educationally focused placement in the work environment. The requirements of the job often take priority, and the student may be reluctant to express educational interests that do not meet the employer's goals and objectives. When students believe that their educational needs have been shortchanged, they might come to regret the choice of this type of placement (Bogo, 2010).

In some communities the employment site and the practice site may be the only available placement that meets the student's educational focus. It may be more challenging to find a different social work field instructor, particularly if the student's work supervisor is the only BSW or MSW at the practice site. This might mean shifting job responsibilities for the student, or finding a field instructor outside the practice site. Technology can facilitate securing supervision from neighboring communities through the use of Web-based video conferencing (such as Skype), email, or teleconferencing. At the MSW level it is common practice to allow a student only one of two placements in an employment-based placement. The program needs to clearly articulate related program policy in official documents such as its catalog, Web sites, and field manual.

It is extremely difficult to manage a full-time job, field hours, family responsibilities, self-care, and classroom courses in a forty-hour week. The placement hours can become evening, weekends, and overnight when supervision and client system contacts may be at a minimum. The field liaison and field director need to closely monitor employment-based placements for appropriate educational experiences and ensure that it is not a place where students can just clock their hours. The accreditation standards require that students demonstrate practice behaviors and attain social work competencies. As such, the current standards (CSWE, 2008, AS 2.1.6) can help to mitigate some of the problems related to employment-based placements.

### International Placements

For properly prepared students, international placements can enrich the students' understanding of the effects of globalization, cross-cultural factors, and international practice. A field director who is developing international placements for the first time must be able to answer important questions in the affirmative before launching international placements. Is the infrastructure in place to support such placements, and are there sufficient program and institutional resources available to cover expected and unexpected costs? A thorough reading of the literature and consulting with social work programs that place students internationally are critical steps in the preparation phase. International placement decisions are different from local placements in terms of the level of scrutiny of the students selected and practice sites utilized. The students' ability to be safe, learn, and cope with stress, oftentimes without peers, friends, or family nearby, are considerations in these placement decisions (Nuttman-Shwartz & Berger, 2012).

Field directors need to negotiate the factors considered in placement decisions with an extra layer of complexity: cultural expectations, time zones, language constraints, limited resources in the host country, and variable characteristics of any international social work partner schools. Budget constraints, language proficiency, the student's level of cultural awareness, and the availability of a contact person in the country all affect feasibility of international placements (Panos, Cox, Pettys, & Jones-Hart, 2004). Nuttman-Shwartz and Berger (2012) describe a model for effective international placements that includes three phases: a preparatory phase where students are prepared and educated about the culture and customs of the country; a study-abroad phase that includes the need for support; and student return, at which time there will be a debriefing.

Programs that have international work as part of their mission have reciprocal relationships with social work schools and field sites in other countries that provide placement resources and on-site contact persons who understand the educational needs of BSW and MSW students. Web-based technology (e.g., Web-based video conferencing, discussion boards, and email) make it feasible for programs to support student learning and participation in field liaison conferences, seminars, and concurrent online courses. Technology facilitates finding and screening placements, field instructors, and/or contact persons, and connecting with colleagues globally. Many resources are now available to assist a field director in developing international placements that meet CSWE standards, such as the university's international office, international professional contacts, educational exchanges, the Baccalaureate Program Directors and CSWE Listserv, and a growing field literature about international placements.

## Placement Disruption of Students from Field

A student, field instructor, or agency administrator can request that a student be removed from a placement. This request requires the immediate attention of the field director and a thorough assessment of the situation. It is not unusual that each party involved will have a slightly different perspective on the nature of the problem and how the problem can be resolved. After reviewing the issues with all the stakeholders, two clearly written policies will be of great help to the field director: one related to re-placements, and the other to student termination.

Due to concerns with a student, field instructor, or agency, any of the parties can initiate a request for re-placement. A placement may be salvaged if the disruption is due to field instructor turnover or what seems like a lack of learning opportunities. Before hastening to take a student out of a practice site due to a lack of learning opportunities, it might be more productive for the liaison to work with the field instructor to develop the opportunities than it would be to re-place a student. The practice sites often have the experiences the student needs but may not be able to creatively see beyond the services they traditionally offer. Group work services are an example of this situation. Practice sites may not provide groups, although clients may benefit from participation in groups. Exploration by the liaison or field director can help the placement site begin group work services via student leadership or coleadership that are of a time-limited nature.

If the field instructor leaves the practice site during a placement and there are no qualified social workers able to provide field instruction to the student, alternatives to re-placement exist. The field director can screen and secure a task supervisor in the agency while a faculty member or an external supervisor provides social work supervision. Depending on how long the student has been in placement, putting in place an alternative supervision plan can be more efficient than a re-placement.

Each year there will be a number of students whom the field office will need to re-place. If the issues are not related to the student, but it would still be inappropriate for the student to continue at the site, then a re-placement occurs. This means that the placement process begins again until a suitable field instructor and practice site are found. Re-placements cause disequilibrium in the entire cohort class. The field director must keep information confidential about re-placements; students, however, have an extensive information network that can quickly start the rumor mill. Loss of agency funding, unethical violations of practice, boundary violations involving the student by practice site personnel, or disregard of school policies (e.g., mandating that students drive clients in their own vehicles if this is not permitted by the school) would constitute valid reasons to re-place a student.

Placement disruptions frequently occur due to students' inability to meet minimum professional performance standards, difficult student-field instructor relationships, and unethical actions by a student. After an assessment of the situation, including discussions with the field instructor, faculty liaison, and student, the field director makes the decision whether to re-place the student or move toward terminating the student from the program. The latter decision has serious implications and is usually made in consultation with the program director, student's advisor, and, in some cases, the university legal counsel. Issues to consider before making a decision involve the student's ability to reflect on his or her role in the problem and willingness to seek help in addressing the problem, and the academic and psychological health of the student to handle the stresses of micro, mezzo, and macro systems operating in practice sites.

If the decision is to re-place the student, veteran field directors will attest that students who struggled in one placement blossomed in another with a different population and a new supervisor. It is important that the reasons for a new placement be documented and shared with the student and new field instructor, and that the challenges faced by the student are incorporated into the new learning agreement. The process for a second placement is more focused on a field instructor who can assist the student with specific learning needs and is able to provide more-intense supervision. A student is occasionally not able to succeed in a second placement, and the field director initiates student termination from field (and possibly from the program, depending on the circumstances). This is one of the most difficult tasks for a field director but is a part of gatekeeping responsibilities. It is helpful to keep in mind that client systems require a knowledgeable, ethical, competent worker/student. The care and safety of client systems is of utmost importance.

The requirement for programs to develop policies and procedures for terminating a student from field and the program is found in EPAS AS 5.7 (CSWE, 2008). An appeal process is part of termination from field and is a required part of due process. Clearly delineated steps with timelines help keep the process moving. Programs need to decide if students who have been terminated are permitted to reapply for program admission and, if so, the timeframe, and the student's obligations (and documentation) prior to reapplication.

## Special Considerations
### Accommodations for Disabilities

Students who are registered with the Office of Disability Services on campus are required to provide a letter to classroom instructors identifying what accommodation the student needs in order to achieve the goals and competencies identified for classroom courses. Accommodations can range from needing extra time for papers and exams; taking exams in a quiet room; requiring a note taker in class; attending class with a guide dog or an interpreter; and/or including a personal assistant to accompany the student to and from class. Providing reasonable accommodations is required by the Americans with Disabilities Act of 1990 legislation. Universities respond to academic requests with a repertoire of individualized accommodations that they have perfected since that legislation was passed. Although some accommodations may be complex and costly, the environment remains relatively stable.

The field learning environment is very different from the classroom; an accommodation specialized to the practice setting will be most useful. The process for identifying their needed accommodations is an important professional skill for students. When a student has disclosed a physical, learning, cognitive, or mental health disability and needs an accommodation in field, assistance from Disability Services in order to place the student may not be sufficient. Devising a plan that also includes the student and potential field instructor can lead to future cooperation if the plan needs adjustment. It is important to give students the opportunity to disclose their disability to the field director in order for the field director to clearly understand the needs of the student and determine which agency is best suited to provide the accommodation. The student and potential field instructor can then work together to incorporate the accommodation into the learning contract with appropriate assignments. A statement is often included in the field application that asks students to share information that could impede a placement decision, the success of a placement, and whether an accommodation is needed.

In addition to the above challenge, field directors are faced with competing demands in carrying out placement decisions for students with requested accommodations. It is important to support the career goals and advocate for the rights of the student and, at the same time, the field director and field instructor must assess if the student can use good judgment, and work and communicate with people, and function under pressure. These are essential functions of most social work jobs. These factors can be defined as qualification standards for placement of all students. Students have the right to not disclose a disability. If the student does not disclose a disability and an issue arises in the field, the placement would be handled in a similar manner as other students with behavioral or academic difficulties.

### Behavioral or Academic Difficulties

If the field director and/or classroom faculty have concerns about a student's academic performance, they must follow the program's policies and procedures on student development. These include meeting with the student to discuss the concerns, setting up a behavioral contract, or delaying placement of the student until the concerns have been addressed. If the field director determines that the student has the potential to fulfill the essential functions in field, the student can be placed with a contract or monitoring by liaison. After putting in place as many supports for the student as possible, the decision to place a student can be successful. Other times, the student may not be able to carry out the essential functions or attain a passing level of competency. Over the span of a career, all field directors make successful and unsuccessful placement decisions with students who present challenges. Experience as a field director can tip the scale toward the more successful decisions.

### International, English Language Learners, and Bilingual Students

Field directors and international students should consult with the university office responsible for international students to ensure that the required practicum is not interpreted as off-campus employment. A work authorization from the university office is required if there is a payment by the field practice site, including mileage reimbursement, made to the student. To discern if this work authorization is needed, students must present a letter to the International Student Office from the agency and the field director stating that the student has been accepted for field placement and that the course is required. This must take place prior to beginning the placement. A question on the field application regarding student visa status alerts the field director and student to initiate this process.

International students will have either an F-1 or J-1 visa. The F-1 visa is known as the student visa. Students with this type of visa are completing their degree at the institution and plan to graduate. This visa allows a student to work for up to one year with a work authorization. A J-1 visa is for exchange students studying at the university on a temporary basis for up to one year, who will not graduate from the institution. These students are not permitted to have paid employment.

Bilingual students often request a setting where their language skills can be utilized. Native speakers may be fluent in day-to-day language but may not be familiar with terminology used in human service settings (Engstrom, Min, & Gamble, 2009). Students learning a second language may have difficulty communicating with the fluency needed in social work practice settings. Field instructors need to determine the students' language ability and be able to provide adequate supervision for these students. Engstrom et alia (2009) found that a great deal of a bilingual student's time was spent interpreting for workers in lieu of practicing educational competencies.

Directors of field should exercise caution with placement decisions when a practice setting requests bilingual students in order to fill a gap in services. A practice site should be able to continue to provide services to a client when the bilingual student completes the practicum; students need to work with a variety of client systems and not just the one client that requires a particular language.

### Dual Relationships

The NASW's *Code of Ethics* 1.06 (2008) exhorts social workers to avoid engaging in dual relationships. Students need to understand what constitutes a dual relationship and why the faculty liaison or field director must be made aware when a dual relationship exists between a student and someone at the practice site. The relationships include but are not limited to these:

• The student was (or is) a client of the practice site.

• Relatives or friends of the student are clients or employees of the practice site.

• There are outside friendships between the student and practicum site employees or clients.

• The student is related to someone either by blood or clan at the practice site.

• The practice site served as an employment site in the past.

Dual relationships are unavoidable in some communities. This may be especially true in rural areas (Pugh, 2007) or where students are placed in their hometown.

Dual relationships between a student and field instructor can cause problems with professional boundaries and with the student's acceptance of supervision and feedback. Strom-Gottfried (2000) found that dual and boundary difficulties in the field results in diminishing experiences due to unequal power relationships. If the field director is alerted to a dual relationship between student and anyone in the agency when the placement is made, the student is usually re-placed. Avoiding dual relationships can protect the student, field instructor, client, and agency. Field directors are advised to develop policies related to dual relationships and the actions to address the situation. In all practice sites, however, it is the field instructor's responsibility to help students learn professional and ethical boundaries with all client systems, other professionals, and the field instructor. With the field instructor's help, a student can set and maintain appropriate professional relationship boundaries (Congress, 2002).

### Criminal Backgrounds

An often-debated topic for field directors is whether criminal background checks should be required. The CSWE standards do not address criminal background checks, giving programs the opportunity to establish their own policies. If background checks are required, the field director needs to develop policies and procedures to help guide the program, field sites, and how to handle the placements of those students who have a criminal background. When placing a student who has a felony conviction, the field director will need to request that the student provide an official document with the nature of the offense, the timeframe and context of the offense, the state of adjudication, and the outcome (i.e., the plea, and the finding and length of sentence). It is important to determine if the student is still under court supervision, or if a trial will take place during the academic year. Some programs handle the placement of students with criminal histories by not placing any student with a felony. Other programs believe everyone deserves a chance to prove themselves and work with agency partners until a placement is found. Schools also may individualize the response to students who seek placements but have criminal backgrounds. State licensure regulations should be made clear to students in any case.

Multiple agencies perform background checks but not all provide the same information. A national background check provides information about offenses from every state where the student has lived. Some programs require only a state patrol check from their own state. In some programs, students pay for the background checks, while in others the practice site will pay. The requested background criminal history must be stored in a very secure place. Archiving or destroying these records depends on state and university policy. A field director who works in a program that requires criminal background reports would be well advised to have an early conversation with the university legal counsel in order to more fully understand the requirements of the state where the school is located in relation to:

- how criminal background checks are requested and who is permitted to make such requests;

- who is responsible for ensuring confidentiality of the criminal background report;

- who may review the report (i.e., whether an administrative assistant can open the report and read it);

- what information can be shared and with whom, if the student has (or has not) signed informed consent;

- where the reports are stored and who has access;

- whether the state has a law about how long reports should be retained; and

- how the reports are destroyed.

## Conclusion

Without excellent practicum sites and master-teacher field instructors, the job of the field director becomes one of running hard just to catch up. Developing policies, procedures, and forms that capture the required information to make an informed placement takes time and some experience. It is important to ask others for feedback and advice. Refining any management system is best done with input from others, both internal and external to the system. If the placement process is cumbersome, or results in chaos in the community, it is time to experiment with a new model and procedures that include an effective evaluation plan.

There will be situations that adversely affect the field directors' ability to complete the placement process. There is no best way to place students. Some models are used more than others, but not because they have been shown to be better or because they contribute to student outcomes, but rather because programs inherited them, or they are what all the social work programs do in the local area or field consortium, or because they work.

When students casually meet, their first question to each other is, "Where is your placement?" Supporting students during this stressful time, as field placement decisions are being made, will reap benefits to all stakeholders.

## Essential Readings

Dalton, B., Stevens, L., & Mass-Brady, J (2011). "How do you do it?" MSW field director survey. *Advances in Social Work, 12*(2), 276–288.

Gibbs, P., & Blakely, E. H. (Eds.). (2000). *Gatekeeping in BSW programs.* New York: Columbia University Press.

Raskin, M. S. (1985). Field placement decisions: Art, science or guesswork? *Clinical Supervisor, 3*(3), 55–67.

## References

Americans with Disabilities Act of 1990, PL 101–336, 42d Cong., § 1201.

Barretti, M. A. (2007). Teachers and field instructors as student role models: A neglected dimension in social work education. *Journal of Teaching in Social Work, 27*(3/4), 215–239.

Bogo, M. (2010). *Achieving competence in social work through field education.* Toronto, ON: University of Toronto Press.

Congress, E. P. (2002). Social work ethics for educators: Navigating ethical change in the classroom and in the field. *Journal of Teaching in Social Work, 22*(1/2), 151–166.

Council on Social Work Education (CSWE). (2008). *Educational policy and accreditation standards* (rev. March 27, 2010/updated August 2012). Alexandria, VA: Author. Retrieved from http://www.cswe.org/Accreditation/41865.aspx.

Dalton, B., Stevens, L., & Maas-Brady, J. (2009). Surveying the BSW field director. *Journal of Baccalaureate Social Work, 14*(2), 17–29.

Dalton, B., Stevens, L., & Maas-Brady, J (2011). "How do you do it?" MSW Field Director Survey. *Advances in Social Work, 12*(2), 276–288.

Dettlaff, A. J. (2005). The influence of personality type on the supervisory relationship in field education. *Journal of Baccalaureate Social Work, 11*(1), 71–86.

Engstrom, D. W., Min, J. W., & Gamble, L. (2009). Field practicum experiences of bi-lingual social work students working with limited English proficiency clients. *Journal of Social Work Education, 45*(2), 209–224.

Family Educational Rights and Privacy Act (FERPA), 20 U.S.C. § 1232g; 34 C.F.R. pt 99 (1974).

Fortune, A. E., McCarthy, M., & Abramson, J. S. (2001). Student learning processes in field education: Relationship of learning activities to quality of field instruction, satisfaction, and performance among MSW students. *Journal of Social Work Education, 37*(1), 111–124.

Gibbs, P., & Blakely, E. H. (Eds.). (2000). *Gatekeeping in BSW programs.* New York: Columbia University Press.

Knight, C. (1996). A study of MSW and BSW students' perceptions of their field instructors. *Journal of Social Work Education, 32*(3), 399–414.

National Association of Social Workers (NASW). (2008). *Code of ethics of the National Association of Social Workers.* Washington, DC: Author.

Nuttman-Shwartz, O., & Berger, R. (2012). Field education in international social work: Where we are and where we should go. *International Social Work, 55*(2), 225–243.

Panos, P. T., Cox, S. E., Pettys, G. L., & Jones-Hart, E. (2004). Research notes: Survey of international field education placements of accredited social work education programs. *Journal of Social Work Education, 40*(3), 467–478.

Pugh, R. (2007). Dual relationships: Personal and professional boundaries in rural social work. *British Journal of Social Work, 37*(8), 1405–1423. doi:10.1093/bjsw/bcl088.

Raskin, M. S. (1985). Field placement decisions: Art, science or guesswork? *Clinical Supervisor, 3*(3), 55–67.

Strom-Gottfried, K. (2000). Ethical vulnerability in social work education: An analysis of NASW complaints. *Journal of Social Work Education, 36*(2), 241–252.

Wayne, J., Bogo, M., & Raskin, M. (2010). Field education as the signature pedagogy of social work education. *Journal of Social Work Education, 46*(3), 327–339.

Wilson, S. (1981). *Field instruction techniques for supervisors.* New York: The Free Press.

# 6

# Training and Supporting Field Instructors

*Carolyn Knight*

Field instruction is an indispensable element of the social work student's education. An essential aspect of the successful field placement, and a consistent theme in the literature, is the working relationship between the student and field instructor (Bennett, Mohr, Deal, & Hwang, 2013; Ornstein & Moses, 2010). This chapter presents the nature of this relationship, including stages of development and associated tasks and skills. Included are suggestions for how field directors can orient, train, and support field instructors in their role as educators, consistent with the Council on Social Work Education (CSWE) 2008 Educational Policy and Accreditation Standards (EPAS) Accreditation Standard (AS) 2.1.7: "The program discusses how its field education program provides orientation, field instruction training, and continuing dialogue with field education settings and field instructors" (p. 9).

## The Field Instructor Role

Unlike staff supervision, the field instructor balances organizational priorities and responsibilities against accountability to the social work program. "Field instructors guide students through the practicum. They have primary responsibility for linking the student to the setting; teaching, coordinating, and evaluating the student's learning; ensuring that the agency's service standards are met; and liaising with the university" (Bogo, 2005, p. 164).

The field instructor will provide direct instruction to the student regarding the skills, knowledge, and values of the social work profession. Equally important, field instructors serve as influential role models to the student, demonstrating through their actions what it means to be a competent, practicing social worker (Knight, 2001; Miehls, Everett, Segal, & duBois, 2013; Mumm, 2006). Serving as a role model is not limited to the instructor's interactions with clients and colleagues; many of the skills of field instruction are comparable to, and reflect, those that professional social workers use with clients (Shulman, 2008).

Field instruction has a clear beginning, middle, and end, which is different from staff supervision. The nature of the relationship between student and field instructor changes over time, as each develops greater comfort with the other and as the student's learning needs evolve (Deal, 2002; Knight, 2001; Ladany, Marotta, & Muse-Burke, 2001). As this process continues, there are implications for educating field instructors that require responses from the field director.

## Engagement Phase of Field Instruction
### Clarifying Role and Expectations

The student will approach the practicum experience with a mixture of fear, excitement, and anticipation. The instructor's ability to tune in (Shulman, 2008) to the student's feelings enhances the likelihood that successful engagement will occur. An important way in which field instructors can respond to the student's early concerns is to clarify their role and what they expect of the student, as well as what the student can expect from them (Knight, 2004; Miehls et al., 2013). In addition, the student should be encouraged to articulate what she or he expects of the instructor and of the learning experience that is about to begin. This process addresses any misconceptions that students might hold about their role or that of their field instructor.

The skill of clarifying role and purpose helps engage the student in a working relationship (Bogo, 2005; Knight, 2000). The discussion affirms for students that they will have an active role to play in the learning process, a role that may differ from their generally passive role in the classroom. Furthermore, it sets the tone for the supervisory relationship, a relationship in which the instructor will ask the student to take responsibility for his or her learning, and to bring learning needs, questions, and concerns to supervisory conferences. Written learning agreements (sometimes called contracts or plans) have the benefit of making explicit the school's expectations for the student.

In many programs students are required, with the assistance of their field instructor and faculty liaison, to complete written learning agreements in which they identify their assignments and activities to meet the practice behaviors (Dalton, Stevens, & Maas-Brady, 2009). Such written agreements, however, cannot take the place of explicit discussion of how the field instructor and student will work together throughout the academic year.

It also is important for students to understand precisely what their role will be within the practice setting. This is consistent with research that suggests that advance preparation for what the student will experience in the field practicum enhances satisfaction with the experience (Kanno & Koeske, 2010). Students will approach their field placement with preconceived, often erroneous, notions of what a social worker does. For example, they are likely to assume that they will sit in an office and clients will come to them willingly for hour-long sessions. In many, if not most, settings the social worker's role and actions are far removed from this stereotype. This is especially true for macro placements.

A critical aspect of clarifying expectations is setting up a supervisory schedule that balances the student's need for direction against the student's need to develop autonomy and experience a sense of self-efficacy. It is generally accepted that one hour of designated supervision per week is appropriate and provides maximum benefits to students. Students continue to value weekly supervision throughout the placement, even though field instructors often spend less time with their student as the placement progresses (Knight, 2001). The field instructor's availability on an as-needed basis also is helpful to students, particularly in the early phase of work. The field instructor, however, must recognize that being too available to students negatively affects students' feelings of self-efficacy (Knight, 2001).

Another decision that the field instructor should make and clarify with the student is the nature of the supervision that he or she will provide. Typically, field instructors provide their students with individual supervision (Bogo, 2005). There is no clear difference in the benefits associated with individual versus group supervision (Gillam & Crutchfield, 2001; Ray & Altekruse, 2000). At least in the early phase of the field practicum, however, students are likely to experience more anxiety about group supervision and may be more comfortable discussing their cases honestly in individual supervision (Bogo, Globerman, & Sussman, 2004b; Walter & Young, 1999).

Field instructors will need clarification from the social work program on expectations with respect to how many assignments there should be, and how often students must submit assignments such as video- or audiotaping of their work with clients, field logs, case presentations, and process recordings. Process recordings are considered a staple of student supervision (Black & Feld, 2006). While students do not necessarily like completing process recordings, they have been found to be beneficial and to enhance learning (Abramson & Fortune, 1990; Knight, 2000, 2001). Field instructors should clarify if they will be requiring students to engage in learning activities in addition to those required by the program.

The field director's role in the initial stage of field instruction is to provide field instructors with orientation and training regarding the school's requirements on supervision, learning agreements, and field assignments. Those assignments designed by the social work program provide an opportunity for students to demonstrate evidence of their competency. The field director can help ease field instructors' and students' anxieties during the engagement phase by clarifying roles and expectations. This finding is supported by at least one study that suggests that field instructors' preparation in advance of the field practicum experience is associated with greater student satisfaction (Kanno & Koeske, 2010).

### Orienting the Student

Orienting the student to the practice setting and the nature of the work is another critical task in the engagement phase. The field director should urge field instructors to limit the amount of information provided to the student since too much information too quickly may serve only to increase anxiety (Gelman, 2011). Numerous activities can be used to orient the student. One activity that has been found to be helpful, particularly for first-time field students, is helping them understand how the practice setting really works (Knight, 2000). Students can read policy manuals and case files or interview key individuals within the organization, and must be acquainted with safety procedures. One creative strategy is to require students to participate in a scavenger hunt in which they must find answers to questions about the organization, community, social welfare policies, programs, services, and the like.

The student can shadow the field instructor or other staff members as they go about their work. This strategy is particularly beneficial in helping students become acclimated to the setting and the work (Fortune, McCarthy, & Abramson, 2001). It is important to clarify for students what their role would be in shadowing (e.g., silent observer or active participant) and to provide them with a clear and timely transition to their own cases, groups, and/or macro projects. Shadowing others, however, can prolong the student's dependence on the field instructor and discourage autonomous behavior (Ladany & Friedlander, 1995). Students' learning is enhanced, though, when they work alongside their field instructor and when both take on professional roles with client systems (Mumm, 2006). This form of working together can be a way to acclimate the student to social work in the practice setting and can be used by the field instructor to pave the way for student behavior that is more autonomous.

The beginning phase of the field placement sets the stage for the rest of the student experience. Orienting students to the practice setting, clients, and community is an important job for the field instructor. The field director needs to place special emphasis on the orientation of students when training field instructors, for example by providing a student orientation checklist that includes the local context and the necessary components of orientation as it relates to the engagement phase.

### Assessing Student Learning Style

It is important to the engagement phase for field instructors to ascertain the student's unique learning needs. Students can be classified according to the ways in which they prefer to interact with their learning environment. Kolb (1984) identifies four styles of learning that are particularly useful for field instruction. Some students are more concrete and learn best through doing. In contrast, others will learn best if they are encouraged to reflect on their doing. Still other students are more abstract in their approach to learning and benefit from opportunities to explain the rationale for their actions. Finally, some students will learn best through active experimentation in which they apply previous learning to their actions.

Field instructors should understand that students learn at different paces and in different ways. One set of variables that is especially important to consider for field instruction is the student's previous experience. Students new to the field practicum generally are more concrete learners, at least in the beginning weeks of the placement, whereas students with previous field experience may be able to adopt a more abstract approach to their learning even from the beginning of a new practicum experience (Everett, Miehls, duBois, & Garran, 2011; Knight, 2000, 2001; Reichelt & Skjerve, 2000).

Field directors can help the field instructor understand learning styles in the orientation and training they provide. Providing resources to field instructors and students to understand their particular learning styles supports the supervisory relationship. Dettlaff (2003) includes a learning style module in his field instructor training program, and a Web search yields numerous online learning style assessment tools.

### Assessing Personality Type

Field instructors should take into account the influence that the personality type of the student and the field instructor has on the supervisory relationship. Students and field instructors do not need to be matched along personality dimensions. Rather, field instructors must first be aware of their own personality traits, followed by the need to "develop an understanding of how to respond effectively to students of different personality types. This understanding of differences and the ability to respond to [them] may lead to a more effective supervisory relationship, and as a result, an enhanced learning experience" (Dettlaff, 2005, pp. 82–83).

A useful conceptualization is the Myers-Briggs Type Indicator® and its four personality dimensions: extraversion–introversion, sensing–intuition, thinking–feeling, and judging–perceiving (Dettlaff, 2005). Whatever conceptualization is utilized, it is important for field instructors to consider the student's personality style and how it interacts with their own (Ornstein & Moses, 2010). For example, research using the Myers-Briggs inventory indicates that the working relationship between student and field instructor is enhanced when both students and field instructors are similar on the extraversion–introversion and sensing–intuition dimensions (Dettlaff, 2005). Personality traits influence the supervisory relationship. The field director should consider providing training, Internet-based assessments, and articles to field instructors as a way to enhance the supervisory relationship.

### Engaging Diversity and Differences

Field instructors must be aware of, and able to respond to, students' questions and concerns about their working relationship based on diversity and differences. These topics remain relatively taboo for discussion (Duan & Roehlke, 2001). Such a conversation between student and field instructor, however, mirrors the type of discussion that students should have with clients who differ from them in ways that are both obvious and subtle and that can inhibit the client's ability to connect with the student. Open discussion regarding difference also models students' engagement on the macro level with policy and community practice where diversity and differences exist. This reflects EPAS AS 3.1.1: "The program describes the specific and continuous efforts it makes to provide a learning environment in which respect for all persons and understanding of diversity and difference are practiced" (CSWE, 2008, p. 11).

As part of their training, field directors can ask field instructors to consider the impact on their students' educational experience of culture, ethnicity, gender, class, sexual orientation, and age characteristics (Marshack, Hendricks, & Gladstein, 1994). As these authors note, just raising the topic for conversation legitimizes its importance and encourages field instructors to be sensitive to and address how these differences play out in the supervisory relationship. Rich resources exist to help the field director craft diversity training, such as *Educating for Cultural Competency: Tools for Training Field Instructors* (Armour, Bain, & Rubio, 2006).

### Providing Direction and Advice

Students, particularly those new to the field experience, will need and expect specific guidance as they begin their work with client systems and as social work professionals. The field instructor's willingness to discuss in depth the student's cases or projects will be most important in the beginning phase of student placement (Knight, 2001). In addition, the instructor's willingness to systematically examine the student's concerns, known as "partializing concerns" in the practice literature (Shulman, 2008), has its greatest impact on the instructor's effectiveness in the beginning phase.

The field instructor will need to balance providing direction against encouraging and expecting the student to engage in independent action. "Students may approach their new responsibilities with ambivalence and trepidation. It should be assumed that . . . until [students] actually begin to interact with clients, they will remain . . . unsure of their abilities. As the supervisor provides structure and direction to the experience, the student's anxiety is lessened, creating an opportunity for the student to begin to act independently" (Knight, 2004, p. 115). Thus, the field instructor can view advice giving in the early phase as a necessary precursor to the student's ability to act autonomously.

Field directors should address partializing concerns and advice giving in training field instructors during this beginning phase. These skills could reduce the sink-or-swim method used by some supervisors at a time when students are highly anxious.

**Providing Support**

In order for students to engage in the working alliance with and learn from the field instructor, they must believe that the supervisor cares about their learning needs and well-being (Fortune et al., 2001; Knight, 2001; Strozier, Barnett-Queen, & Bennett, 2000). In many ways, this is akin to what clients must experience with their worker: that the worker is on their side and cares about them (Shulman, 2008). As Bennett (2008) notes, "The supervisor's ability to develop positive relationships with supervisees has been reported as the principal characteristic that social work students value" (p. 97).

Field instructors demonstrate their support of the student as they prepare the student for the year or semester ahead and provide the information needed to hit the ground running. Creating a supportive environment does not mean developing a friendship with the student, and it is not an end in and of itself (Ornstein & Moses, 2010). It means creating a working alliance with clear expectations that places a priority on the student's learning needs, reflects the student's personality, and takes into account the impact of diversity and differences. Just as the field instructor supports the student's learning needs, field directors offer support to field instructors to accomplish tasks during this engagement phase.

## Orientation of New Field Instructors

Field instructors need and benefit from orientation and training facilitated by the field director and staff. While not universal, orientation for new and experienced field instructors at the start of the academic year is typical. In many programs, orientation is mandatory, at least for new field instructors (Dalton et al., 2009). Field instructors will benefit most from concrete, specific instruction about their role and its tasks and responsibilities rather than abstract presentations in which the link to their field responsibilities is unclear (Bogo, 2005; Kanno & Koeske, 2010). Field directors must consider the time constraints field instructors are faced with and provide targeted, concise training that provides, if at all possible, incentives such as continuing education units and lunch. One approach is providing online training to field instructors; this has several advantages, including convenience and limited time commitments (Dedman & Palmer, 2011).

Field directors can make use of the curriculum resources published specifically for training field instructors in their role as social work educators such as *Learning to Teach, Teaching to Learn: A Guide for Social Work Field Education* (Hendricks,

Finch, & Franks, 2005), *The Practice of Field Instruction in Social Work: Theory and Process* (Bogo & Vayda, 1998), and *From Mission to Evaluation: A Field Instructor Training Program* (Dettlaff, 2003).

Although there are few empirical studies on field instructor orientation and training programs, field instructor satisfaction is associated with structured training programs, active learning strategies, and small peer collaborations (Bogo, 2005). There are many variations on field instructor orientation and training, such as whether training is required, how much time should be allocated to that training, and specific delivery methods. Increasingly, field instructor training is delivered in a collaborative arrangement with other social work programs or with the use of Web-based technology as a way to stretch limited time and financial resources.

### Overview of the Academic Program

An orientation for field instructors begins with an overview of the entire academic program, including goals, objectives, and desired educational outcomes. The field director, via training and the field manual, should provide specific information about the courses students already have taken and will take during the field practicum. Course syllabi, assignments, and readings from the program curriculum can be especially helpful to field instructors as they assist students in applying theory and research to their practice.

The director of field must also undertake a specific discussion of desired educational outcomes envisioned by the social work program, and required by EPAS. This discussion includes suggestions for how field instructors can create learning opportunities that allow students to acquire and demonstrate specific competencies. This is consistent with EPAS AS B2.1.2: "The program discusses how its field education program provides generalist practice opportunities for students to demonstrate the core competencies" and EPAS AS M2.1.2: "The program discusses how its field education program provides advanced practice opportunities for students to demonstrate the program's competencies" (CSWE, 2008, p. 9).

### Clarify Expectations

Just as students benefit from obtaining a clear understanding of what instructors will expect of them, field instructors need clarification on the academic program's expectations. The field director should be prepared to specify what is required. For example:

- Amount of supervision

- How many hours the field instructor must be on site with the student

- Timing, nature, and deadlines associated with student evaluation

- Documentation of student hours

- Role and responsibilities of field instructors and task supervisors, if relevant

- Role and responsibilities of the faculty field liaison and field director

- Role of field seminar, if applicable

- Policies regarding problematic students

- Requirements regarding process recordings, case presentations, video and audio recordings, and portfolios

- Policies regarding student absences

- Policies regarding ethics violations

- Policies regarding safety and risk management

In an era of shrinking resources and time constraints, the field director should consider ways to support field instructors as they assume their role. He or she may encourage field instructors to consider group supervision. Advantages include the opportunity for students to learn not just from the field instructor, but also from one another, and the potential for the group to normalize students' feelings, experiences, and reactions. Yet field instructors also must be aware of the drawbacks of group supervision, which include the potential for insufficient attention to be paid to the unique learning needs of each student. Students' previous experience with one another, their reactions to one another's competence, and their ability to function as members of a group can have a significant impact on the effectiveness of group supervision (Bogo et al., 2004b).

The field instructor will need to have a solid understanding of basic group work principles and skills in order to balance the learning needs of individual student members with the needs of the group as a whole, and be able to respond appropriately to group dynamics and processes (Bogo, Globerman, & Sussman, 2004a). The field director can assist in this regard by providing training on core group work principles and how they can be utilized in supervision (Knight, 2009; Wayne &

Cohen, 2001). An outside consultant with expertise in group work can supplement the basic training.

Time constraints also may hamper field instructors' willingness and ability to require process recordings, regardless of the social work program's requirements. The educational benefit of process recordings lies not only in what the student writes, but also in what the field instructor does with those recordings (Knight, 2000). The field instructor and the field director must be realistic regarding requirements in this area, limiting the number of process recordings to be submitted to what they will actually read. The field director can assist the field instructor by having clear formatting guidelines for process recordings whether on a micro, mezzo, or macro level (Medina, 2010). As a time-saving strategy, the field instructor can be encouraged to require students to process record only parts of a session (e.g., the most difficult part of the interview or the beginning or ending of a group session or community meeting). The field instructor can explore other techniques for monitoring student progress, such as video and audio recordings, case presentations, and the use of live supervision in agencies that have two-way mirrors (Saltzburg, Greene, & Drew, 2010). The field director may need to assist field instructors in how to use these tools in ways that limit time commitment, maximize student learning potential, and decrease student anxiety.

## The Middle/Work Phase of Field Instruction

Between the fifth and eighth week of a concurrent placement, or the third and fourth week of a block placement, the learning needs of students will begin to change as they become comfortable in the setting and in the relationship with the supervisor. This transition also is observed as the student moves from a concrete approach to learning to a more abstract approach; it is likely to occur earlier for experienced students and those who are more emotionally mature (Everett et al., 2011; Knight, 2001). This phase of work is likely to last until close to the end of the practicum.

### Promoting Open Discussion

Unfortunately, students typically do not talk about the subjects that are most critical and important (Ladany, Hill, Corbett, & Nutt, 1996; Pisani, 2005; Rosenberger & Hayes, 2002; Webb & Wheeler, 1998; Yourman, 2003). Reasons for this tendency have to do with the field instructor's authority and administrative responsibilities for evaluating students. It is particularly likely that the student may withhold sensitive information, given the field instructor's evaluative responsibilities.

It is critical that field instructors create an environment in which the student believes it is acceptable to talk openly about the issues and concerns faced in the work with clients. This task of sharing concerns will come into play well before the middle phase. As field instructors engage in the activities outlined in the beginning phase, they are creating the sort of environment that will allow the student to talk openly. Open discussion in the middle phase is of particular importance, since it is at that time that students are likely to encounter their greatest challenges with client systems and to engage in more-autonomous practice.

Field instructors can affectively tune in, asking the student about personal reactions to the work, since this is an area that students and field instructors appear reluctant to discuss (Fontes, 1995). Similarly, Davis (2002) urges supervisors to listen without judgment, which, in turn, encourages honest reflections from students. When students perform social work roles like counseling, the field instructor can address topics that are more taboo, such as countertransference and indirect trauma, in a way that minimizes their impact on students and in the working alliance with clients (Knight, 2010). Field instruction is not therapy, but the field instructor must be willing to address the student's personal issues if these manifest themselves in relationships with client systems.

The field instructor must continue to address obstacles and issues that surface in the relationship with the student (Ornstein & Moses, 2010). Field instructors typically are not comfortable engaging in this type of discussion, but it may be necessary in those cases where cultural differences (e.g., race, ethnicity, and sexual orientation) interfere with the supervisory relationship and/or the student's interactions with client systems (Armour, Bain, & Rubio, 2004; Messinger, 2004). As field instructors address these topics directly, they serve as an important model to their students, demonstrating how to raise these very same issues with clients in a way that promotes the work.

At this stage of the working relationship, the field director puts in place a mechanism that promotes open discussion between field instructor and student regarding the challenges and successes in working with client systems. The mechanism could be a liaison visit or phone call, an assessment tool of the working relationship, or a documented discussion.

**Engaging in Ethical Self-Disclosure**

The field instructor can use self-disclosure to enhance the working alliance with the student, promote honest discussion, and convey supportive understanding. The instructor's willingness to share thoughts and feelings about the student, the student's work, and the supervisory relationship fosters the supervisory alliance and leads to an environment in which the student is more likely to be open and honest (Nelson, Barnes, Evans, & Triggiano, 2008). Supervisor self-disclosure that deals with a practice mistake or challenge is particularly likely to facilitate honest discussion (Ladany & Lehrman-Waterman, 1999). When supervisors disclose mistakes they may have made in the supervisory relationship itself, they minimize the negative impact of the error and also encourage the supervisee to be more open (Gray, Ladany, Walker, & Ancis, 2001). Appropriate use of self-disclosure also demonstrates for the student how self-disclosure is used in work with client systems (Ganzer & Ornstein, 1999).

The need for field instructors to attend to boundaries is an especially relevant ethical consideration with regard to self-disclosure. For example, two of the most *un*helpful supervisory behaviors are disclosing, or requiring the supervisee to self-disclose, information that is too personal in nature and moves the supervisory relationship into a therapeutic one (Gray et al., 2001; Heru, 2006). It may be necessary for the field director to directly address this issue with field instructors. To some extent, the orientation and training topics that have already been mentioned should assist field instructors in adhering to ethical considerations. Ironically, the parallel process can lead the field instructor to inadvertently engage in boundary violations, treating the student as a client, and not as a supervisee. This is particularly likely to happen in cases where the student is experiencing difficulties in the field and/or personal problems. It may be tempting for the field instructor to transition into the role of social worker, providing therapeutic support to the student. It is critical that the field director emphasize the educational aspects of the working relationship between student and field instructor.

Given that field instructors serve as role models for their students, it is advisable that field directors facilitate opportunities to refresh and refine their understanding of the ethical mandates of the social work profession and their practice as educators. Offering a workshop on ethical considerations not only enhances the field instructors' educational responsibilities, but provides them with needed continuing education units in ethics, a requirement now in place in many states.

## Linking Theory to Practice

It is in the middle phase of the supervisory relationship that the field instructor is most likely to promote abstract, reflective learning, and to require the student to engage in independent practice. For more-advanced students, this skill may come into play earlier, but for all students a demand for work (Shulman, 2008) that requires them to apply their classroom learning is critical to maximizing the educational opportunities afforded by the practicum experience.

Linking theory to practice requires that the field instructor be familiar with the student's learning in the classroom, assist the student in applying classroom learning to practice experiences, and provide specific examples of how theoretical material applies to real-life practice situations (Bogo, 2005; Choy, Leung, Tam, & Chu, 1998; Knight, 2000). The field instructor must help students to "reconcil[e] the theory application imagined by professors with constraints known by experienced supervisors" (Forte & LaMade, 2011, p. 73). In supervision, the field instructor can ask students to identify theory and research that guide their practice interventions. Students are likely to have difficulty with this request, at least early on, since many will struggle with understanding the connection between what they are learning in the classroom and what they are doing in the field (Carey & McCardle, 2011).

This is likely to be one of the more challenging tasks in which field instructors will engage. Critical to supporting the field instructors in this task is training by field directors in integration of theory and practice. Field directors must be versed in theory and research that are relevant to the practice setting and to the theory and research that the student is learning about in the classroom. In some schools of social work, the field director is not a member of the curriculum committee. That field directors need to be well versed in the total curriculum is a strong argument for them to be on curriculum committees and teach social work courses. Field instructors may need assistance in identifying their own theoretical and evidence-based foundation. Given the numerous responsibilities that field instructors must juggle and constraints on their practice and supervision imposed by their practice setting, it may be unrealistic to assume that these individuals are operating from a clear theoretical and, particularly, evidence-based foundation (Forte & LaMade, 2011; Mullen, Bledsoe, & Bellamy, 2008; Ruffolo, Savas, Neal, Capobianco, & Reynolds, 2008).

Unlike their academic counterparts, practicing social workers have limited access to bibliographic databases and make limited use of evidence-based interventions

(Edmond, Megivern, Williams, Rochman, & Howard, 2006; Osterling & Austin, 2008; Rubin & Parrish, 2007; Smith, Cohen-Callow, Harnek Hall, & Hayward, 2007). The field director can provide training in the principles of evidence-based practice. As noted earlier in the orientation to the practicum, the field director or practice faculty should introduce field instructors to the theoretical models utilized by the social work program and taught to students. As an incentive to participate, and as a way to encourage theory and evidence-based practice, field directors might consider arranging library privileges that allow field instructors access to relevant databases.

### Evaluating the Student's Competence

One of the most difficult and challenging tasks for the field instructor is performance evaluation of the student. For many field instructors, this skill is unfamiliar and inconsistent with their self-perceived role as social workers (Munson, 2002). This task will surface in the beginning phase, but it will be less central to the work, given the student's newness to the setting. It is in the middle phase, when the student engages in more-autonomous practice, that providing constructive feedback and evaluating the student's work becomes a main responsibility of the field instructor.

Students welcome and value feedback (Bogo, 2005). However, criticism that is not balanced with positive feedback, or that is provided in an unsupportive and authoritarian manner and without advanced preparation or specific suggestions for change, is unlikely to be helpful or lead to positive growth (Abbott & Lyter, 1998; Giddings, Vodde, & Cleveland, 2003).

The field instructor must be prepared to cite specific instances in which the student performed well or needed to have considered alternative courses of action. Students also benefit from feedback that encourages self-criticism (Abbott & Lyter, 1998; Fortune et al., 2001; Ladany et al., 2001). The field instructor should require that the student engage in self-assessment, preferably in advance of the field instructor's feedback. For example, during supervision the field instructor can first ask the student to identify successful interventions and areas for growth, and to provide suggestions for how to achieve that growth. Field instructors can then provide feedback.

Given the difficulties field instructors experience assuming student evaluation responsibilities, the field director should be prepared to provide guidance in this area. The problems faced by field instructors are compounded when there are no objective, standardized outcome measures to assess student performance (Bogo, 2005, 2010). In most instances, the field office develops its own evaluation form and outcome variables based on competencies and practice behaviors. In order for field instructors to effectively engage in evaluation of the student they must understand what each outcome measure means. They also must understand what the criteria are for successful (and unsuccessful) mastery. This can be accomplished by providing the instructor with examples of highly competent, competent, and incompetent behaviors. The more concrete and specific the criteria, the more helpful these will be to the field instructor (Sowbel, 2011).

### Assuming Gatekeeping Responsibilities

All field instructors will engage in evaluation and provide their students with constructive criticism. There will be times, however, when the field instructor and the social work program will need to take additional steps to ensure that a student who is deemed inappropriate for the social work profession is prevented from entering it. Gatekeeping is one of the most difficult tasks that the supervisor can assume (Bogo, Regehr, Power, & Regehr, 2007). From the field instructor's perspective, the tasks associated with addressing the problematic student are in contrast to the profession's values and commitment to empowerment and strengths-based practice (Abbott & Lyter, 1998). The gatekeeping responsibility, however, is critical to the well-being of clients and to the integrity of the social work profession itself.

The challenges associated with dismissing a student often fall to field instructors, since they, more than classroom instructors, are likely to see manifestations of the student's inappropriateness in interactions with client systems and under supervision. This underscores the importance of the field instructor maintaining regular supervision with the student and, as discussed, engaging in ongoing evaluation. Field directors must develop and disseminate clear evaluation guidelines, gatekeeping policies, and related practices that are specific and supported by their academic institution.

Field instructors typically do not feel supported by the social work program in cases where the student is performing poorly in field (Bogo et al., 2007). "Giving negative feedback and continuing to teach in a deteriorating and tense relationship . . . was highly stressful and instructors described their experience as 'tedious, the repetition in teaching the same thing again and again with no change in the student's behavior was draining'" (Bogo et al., 2007, p. 110). Given these difficulties, it is incumbent on the field director to provide the field instructor with needed support and guidance.

Training by the field director should clarify the policies and processes for addressing problematic students. If a problem arises, it is more likely to be successfully resolved if the field instructor knows in advance what steps to take. It will be easier for the field instructor to be proactive if the academic institution has provided clear guidelines for acceptable and unacceptable performance. The more clear-cut the standards for performance, the more clear-cut will be the decisions for removal (Urwin, Van Soest, & Kretzschmar, 2006).

## The Ending Phase of Field Instruction

During the last several weeks of the placement, the student's work will start to wind down, and the relationship with the field instructor will change yet again. Field directors prepare all parties for termination through training and program structures such as evaluations, final faculty liaison visits, and end-of-year celebrations.

### Helping the Student End with the Field Instructor

Probably the most critical task in the ending phase of work is assisting the student in terminating with all client systems. The manner in which the field instructor ends with the student sets the stage for and models how the student will terminate with clients. At the outset of the placement, the student knows that work with the field instructor and the client will end. Field instructors should plan with the student for this ending. As with clients, this planning means deliberately raising the prospect of ending and reaching for the student's feelings about it (Shulman, 2008). Students will probably struggle with putting into words their feelings about ending, given cultural prohibitions that encourage avoidance of this issue (Gelman, 2009; Walsh, 2002).

Students are not just ending with their field instructor, but they are also ending with client systems and staff in the practice setting. Furthermore, some students are ending their formal education. Taken together, these factors may explain why students find it so difficult to talk about termination. This discussion is important because "endings provide both supervisor and student with the opportunity to reflect on and learn from their time together and to discuss what went right and what went wrong" (Knight, 2004, p. 122).

Field instructors must be prepared to talk honestly about how they and the student worked together, and to solicit the student's views about the learning environment within the practice setting and the supervision that was provided. If the field instructor has created the sort of learning environment in which honest discussion takes place, the feedback received in the ending phase may not be altogether new, but it will provide both student and field instructor with a sense of closure and the instructor with valuable information for future use. In those instances where the ending is under difficult circumstances, such as the student's removal from the placement, the need for honest discussion is even more critical.

Field instructors also should provide the student with a final performance summary. This will involve the formal evaluation process required by the social work program. It should involve field instructors' summary of the student's strengths, areas for growth, and suggestions for future career plans. This feedback should focus not only on the student's work with clients and colleagues, but also on the student's use of supervision.

Field instructors may need to consider what, if any, relationship they wish to maintain with the student once the placement ends, and to clarify these expectations. In some instances, students may continue on in the placement in a staff position that may or may not involve professional contact with the field instructor. In others, student and field instructor may agree to keep in touch on a professional basis; for example, the field instructor may serve as a reference for the student.

### Helping the Student End with Client Systems

It is particularly important for field instructors to assist students in terminating with all their clients. Students often do not receive adequate classroom preparation for how to effectively terminate with clients and find this task particularly challenging (Gelman, 2009). This process can lead to feelings of guilt at "abandoning" clients and to worry over their fate (Baum, 2004).

Clients and students are likely to avoid discussing planned endings. In those cases where the ending is unplanned, students may struggle with feelings of frustration, anger, guilt, and self-doubt. It is important for field instructors to engage in the affective tuning in discussed above, inquiring of the student's feelings about endings with clients. As students come to terms with these feelings, they will be in a better position to engage in the professional actions required for endings. Students often wish to continue to see clients on a volunteer or informal basis. This underscores the need for the field instructor to explore with the student the feelings behind this desire, and to reinforce professional boundary considerations.

## Conclusion

The field instructor and field director are partners in the education of the social work student. This chapter has examined the role of the field instructor as an educator, as well as the skills in each stage in the working relationship between student and instructor. While the orientation and training of field instructors is mandated, the content is left to each social work program to establish. This chapter includes guidance on how field directors can support field instructors as they assume an educator role in socializing students into the profession.

## Essential Readings

Bogo, M. (2010). *Achieving competence in social work through field education.* Toronto, ON: University of Toronto Press.

Dettlaff, A. (2003). *From mission to evaluation: A field instructor training program.* Alexandria, VA: Council on Social Work Education.

Hendricks, C. O., Finch, J. B., & Franks, C. (2005). *Learning to teach, teaching to learn: A guide for social work field education.* Alexandria, VA: Council on Social Work Education.

Kolb, D. (1984). *Experiential learning: Experience as the source of learning and development.* Englewood Cliffs, NJ: Prentice-Hall.

## References

Abbott, A., & Lyter, S. (1998). The use of constructive criticism in field supervision. *Clinical Supervisor, 17*(2), 43–57.

Abramson, J., & Fortune, A. (1990). Improving field instruction: An evaluation of a seminar for new field instructors. *Journal of Social Work Education, 26*(3), 273–286.

Armour, M., Bain, B., & Rubio, R. (2004). An evaluation study of diversity training for field instructors: A collaborative approach to enhancing cultural competence. *Journal of Social Work Education, 40*(1), 27–38.

Armour, M. P., Bain, B., & Rubio, R. (2006). *Educating for cultural competence: Tools for training field instructors.* Alexandria, VA: Council on Social Work Education.

Baum, N. (2004). Social work students' treatment termination as a temporary role exit. *Clinical Supervisor, 23*(1), 165–177.

Bennett, C. S. (2008). Attachment-informed supervision for social work field education. *Clinical Social Work Journal, 36*(1), 97–107.

Bennett, S., Mohr, J., Deal, K., & Hwang, J. (2013). Supervisor attachment, supervisory working alliance, and affect in social work field instruction. *Research on Social Work Practice, 23,* 199–209.

Black, P., & Feld, A. (2006). Process recording revisited: A learning-oriented thematic approach integrating field education and classroom curriculum. *Journal of Teaching in Social Work, 26*(3/4), 137–153.

Bogo, M. (2005). Field instruction in social work: A review of the research literature. *Clinical Supervisor, 24*(1/2), 163–193.

Bogo, M. (2010). *Achieving competence in social work through field education.* Toronto, ON: University of Toronto Press.

Bogo, M., Globerman, J., & Sussman, T. (2004a). Field instructor competence in group supervision: Students' views. *Journal of Teaching in Social Work, 24*(1/2), 199–216.

Bogo, M., Globerman, J., & Sussman, T. (2004b). The field instructor as group worker: Managing trust and competition in group supervision. *Journal of Social Work Education, 40*(1), 13–26.

Bogo, M., Regehr, C., Power, R., & Regehr, G. (2007). When values collide: Field instructors' experiences of providing feedback and evaluating competence. *Clinical Supervisor, 26*(1/2), 99–117.

Bogo, M., & Vayda, E. J. (1998). *The practice of field instruction in social work: Theory and process.* Chichester, NY: Columbia University Press.

Carey, M., & McCardle, M. (2011). Can an observational field model enhance critical thinking and generalist practice skills? *Journal of Social Work Education, 47,* 357–366.

Choy, B., Leung, A., Tam, T., & Chu, C. (1998). Roles and tasks of field instructors as perceived by Chinese social work students. *Journal of Teaching in Social Work, 16*(1/2), 115–132.

Council on Social Work Education (CSWE). (2008). *Educational policy and accreditation standards* (rev. March 27, 2010/updated August 2012). Alexandria, VA: Author. Retrieved from http://www.cswe.org/Accreditation/41865.aspx.

Dalton, B., Stevens, L., & Maas-Brady, J. (2009). Surveying the BSW field director. *Journal of Baccalaureate Social Work, 14*(2), 17–29.

Davis, B. (2002). Group supervision as a learning laboratory for the purposeful use of self in child protection work. *Journal of Teaching in Social Work, 22*(1/2), 183–198.

Deal, K. (2002). Modifying field instructors' supervisory approach using stage models of student development. *Journal of Teaching in Social Work, 22*(3/4), 121–137.

Dedman, D., & Palmer, L. (2011). Field instructors and online training: An exploratory survey. *Journal of Social Work Education, 47,* 151–161.

Dettlaff, A. (2003). *From mission to evaluation: A field instructor training program.* Alexandria, VA: Council on Social Work Education.

Dettlaff, A. (2005). The influence of personality type on the supervisory relationship in field education. *Journal of Baccalaureate Social Work, 11*(1), 71–86.

Duan, C., & Roehlke, H. (2001). A descriptive 'snapshot' of cross-racial supervision in university counseling center internships. *Journal of Multicultural Counseling and Development, 29*(2), 131–146.

Edmond, T., Megivern, D., Williams, C., Rochman, E., & Howard, M. (2006). Integrating evidence-based practice and social work field education. *Journal of Social Work Education, 42*(2), 377–396.

Everett, J., Miehls, D., duBois, C., & Garran, A. (2011). The developmental model of supervision as reflected in the experiences of field supervisors and graduate students. *Journal of Teaching in Social Work, 31*(3), 250–264.

Fontes, L. (1995). Sharevision: Collaborative supervision and self-care strategies for working with trauma. *Family Journal, 3*(3), 249–254.

Forte, J., & LaMade, J. (2011). The center cannot hold: A survey of field instructors' theoretical preferences and propensities. *Clinical Supervisor, 30*(1), 72–94.

Fortune, A., McCarthy, M., & Abramson, J. (2001). Student learning processes in field education: Relationship of learning activities to quality field instruction, satisfaction, and performance among MSW students. *Journal of Social Work Education, 37*(1), 111–124.

Ganzer, C., & Ornstein, E. (1999). Beyond parallel process: Relational perspectives on field supervision. *Clinical Social Work Journal, 27*(3), 231–246.

Gelman, C. (2009). MSW students' experience with termination: Implications and suggestions for classroom and field instruction. *Journal of Teaching in Social Work, 29*(2), 169–187.

Gelman, C. (2011). Field instructors' perspectives on foundation year MSW students' preplacement anxiety. *Journal of Teaching in Social Work, 31*, 295–312.

Giddings, M., Vodde, R., & Cleveland, P. (2003). Examining student-field instructor problems in practicum: Beyond student satisfaction measures. *Clinical Supervisor, 22*(2), 191–214.

Gillam, S., & Crutchfield, L. (2001). Collaborative group supervision of practicum students and interns. *Clinical Supervisor, 20*(1), 49–60.

Gray, L., Ladany, N., Walker, J., & Ancis, J. (2001). Psychotherapy trainees' experience of counterproductive events in supervision. *Journal of Counseling Psychology, 48*(4), 371–383.

Hendricks, C. O., Finch, J. B., & Franks, C. (2005). *Learning to teach, teaching to learn: A guide for social work field education.* Alexandria, VA: Council on Social Work Education.

Heru, A. (2006). Psychotherapy supervision and ethical boundaries. *Directions in Psychiatry, 26*(1), 79–88.

Kanno, H., & Koeske, G. (2010). MSW students' satisfaction with their field placements: The role of preparedness and supervision quality. *Journal of Social Work Education, 46*, 23–38.

Knight, C. (2000). Engaging the student in the field instruction relationship: BSW and MSW students' views. *Journal of Teaching in Social Work, 20*(3/4), 173–201.

Knight, C. (2001). The process of field instruction: BSW and MSW students' views of effective field supervision. *Journal of Social Work Education, 37*(2), 357–379.

Knight, C. (2004). Modeling professionalism and supervising interns. In M. Austin & K. Hopkins (Eds.), *Supervision as collaboration in the human services: Building a learning culture* (pp. 110–124). Thousand Oaks, CA: Sage.

Knight, C. (2009). The use of a workshop for field instructors to enhance students' experience with group work in the field practicum. *Social Work with Groups, 32*(3), 230–242.

Knight, C. (2010). Indirect trauma in the field practicum: Secondary traumatic stress, vicarious trauma, and compassion fatigue among social work students and their field instructors. *Journal of Baccalaureate Social Work, 15*(1), 31–52.

Kolb, D. (1984). *Experiential learning: Experience as the source of learning and development.* Englewood Cliffs, NJ: Prentice-Hall.

Ladany, N., & Friedlander, M. (1995). The relationship between the supervisory working alliance and trainees' experience of role conflict and role ambiguity. *Counselor Education and Supervision, 34*(3), 220–230.

Ladany, N., Hill, C., Corbett, M., & Nutt, E. (1996). The nature, extent, and importance of what psychotherapy trainees do not disclose to their supervisors. *Journal of Counseling Psychology, 43*(1), 10–24.

Ladany, N., & Lehrman-Waterman, D. (1999). The content and frequency of supervisor self-disclosures and their relationship to supervisor style and the supervisory working alliance. *Counselor Education and Supervision, 38*(3), 143–160.

Ladany, N., Marotta, S., & Muse-Burke, J. L. (2001). Counselor experience related to complexity of case conceptualization and supervision preference. *Counselor Education and Supervision, 40*(3), 203–219.

Marshack, E., Hendricks, C., & Gladstein, M. (1994). The commonality of difference: teaching about diversity in field instruction. *Journal of Multicultural Social Work, 3*(1), 77–89.

Medina, C. K. (2010). The need and use of process recording in policy practice: A learning and assessment tool for macro practice. *Journal of Teaching in Social Work, 30*(1), 29–45.

Messinger, L. (2004). Out in the field: Gay and lesbian students' experiences in field placement. *Journal of Social Work Education, 40*(2), 187–204.

Miehls, D., Everett, J., Segal, C., & duBois, C. (2013). MSW students' views of supervision: Factors contributing to satisfactory field experiences. *Clinical Supervisor, 32,* 128–146.

Mullen, E., Bledsoe, S., & Bellamy, J. (2008). Implementing evidence-based social work practice. *Research on Social Work Practice, 18*(4), 325–338.

Mumm, A. M. (2006). Teaching social work students practice skills. *Journal of Teaching in Social Work, 26*(3/4), 71–89.

Munson, C. (2002). *Handbook of clinical social work supervision* (3rd ed.). Binghamton, NY: Haworth Press.

Nelson, M., Barnes, K., Evans, A., & Triggiano, P. (2008). Working with conflict in clinical supervision: Wise supervisors' perspectives. *Journal of Counseling Psychology, 55*(2), 172–184.

Ornstein, E., & Moses, H. (2010). Goodness of fit: A relational approach to field instruction. *Journal of Teaching in Social Work, 30*(1), 101–114.

Osterling, K. L., & Austin, M. J. (2008). Substance abuse interventions for parents involved in the child welfare system: Evidence and implications. *Journal of Evidence-Based Social Work, 5*(1/2), 157–180.

Pisani, A. (2005). Talk to me: Supervisee disclosure in supervision. *Smith College Studies in Social Work, 75*(1), 29–47.

Ray, D., & Altekruse, M. (2000). Effectiveness of group supervision versus combined group and individual supervision. *Counselor Education and Supervision, 40*(1), 19–30.

Reichelt, S., & Skjerve, J. (2000). Supervision of inexperienced therapists: A qualitative analysis. *Clinical Supervisor, 19*(2), 25–43.

Rosenberger, E., & Hayes, J. (2002). Therapist as subject: A review of the empirical countertransference literature. *Journal of Counseling & Development, 80*(3), 264–270.

Rubin, A., & Parrish, D. (2007). Views of evidence-based practice among faculty in master of social work programs: A national survey. *Research on Social Work Practice, 17*(1), 110–122.

Ruffolo, M., Savas, S., Neal, D., Capobianco, J., & Reynolds, K. (2008). The challenges of implementing an evidence-based practice to meet consumer and family needs in a managed behavioral health care environment. *Social Work in Mental Health, 7*(1–3), 30–41.

Saltzburg, S., Greene, G., & Drew, H. (2010). Using live supervision in field education: Preparing social work students for clinical practice. *Families in Society, 91,* 293–299.

Shulman, L. (2008). *The skills of helping individuals, families, groups, and communities* (6th ed.). Belmont, CA: Thomson Brooks/Cole.

Smith, C., Cohen-Callow, A., Harnek Hall, D., & Hayward, R. A. (2007). Impact of a foundation-level MSW research course on students' critical appraisal skills. *Journal of Social Work Education, 43*(3), 481–495.

Sowbel, L. (2011). Gatekeeping in field performance: Is grade inflation a given? *Journal of Social Work Education, 47,* 367–377.

Strozier, A., Barnett-Queen, T., & Bennett, C. (2000). Supervision: Critical process and outcome variables. *Clinical Supervisor, 19*(1), 21–39.

Urwin, C., Van Soest, D., & Kretzschmar, J. (2006). Key principles for developing gatekeeping standards for working with students with problems. *Journal of Teaching in Social Work, 26*(1/2), 163–180.

Walsh, J. (2002). Termination and your field placement. *New Social Worker, 9*(2), 14–17.

Walter, C., & Young, T. (1999). Combining individual and group supervision in educating for the social work profession. *Clinical Supervisor, 18*(2), 73–89.

Wayne, J., & Cohen, C. (2001). *Group work education in the field.* Alexandria, VA: Council on Social Work Education.

Webb, A., & Wheeler, S. (1998). How honest do counsellors dare to be in the supervisory relationship?: An exploratory study. *British Journal of Guidance and Counselling, 26*(4), 509–524.

Yourman, D. (2003). Trainee disclosure in psychotherapy supervision: The impact of shame. *Journal of Clinical Psychology, 59*(5), 601–609.

# 7

# Facilitating Student Learning between Classroom and Field

*Julia K. Moen, Denice Goodrich Liley, and Sheila R. Dennis*

Since its inception, social work education has embraced the position that both classroom and field instruction are vital to professional education. The apprenticeship training model that began in 1898 evolved into a uniform approach to field education that is coordinated, monitored, and evaluated based on criteria by which all students demonstrate the achievement of program competencies. The Council on Social Work Education (CSWE) now evaluates social work programs on student learning outcomes framed as professional competencies. The shift from content- to competency-based learning has reinforced the enduring charge to fuse "the theoretical and conceptual contribution of the classroom with the practical world of the practice setting" (CSWE, 2008, Educational Policy [EP] 2.3, p. 8). Field directors are integral to inspiring students' growth toward professional competence by threading pedagogical standards throughout the field delivery process. This chapter introduces field directors to various field education delivery approaches that promote the integration of classroom knowledge and field practice.

A constellation of theories and perspectives underlying an effective teaching–learning process in field education sets the stage for the chapter. This chapter includes a theoretical framework for integrating theory and practice to guide field educators (directors, liaisons, agency-based field instructors, teaching coordinators) in the arduous task of linking structured classroom learning to the ambiguities and complexities inherent in the practice setting. The next section will outline predominant curricular structures that social work programs employ to deliver field education. Finally, the chapter emphasizes the central role of the field liaison and the importance of the field seminar as a vehicle for integrative learning.

## Selected Practice Perspectives, Theories, and Models on Teaching and Learning

The charge for field educators to foster a learning process that promotes the integration of knowledge and practice emanates from the early articulations of social work education. Bertha Capen Reynolds (1942), a pioneer of social work education, exhorted educators to shift focus from the intended content to the learner's relationship with the content's integration and application. Similarly, Charlotte Towle (1954) affirmed a student-centered approach to teaching and learning, and established a foundation for the application of learning theories in social work education. This call is especially meaningful for the field practicum in social work since the profession seeks to establish teaching and learning norms characteristic of a signature pedagogy in professional education (Shulman, 2005).

Learning theories provide the conceptualization of the teaching–learning enterprise and are useful for illuminating how students become competent professional social workers through their classroom and field experiences. By knowing how to optimize learning, field directors can construct and reinforce effective learning environments. Theories and perspectives most closely aligned with field education that this chapter spotlights include adult learning theory, experiential learning, deep and surface learning, the centrality of reflection and assessment, and a theoretical model to promote integration in field education.

### Adult Learning Theory

Underpinning the web of theories informing field education is adult learning theory, which Malcolm Knowles pioneered (1972). Applying a humanistic framework, Knowles sought a theoretical lens that could more effectively capture the complexity of the interplay between adult learners and their environments. Adult learning theory is based on the assumptions that adults are collaborative, intrinsically motivated to learn, self-directed, and inclined toward a problem-centered rather than subject-oriented approach. Adults value their life experiences and relate new learning to their existing systems of meaning. Consequently, adult learners embrace their individual voice and expression in the learning process and are thus motivated to interweave new learning with life experiences, reconfiguring their interpretive lenses through which they view the world.

## Experiential Learning

Building on the principles of adult learning theory, Kolb's experiential learning cycle is often referenced as a guiding model for conceptualizing the learning process; field directors typically orient field instructors and students to this model. Kolb (1984) outlined a four-step experiential learning cycle of (1) concrete experience, (2) reflective observation, (3) abstract conceptualization, and (4) active experimentation. Prompted by individual intrinsic motives and learning styles, a student engages with this cyclical model for learning, entering into the various stages at different points in the cycle. The cycle entails an interactive, reflective process of challenging previously held views about an experience. A new conceptualization based on the reflective tension emerges, from which the student then experiments to birth a modified concrete experience. This transformative process inspires the habit of engagement and inquiry for perpetual learning in the practice setting.

There are numerous examples of how this cycle is applied in the field practicum. Students learn about concepts in the classroom and only truly "get it" after engaging in "real" practice with client systems, and observing, coworking, and having reflective discussions with field educators. In a study about the methods field instructors use to teach practice skills, "students report that discussion, modeling, and cocounseling were most helpful to their learning" (Mumm, 2006, p. 71). Kolb's experiential learning cycle, as illustrated by figure 7.1, is consistent with Bogo and Vayda's Integration of Theory and Practice (ITP) loop model (1998) and prescribes the best strategies for field educators to enable students to integrate theory with practice.

## Deep and Surface Learning

In their classic research on how students approach learning, Marton and Säljö (1976) set forth the deep and surface learning premise that there are qualitative differences in how students learn. Deep learning, anchored in a constructivist orientation (Biggs & Tang, 2007), is based on students actively pursuing meaning in the learning encounter. Students aspiring to deep learning seek to understand new ideas, partner with teachers/mentors, and generate new conceptual frameworks. Learning occurs when students inject new insight into their existing systems of meaning and transform cognitive schemas. Students' perspectives are refined and

**Figure 7.1. Kolb's Experiential Learning Cycle (1984)**

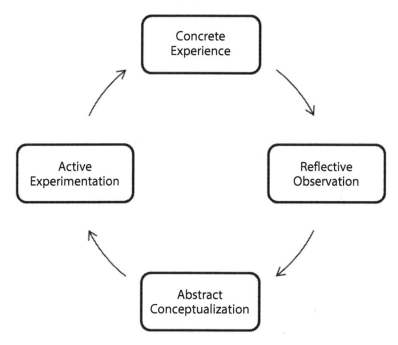

modified, which leads to learning that endures and that the students can use in professionally appropriate ways, such as ethical decision making or communicating with clients.

Conversely, surface learning entails a process that is passive and reproductive. Surface learning is more likely to occur when workload and/or assessment in field education are excessive (Gardiner, 1988; Light, Cox, & Calkins, 2009). An extension of surface learning is strategic learning, a surface learning approach where students engage only to the extent that they achieve assessment outcomes. Students ascribing to a strategic learning approach are extrinsically motivated to meet course requirements rather than intrinsically compelled toward genuine engagement with the learning phenomenon, as is the case with deep learning. Both surface and strategic learning approaches are characterized by externalized, content-based processes that do not penetrate a student's perspective in a manner that generates transformative learning (Entwistle & Ramsden, 1983; Light et al., 2009). A field educator can promote deep learning by providing plenty of opportunities for practice with focused and supportive feedback.

Expanding on deep learning, the relatively new field of neuroscience research is validating many learning theories and influencing educators by providing research-informed, brain-based learning strategies that bridge pedagogy with biology. Zull (2002) describes teaching as "the art of changing the brain" (p. 5) by creating "interactions with the physical world that produce learning" (p. 245). As students develop habits of learning through reflection and experience, regions in the brain are activated, prompting a physical change within the brain (Zull, 2002). Role plays, case-based learning, and simulations use these strategies to reinforce student learning. *How the Brain Learns* (Sousa, 2006) and *12 Brain/Mind Learning Principles in Action* (Caine, Caine, McClintic, & Klimek, 2005) are two resources that could be useful for field directors in understanding the explosion of research on the brain and the biology of learning.

Applying a theoretical framework when designing and delivering field education enhances students' learning and strengthens all facets of field education. By prompting students throughout the field practicum to engage in meta-learning (e.g., thinking about their learning from a theoretical perspective), field educators encourage students to be active learners. Furthermore, field directors take a leadership role in educating field instructors on theoretical approaches to students' experiential learning in practice settings.

### Reflection: The Engine for Integrative Learning Outcomes

While the call for reflection is a persistent theme in the literature and in field education, it remains unclear how meaning reflection occurs (Clare, 2007). The process of student reflection is complex (Kegan, 1994, as cited in Grossman, 2009). Reflection that generates meaningful learning is not merely a recall of experience, but is the active process of analysis, synthesis, and evaluation prompting change (Dewey, 1933). Strategies to inspire reflection must be flexible, sensitive to the learner's social and cultural context, and directed (Boud & Walker, 1998; Dewey, 1933). Simply inserting time for reflection may carve out a break from a demanding course schedule but may not yield reconfigured conceptualizations. Through a critically reflective process, students fashion new cognitive schemas that meld with their existing conceptual frameworks (Grossman, 2009; Light et al., 2009). From this reflective interplay, a transformation of the learner's meaning system emerges, laying the groundwork for future learning.

Teaching students how to engage in reflection has direct application to practice and relates to adaptive anxiety, which Shulman asserts is a required feature of learning in a signature pedagogy. "Uncertainty, visibility, and accountability inevitably raise the emotional stakes of the pedagogical encounters" (Shulman, 2005, p. 57). In his definitive work on reflective practice, Schön (1983, 1987) postulated that the uncertainty inherent in practice encounters with clients requires practitioners who can reflect in and on practice, producing new practice knowledge on which subsequent practice decisions may be constructed. Schön's premise entails an artistic approach to practice that engages the practitioner's tacit knowledge (Polanyi, 1967), which emerges in the practice moment. Reflective practice fuses the student's objective understanding of scientifically derived knowledge from the classroom experience with the creative application of an internal knowledge system that emerges in the complexity of unique practice encounters. The ability to actively reflect on practice situations is what distinguishes social workers' instruction from a technical rational approach, which is merely the application of externalized knowledge (Bogo, 2010). It is essentially the ability to respond creatively to diverse and ambiguous events in the here and now that showcases the professional nature of social workers. Furthermore, reflecting on these decisions solidifies new cognitive templates for future practice.

Adult learning strategies that promote transformative learning through reflection include creating time and a safe space for students' unique voices (Bogo & Vayda, 1998; Drisko, 2000, as cited in Hendricks, Finch, & Frank, 2005), avoiding content overload (Light et al., 2009), and devising evaluative strategies that facilitate qualitative responses. When evaluating student learning, field educators who ascribe to a constructivist teaching approach encourage students' different interpretive responses to practice encounters. By designing field assignments (e.g., student learning agreements) that invite students' individuality and allow for multiple ways of learning, field educators may contribute to a reflective process (Biggs & Tang, 2007). The field seminar is a setting that is conducive to engaging students in the reflective process, allowing time and space for students to collectively examine current practice encounters in light of past experiences and acquired classroom knowledge. Finally, educating field instructors and liaisons on the essential role of reflection in field education is integral to supporting a systematic approach that requires student reflection.

## The Importance of Assessment to Promote Learning

Formally instituted with the 2008 Educational Policy and Accreditation Standards (EPAS), the competency-based learning approach has heralded a paradigm shift in capturing student learning outcomes for social work (Holloway, Black, Hoffman, & Pierce, n.d.). The amplified assessment structure provides an opportunity for social work educators to more closely align field education with signature pedagogy criteria. Standardizing learning outcomes of competencies and practice behaviors is intended to ensure the quality of social work graduates and establish the kind of habitual professional activities underscored by Shulman (2005). A field educator, however, may encounter tension when seeking to embrace students' individualized learning experiences in field education while assessing for predetermined learning outcomes. Social work education is in a season of change, and field programs must pay close attention to formulating assessment approaches that nurture student learning in a competency-based curricular structure.

The literature reveals a strong theme that learning is intimately connected with assessment since the assessment requirements define for the learner what learning is valued (Havnes, 2004). Assessment drives student learning (Shepard, 2000). Boud and Falchikov (2006) argue that higher education, with its traditional assessment mechanisms, has historically fostered transmissional learning and perfunctory student engagement. To foster participatory learning that more closely reflects learning in real-world settings, field educators should consider a collaborative approach to assessment that incorporates students' voices in the assessment process (e.g., portfolios and self-assessments), promoting critical thinking and self-reflection (Crisp & Lister, 2002, as cited in Theriot, Johnson, Mulvaney, & Kretzschmar, 2006; Boud & Falchikov, 2006). Overassessing in field education can inadvertently promote surface learning instead of engaging with the transformation of students' meaning-making systems (Light et al., 2009). Effective field assessment entails alignment with what and how we want students to learn, and it requires that students have adequate time and space for the assessment process to become meaningful to them.

### Theoretical Model to Promote Integration in Field Education

The Integration of Theory and Practice Loop Model (ITP), developed by Bogo and Vayda (1998), is a prominent and contemporary social work model to assist field educators in examining practice and articulating feedback to students (see figure 7.2). ITP is a framework that unites social work theory taught in the classroom to actual practice. The model, applicable to all levels of practice, looks at the entire

**Figure 7.2. Bogo and Vayda's Integration of Theory and Practice Loop Model (1998)**

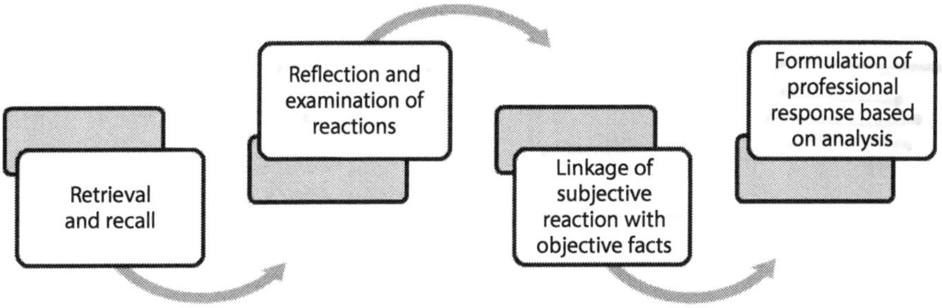

*Source*: Adapted from Bogo & Vayda (1998).

process of a practice situation and breaks it down into four phases: (1) retrieval and recall, (2) reflection and examination of reactions, (3) linkage of subjective reaction with objective facts, and (4) formulation of professional response based on analysis. The ITP model helps to demystify the process of theory and practice integration in the practice setting.

Field directors may employ the model as a guiding tool for training field educators on the model's use in supervision, integrative seminars, and student assignments (e.g., micro and macro case presentations, process reports, field logs). For example, in preparing students to make case presentations (Boisen & Syers, 2004), field educators guide students through a structured series of questions to enhance their ability to analyze their work with clients and systematically integrate theory and practice.

## Field Program Models and Structural Approaches

Assumptions about how students learn shape field curriculum design and implementation. Various field models exist, and the implementations of these structures influence student learning and professional socialization. A field director typically inherits an existing field model that encompasses structural arrangements, which include timing, sequencing, field seminar courses, and course requirements. Field directors are encouraged to use research to advocate for field program improvements or to sustain existing program elements that are effective.

Concurrent field delivery models entail students taking classes alongside the field practicum, typically over the course of two semesters. Conversely, a block placement is an immersive field practicum in one setting that usually occurs throughout one semester. Rotational placements occur when a field practicum comprises multiple practice settings, giving the student exposure to varied experiences (Birkenmaier, Curley, & Rowan, 2011). Programs also delay the entry of students into the field, by a month or a semester, for reasons such as the need for more educational preparation before the student works with clients. Scant research exists to guide programs in what model to adopt, and a program's choice of a field delivery model is typically driven by institutional need rather than a theoretically grounded approach that best supports students' learning (Theriot et al., 2006).

Predicated on the belief that a concurrent model facilitates the link between the field and classroom learning contexts, programs often embrace a concurrent model, where students are in field and coursework simultaneously. One study offered evidence that the concurrent model was more effective than a block model for student learning (Fortune, 1994). In contrast, Theriot et al. (2006) offer empirical evidence that suggests there is no significant difference in the effectiveness of block and concurrent models. Despite the incongruous outcomes of the studies investigating the effectiveness of these two primary delivery models, there is evidence to support the efficacy of a concurrent rotational model where students rotate through various placements, a distinctive feature of the Hartford Partnership Program for Aging Education. Birkenmaier et al. (2011, p. 325) reported positive knowledge outcomes for students in this program model, and very high student satisfaction. The study did not measure student competence, however. There remains a persistent need for more empirical evidence to guide social work programs in structuring field delivery in a way that optimizes students' learning.

Sheafor and Jenkins (1982) noted "three approaches to experiential learning that characterize social work field instruction: the apprenticeship, the academic, and the articulated orientations" (p. 13) (see figure 7.3). Field education today resembles variations of the three approaches, each rooted in the history of social work. First, the apprentice approach is the earliest model and positions the practicum toward the beginning of the education process. The curricular emphasis is on developing an experiential base so when students learn classroom theories they have practice examples on which to apply that theory. Implementation of this structure relies on faculty who match the experiential base of each student with teaching of theory in the classroom and field instructors who have an adequate knowledge base. The field liaison is more of a consultant to the agency, and the field instructor and student assume primary responsibility for integration of classroom and field learning.

**Figure 7.3. Apprentice, Academic, and Articulated Approaches to Field Delivery**

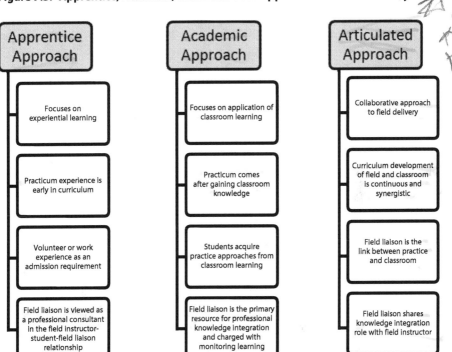

*Source*: Adapted from Sheafor & Jenkins (1982).

In the academic approach, knowledge is the focus of the learning encounter. The classroom is a central feature in this model, and the practicum is perceived as a laboratory where students apply knowledge gained from the classroom. The learning emphasis is placed on the student, and program faculty and liaisons become a primary resource for the student. The field instructor is present merely to facilitate the experience in the practicum.

Of the three structural models, Sheafor and Jenkins (1982) assert that the articulated approach provides the most collaborative field education delivery method. The articulated model facilitates an instructional partnership between the field liaison and field instructor while they assist students to integrate theory into practice. It uses the themes emerging in the field setting to continuously inform the program's curriculum. From this participatory approach, a synergistic exchange among the student, field instructor, and field liaison naturally emerges.

It is valuable for field directors to understand the chosen field delivery model of their program since it reflects the program's history and philosophical orientation toward field education. The selected model will influence decision making around field education and how a program appropriates resources and defines the role of the field liaison. The evolution of assessment in field education will also shape a program's approach to field delivery in the future, given the call for more congruence between the classroom and field components of the curriculum. The articulated approach, a planned linkage between classroom and field, most resonates with the purposes of field education today.

Two field educators are vital to student learning in an effective field education delivery model: the field instructor and the field liaison. Student satisfaction with field learning has been most associated with the relationship each student has with his or her field instructor (Alperin, 1998; Raskin, 1989). Bogo (2005), in a synthesis of forty empirical field studies, noted that

> a constellation of field instruction factors emerges, with some supporting evidence that they are valued by students. Field instruction is valued when it includes: (1) instructor behavior and characteristics that offer support, including providing balanced feedback on students' practice; (2) frequent field instruction sessions of duration; (3) direct learning activities such as observing and working with professional role models; (4) reflective and conceptual learning activities such as providing a conceptual framework for understanding students' practice, assistance in analyzing cases, and integration of theory and practice, including concepts studied in the classroom; and (5) activities that encourage student self-critique. (Bogo, 2005, p. 176)

These factors should be infused throughout field education relationships between student and field instructor and, when feasible, between student and liaison, in integrative field seminars and field conferences.

### The Field Liaison Role: A Bridge to Learning

The field liaison role has existed since the genesis of professional social work education in the early 1900s (Raphael & Rosenblum, 1987). Its early iterations, enduring to the present, encompassed various titles and functions with the primary focus of advocating, consulting, teaching, monitoring, and mediating (Bogo, 2010). The field liaison is the university representative who serves as an intermediary among the agency, social work program, and student. While field instructors hold primary responsibility for student learning in the practice setting, the endemic dilemma of resource scarcity among social service agencies has limited the amount of time they can dedicate to teaching and supervising students. In response, many social work programs have expanded the role of a field liaison to include partnering with field instructors in providing quality instruction. The literature has consistently noted reliance on liaisons to support field instructors in assisting students with the integration of theory with practice, facilitating evaluation, and gatekeeping (Homonoff, 2008).

Field directors typically oversee and/or supervise the work of the liaison; it is imperative for the director to describe the liaison's role, set clear expectations, and establish performance evaluation criteria. In addition, liaisons need adequate instruction to enable them to perform their roles effectively. While the CSWE leaves the definition of the position up to individual social work programs, the literature most often describes the role as an adviser to the student, consultant to the field instructor, mediator between the student and field instructor (and agency), teacher, and advocate (Faria, Brownstein, & Smith, 1988; Ligon & Ward, 2005; Liley, 2006; Lyter, 2005; Raphael & Rosenblum, 1987). The most commonly reported liaison responsibilities can be delineated as follows:

- Facilitating field conferences

- Monitoring student hours, progress, and educational opportunities

- Leading field seminars

- Assisting students in integrating theory and practice

- Fostering dialog and building rapport between school and practice settings

- Evaluating students' performance and gatekeeping

- Evaluating the effectiveness of field instructors and practice settings

Despite this often-referenced list of responsibilities, substantial variation in the role and function of the liaison exists across programs due to factors such as faculty status (e.g., tenure or nontenure), qualifications, job description, and assignments. Program staffing patterns include the use of tenured/tenure-track faculty, adjunct faculty, community practitioners, tutors, and teaching coordinators (Ligon & Ward, 2005). Programs increasingly assign the liaison functions to part-time staff, adjunct faculty, and doctoral students, who may have limited knowledge and influence on curriculum decisions (Burke, Condon, & Wickell, 1999). Tenure-track faculty, especially those at research-intensive universities, have increased demands to carry out research and to publish, and are less likely to serve as liaisons. Regardless of how this position is filled, programs should assess the effectiveness of staffing patterns and performance by eliciting feedback from students and field instructors on an annual basis. The program should recognize and reward liaisons who demonstrate effective teaching and, in some programs, scholarship.

Even with the longstanding tradition of the field liaison's integral presence in social work education, there exists minimal empirical evidence to guide the formulation of educational standards for this central function (Bennett & Coe, 1998; Bogo, 2010). Dennis (2013) sought to better understand the existing evidentiary landscape surrounding the field liaison role by conducting a systematic review of the literature on the field liaison published between 1982 and 2012. The most salient themes emerging from the review include these:

- The existing body of evidence-based knowledge is primarily derived from exploratory studies; almost all the studies are philosophically pragmatic.

- There is a dearth of available research; what exists is not generalizable based on the methodologies employed. Additionally, the current body of scholarship examining the field liaison role is dated, with only four studies in the past decade.

- Scant research exists that addresses how varying contexts (urban, suburban, rural, international, and online) affect the purpose and function of the field liaison role.

- The existing research on the field liaison primarily addresses student and field instructor perceptual satisfaction and is not linked to student performance measures.

- The field liaison role is complex, and there is a plurality of perspectives among social work programs as to how the role should be used to deliver field education.

As social work education continues to formulate sound pedagogical standards, integrate theory and practice, and cultivate synergistic agency-academy partnerships, there is a growing need for a better understanding of how the field liaison role could be most efficaciously used to further student learning. The way programs execute this role varies greatly, and field directors are often positioned to deal with such realities as liaisons who do not make field visits, programs that cut the number of visits due to budget constraints, and field instructors who report liaison performance problems. With the program context evolving, partly due to distance learning options and burgeoning assessment requirements in field education, questions about how to appropriate resources to this critical field educator role will grow in importance.

### Field Conferences: Bridging Conversations

The field liaison, field instructor, and student communicate routinely through regular contact in person and/via the use of technology throughout the practicum. Guided by the standard that states field programs must specify policies and procedures for "maintaining field liaison contacts with field education settings" (CSWE, 2008, Accreditation Standard 2.1.5, p. 9), a common practice is a field conference or liaison site visit. Despite this CSWE mandate, there persists ambiguity in how programs interpret this requirement.

Programs vary in the number of visits that liaisons are required to make per semester. Investigation into this process suggests that field liaisons conduct an average of 2.2 visits a semester in bachelor of social work (BSW) programs (Ligon & Ward, 2005), whereas master of social work (MSW) liaisons visit students slightly less frequently, averaging 1.5 visits per semester (Dalton, Stevens, & Maas-Brady, 2011). Raphael and Rosenblum (1987) recommended an approach that includes four visits per year; more-contemporary field scholars, however, propose a format of one visit to be made in the fall term "followed by other means of communication during the spring term, and planning visits only when indicated by needs" (Lyter, 2005, p. 9). This is commonly referred to as the trouble-shooting model. Regardless of approach, field instructor satisfaction tends to be correlated with the availability of the field liaison throughout the field placement (Bennett & Coe, 1998; Lyter, 2005).

The purpose of the liaison contact is to ensure the quality of the field practicum and field instructor supervision. Topics covered in the visit include the student learning agreements, course assignments, student learning needs, progress toward achieving competencies, application of theory, and persistent challenges (Lyter, 2005). A site visit might also consist of the liaison observing the student in practice, touring the setting, and/or participating in the formal evaluation of the student. If there is a task supervisor (someone who provides supervision in conjunction with the field instructor) working with the student, that person is typically included in the conference. Lyter found that student satisfaction with the liaison role was elevated by field liaison visits associated with a discussion of the student learning agreement, integration of class and field, and attention to the student portfolio.

At the field visit, the liaison should also assess student progress toward developing competencies, and should promote field instruction factors most valued by students in the field instructor–student relationship. A process recording, journal entry, and/or survey, specific to the supervisory relationship at a beginning, middle, or end phase of the practicum experience, can provide valuable information to the liaison. By listening to the student's voice in the process, the liaison may identify specific supervisory training needs, refine the placement or student learning agreement, or determine that the placement is not a good fit for field learning at that time.

## Field Seminar

The field seminar is offered at the MSW and BSW levels of social work education and is acknowledged as a valuable component of a unified curriculum (Birkenmaier, Wilson, Berg-Weger, Banks, & Hartung, 2003; Dalton et al., 2011; Giddings & Vodde, 2003; Jarman-Rhode, McFall, Kolar, & Strom, 1997; Mary & Herse, 1992; Poe & Hunter, 2009). Surveys estimate that close to 96 percent of undergraduate programs (N=191) offer field seminars (Poe & Hunter, 2009), and 81 percent of graduate programs (N=135) include seminars in their curriculum (Dalton et al., 2011). The field seminar is an interactive learning community that typically entails a small group of students who regularly carve out reflective time to discuss field learning as well as to become socialized to the profession. To maximize students' competency, the field seminar requires a well-defined purpose and pedagogical norms. Field directors interested in developing or refining the field seminar will benefit from considering the following aspects: purpose, curriculum location and field delivery model, credit and grading, frequency of meetings, student group composition, instructor, and student assignments (see figure 7.4 and discussion below).

**Figure 7.4. Considerations for Conducting Field Seminars**

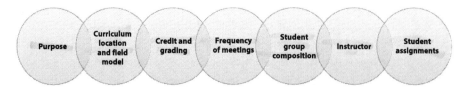

## Purpose

To stretch students' understanding as they interface with practicum experiences, seminars offer a unique curricular "pedagogical space [and a] consistent structure" for transformative reflective processes (Poe & Hunter, 2009, p. 45). Poe and Hunter describe seminars as the primary curricular destination for faculty's opportunity to "guide and observe a student's process of integration, interpretation, and identification" (p. 44). Field directors in the study underscored the primary purposes of the seminar as being (1) "development of professional identity," (2) "development of professional competence," (3) "discussion of ethical issues," (4) "development of generalist perspective," (5) "troubleshooting of problems," and (6) "integration of theory and practice" (Poe & Hunter, 2009, p. 37). Seminars may cover curriculum topics most related to field, such as risk management, safety training, indirect trauma (Cunningham, 2004), self-care, community resources, professional supervision, career planning, life-long learning, and state licensure (Bibus & Boutté-Queen, 2011). Finally, seminars become a potential gatekeeping opportunity for field educators to identify students not suited for the profession.

## Curriculum Location and Field Delivery Model

If one of the purposes of the field seminar is to integrate theory with field experiences, then programs must discern how to best interweave the seminar within the overall curriculum. In many programs, the field seminar is a required course embedded in the field practicum. Other programs locate the seminar within a practice course or concentration, such as mental health, child welfare, gerontology, or policy, or as a capstone course.

The field education delivery model (concurrent, block, rotation, or delayed entry) will also influence the seminars' purpose and curriculum content. For example, in a delayed entry model, where field begins a month or more after the seminar begins, the seminar may be used in the weeks leading up to practicum as a way for the instructor to become acquainted with students, practice simulations, assess skills, and professionally prepare students for field.

## Credit and Grading

Programs vary on how to assign seminar course credit(s), course grading, and course meeting frequency. Students who receive credit for the seminar are more likely to value their participation in it (Birkenmaier et al., 2003). Deciding how students will be graded requires consideration, including whether the seminar is graded as a separate course or is incorporated into the overall field practicum grade. Arguably, faculty can assign A to F grading if students are meeting course objectives and developing competencies.

### Frequency of Meetings

The frequency of meeting for the seminar is commonly determined by the hours and credits assigned. Existing research suggests that undergraduate programs tend to meet more frequently than graduate programs. A study of graduate programs found that 81 percent of respondents reported having academic credit–based field seminars that met on an average only 9.5 times over a semester (Dalton et al., 2011). A similar study on undergraduate programs revealed that BSW programs tend to meet weekly for seminar, as reported by 78 percent of respondents (Poe & Hunter, 2009).

### Student Group Composition

There are several considerations for seminar student composition, including student characteristics, field placement settings, and faculty foci. Different student characteristics are noteworthy when forming a seminar group: (1) traditional students, (2) commuting students, (3) nontraditional students, and (4) a mix of students. Another aspect of student composition is the practice setting. An agency with a number of students may be in one seminar providing opportunity for sharing of common experiences based on the field of practice, such as child welfare, school social work, military social work, mental health, or gerontology. Some programs arrange seminar composition to match the liaison's practice experience, research interests, and established relationships with community service providers.

### Instructor

The question of who holds primary responsibility for facilitating the field seminar relates to its stated purpose, importance in the curriculum, and the content to be delivered (Smith & Faria, 1988). A program's structure, philosophical orientation about field delivery, and available resources typically determine who in the program facilitates the seminar, whether that be full-time tenured or adjunct faculty. Poe and Hunter (2009) noted that when the seminar is facilitated by adjunct faculty it may be more difficult for that faculty to facilitate integration of class and field if the instructors do not have a role in curriculum design and implementation. To fortify the ongoing fusion between the curriculum and field experiences, there are advantages to having full-time teaching faculty facilitate seminars. Possessing insight into the curriculum, these faculty members can help to contemporize the explicit curriculum by transferring classroom knowledge into the field while also using the direct contact with the field to inform the curriculum of changes in the practice realm.

## Student Assignments

A range of activities and assignments to facilitate student learning in field education can often be situated in the field seminar. Poe and Hunter (2009) found similarities in student assignments across the 191 undergraduate programs they surveyed. Assignments queried in their study included learning agreements, reflective writing, process recordings, oral case presentations, written micro and macro case analyses, environmental studies of agencies and communities, policy studies, portfolios, and literature reviews (Poe & Hunter, 2009, p. 41). A study by Dalton (2012) found a similar pattern and use of assignments in MSW programs. It would be valuable to investigate further student learning activities, especially as these activities relate to developing student practice competence (Fortune, McCarthy, & Abramson, 2001; Knight, 2001).

## The Potential Role of Field Seminar in Signature Pedagogy

Field scholars promote the use of educational group structures taught by master teachers as an approach to improving the quality of social work education and contributing to the profession's signature pedagogy (Wayne, Bogo, & Raskin, 2010). The seminar has the potential to offer a consistent structure for students to think critically and reflectively about their practice in an accountable, peer-to-peer manner, while being guided by an experienced field educator. The seminar's educator-facilitator needs to be highly skilled in group work and educational supervision.

Field directors "assist in the development and monitoring of integrative seminars" (Pierce, 2008, p. 9), and can strengthen the role of the seminar as a vehicle for integration of classroom and field by establishing a clearly stated purpose, one that can be operationalized and measured. To increase the seminars' classroom-field integrative effectiveness, the field director should collaborate with field educators on curriculum and student assignments. Designing a meaningful faculty-field-classroom relationship is integral to ensuring a seminar structure that promotes integrative learning.

## Conclusion

Quality social work education is predicated on the intentional blending of classroom and field education, which remains a difficult and elusive task for social work educators. As social work education has evolved into a competency-based model, field education has emerged as the culminating curricular event. Field education's signature status is catalyzing an intensified focus on how it can seek to become more congruent with pedagogical norms characteristic of signature pedagogies in professional education (Wayne et al., 2010). Consequently, the accentuation of assessment in field will likely magnify attention on the delivery of field and how to appropriate needed resources to this essential feature of social work education.

To that end, it is critical to recognize the importance and evolving role of the field liaison in facilitating student learning and supporting field instructors in their educational endeavors. Field conferences and seminars offer engaging opportunities for learning that synthesize theory and practice. The field seminar or integrative seminar course provides a programmatic mechanism for students to develop professional identity and competence, examine ethical and practice issues, integrate theory with practice, and offer mutual support during the field placement (Poe & Hunter, 2009). Through the infusion of creativity, innovation, and collaboration, field directors provide vision for the culmination of this dynamic teaching and learning endeavor in field education. Ultimately, from this collaborative effort competent social workers emerge, equipped with the ability to adapt to an ever-changing practice context.

### Essential Readings

Birkenmaier, J., Wilson, R. J., Berg-Weger, M., Banks, R., & Hartung, M. (2003). MSW integrative seminars: Toward integrating course and field work. *Journal of Teaching in Social Work, 23*(1/2), 167–182.

Bogo, M. (2010). *Achieving competence in social work through field education.* Toronto, ON. University of Toronto Press.

Hendricks, C., Finch, J, & Franks, C. L. (2005). *Learning to teach: Teaching to learn.* Alexandria, VA: Council on Social Work Education Press.

Poe, N. T., & Hunter, C.A. (2009). A curious curriculum component: The non-mandated "given" of field seminar. *Journal of Baccalaureate Social Work, 14*(2), 31–47.

Sheafor, B. W., & Jenkins, L. E. (Eds.). (1982). *Quality field instruction in social work.* New York: Longman.

Wayne, J., Bogo, M., & Raskin, M. (2010). Field education as the signature pedagogy of social work education. *Journal of Social Work Education, 46*(3), 327–339.

## References

Alperin, D. E. (1998). Factors related to student satisfaction with child welfare field placements. *Journal of Social Work Education, 34*(1), 43–54.

Bennett, L., & Coe, S. (1998). Social work field instructor satisfaction with faculty field liaisons. *Journal of Social Work Education, 34*(3), 345–352.

Bibus, A. A., & Boutté-Queen, N. (2011). *Regulating social work: A primer on licensing practice.* Chicago: Lyceum Books.

Biggs, J., & Tang, C. (2007). *Teaching for quality learning at university: What the student does* (3rd ed.). Berkshire, UK: Open University.

Birkenmaier, J., Curley, J., & Rowan, N. L. (2011). Knowledge outcomes within rotational models of social work field education. *Journal of Gerontological Social Work, 55*(3), 321–336.

Birkenmaier, J., Wilson, R. J., Berg-Weger, M., Banks, R., & Hartung, M. (2003). MSW integrative seminars: Toward integrating course and field work. *Journal of Teaching in Social Work, 23*(1/2), 167–182.

Bogo, M. (2005). Field instruction in social work: A review of the research literature 1999–2005. *Clinical Supervisor, 24*(1/2), 163–193.

Bogo, M. (2010). *Achieving competence in social work through field education.* Toronto, ON. University of Toronto Press.

Bogo, M., & Vayda, E. (1998). *The practice of field instruction in social work: Theory and process* (2nd ed.). New York: Columbia University Press.

Boisen, L., & Syers, M., (2004). The integrative case analysis model for linking theory and practice. *Journal of Social Work Education, 40*(2), 205–217.

Boud, D., & Falchikov, N. (2006). Aligning assessment with long-term learning. *Assessment & Evaluation in Higher Education, 31*, 399–413. doi:10.1080/02602930600679050.

Boud, D., & Walker, D. (1998). Promoting reflection in professional courses: The challenge of context. *Studies in Higher Education, 23*(2), 1–16.

Burke, S. G., Condon, S., & Wickell, B. (1999). The liaison role in schools of social work: A break with the past. *Clinical Supervisor, 18*(1), 203–210.

Caine, R. N., Caine, G., McClintic, C., & Klimek, K. (2005). *12 brain/mind learning principles in action.* Thousand Oaks, CA: Corwin Press.

Clare, B. (2007). Promoting deep learning: A teaching, learning and assessment endeavour. *Social Work Education, 26*, 433–446. doi:10.1080/02615470601118571.

Council on Social Work Education (CSWE). (2008). *Educational policy and accreditation standards* (rev. March 27, 2010/updated August 2012). Alexandria, VA: Author. Retrieved from http://www.cswe.org/Accreditation/41865.aspx.

Cunningham, M. (2004). Teaching social workers about trauma: Reducing the risks of vicarious traumatization in the classroom. *Journal of Social Work Education, 36*, 27–38.

Dalton, B. (2012). "You make them do what?" A national survey on field seminar assignments. *Advances in Social Work, 13*(3), 618–632.

Dalton, B., Stevens, L., & Maas-Brady, J. (2011). "How do you do it?": MSW field director survey. *Advances in Social Work, 12*(2), 276–288.

Dennis, S. (2013, March). *The Faculty Field Liaison Role: An Evidentiary Examination.* Paper presentation at the Baccalaureate Program Directors Annual Conference, Myrtle Beach, SC.

Dewey, J. (1933). *How we think.* New York: Heath.

Entwistle, N., & Ramsden, P. (1983). *Understanding student learning.* London: Croom Helm.

Faria, G., Brownstein C., & Smith, H. (1988). A survey of field instructors' perceptions of the liaison role. *Journal of Social Work Education, 24*(2), 135–144.

Fortune, A. E. (1994). Field education. In F. J. Reamer (Ed.), *The foundations of social work knowledge.* New York: Columbia University Press.

Fortune, A. E., McCarthy, M., & Abramson, J. S. (2001). Student learning processes in field education: Relationship of learning activities to quality of field instruction, satisfaction, and performance among MSW students. *Journal of Social Work Education, 37*(1), 111–124.

Gardiner, D. (1988). Improving students' learning: Setting an agenda for quality in the 90's. *Issues in Social Work Education, 8*, 3–10.

Giddings, M., & Vodde, R. (2003). A conceptual framework for foundation practicum and seminar: The progressive adaptation model. *Journal of Teaching in Social Work, 23*(1/2), 123–143.

Grossman, R. (2009). Structures for facilitating student reflection. *College Teaching, 47*(1), 15–22.

Havnes, A. (2004). Examination and learning: An activity-theoretical analysis of the relationship between assessment and educational practice. *Assessment & Evaluation in Higher Education, 29*(2), 159–176.

Hendricks, C., Finch, J, & Franks, C. L. (2005). *Learning to teach: Teaching to learn.* Alexandria, VA: Council on Social Work Education Press.

Holloway, S., Black, P., Hoffman, K., & Pierce, D. (n.d.). *Some considerations of the import of the 2008 EPAS for curriculum design.* Retrieved from http://www.cswe.org/File.aspx?id=31578.

Homonoff, E. (2008). The heart of social work: Best practitioners rise to challenges in field instruction. *Clinical Supervisor, 27*(2), 135–169.

Jarman-Rhode, L. J., McFall, J., Kolar, P., & Strom, G. (1997). The changing context of social work practice: Implications and recommendations for social work educators. *Journal of Social Work Education, 33*(1), 29–46.

Knight, C. (2001). The process of field instruction: BSW and MSW student views of effective field supervision. *Journal of Social Work Education, 32*, 399–414.

Knowles, M. S. (1972). Innovations in teaching styles and approaches based upon adult learning. *Journal of Education for Social Work, 8*(2), 32–39.

Kolb, D. A. (1984). *Experiential learning: Experience as the source of learning and development.* Englewood Cliffs, NJ: Prentice Hall.

Light, G., Cox, R., & Calkins, S. (2009). *Learning and teaching in higher education: The reflective professional* (2nd ed.). London: Sage.

Ligon, J., & Ward, J. (2005). A national study of field liaison role in the social work education programs in the United States and Puerto Rico. *Social Work Education, 24*(2), 235–243.

Liley, D. (2006). What do faculty liaisons have to offer? *New Social Worker, 13*(2), 6–7.

Lyter, S. (2005). Social work field liaison agency visits: Factors associated with student performance and satisfaction. *Atre, 28*(2), 1–11.

Marton, F., & Säljö, R. (1976). On qualitative differences in learning: Outcome and process. *British Journal of Educational Psychology, 46*, 4–11.

Mary, N. L., & Herse, M. H. (1992). What do field seminars accomplish? Student and instructor perspectives. *Journal of Teaching in Social Work, 6*(2), 59–73.

Mumm, A. M. (2006). Teaching social work student practice skills. *Journal of Teaching in Social Work, 26*, 71–89.

Pierce, D. (2008). *Field education in the 2008 EPAS: Implications for the field director's role.* Retrieved from http://www.cswe.org/File.aspx?id=31580.

Poe, N. T., & Hunter, C.A. (2009). A curious curriculum component: The non-mandated "given" of field seminar. *Journal of Baccalaureate Social Work, 14*(2), 31–47.

Polanyi, M. (1967). *The tacit dimension.* London: Routledge.

Raphael, F. B., & Rosenblum, A. F. (1987). An operational guide to the faculty field liaison role. *Social Casework, 68*(3), 157–163.

Raskin, M. (1989). *Empirical Studies in Field Education.* New York: Haworth Press.

Reynolds, B. C. (1942). *Learning and teaching in the practice of social work.* New York: Russell & Russell.

Schön, D. (1983). *The reflective practitioner: How professionals think in action.* New York: Basic Books.

Schön, D. (1987). *Educating the reflective practitioner: Toward a new design for teaching and learning in the professions.* San Francisco: Jossey-Bass.

Sheafor, B. W., & Jenkins, L. E. (Eds.). (1982). *Quality field instruction in social work.* New York: Longman.

Shepard, L. (2000). The role of assessment in a learning culture. *Educational Researcher, 29*(7), 1–14.

Shulman, L. S. (2005). Signature pedagogies in the professions. *Daedalus, 134*(3), 52–59.

Smith, H., & Faria, G. (1988). A survey of field perceptions of the liaison role. *Journal of Social work Education, 24*(2), 239–248.

Sousa, D. A. (2006). *How the brain learns.* Thousand Oaks, CA: Corwin Press.

Theriot, M., Johnson, T., Mulvaney, M., & Kretzschmar, J. (2006). Does slow and steady win the race? The impact of block versus concurrent field on BSW students' professional development and emotional well-being. *Journal of Baccalaureate Social Work, 12*(1), 203–217.

Towle, C. (1954). *The learner in education for the professions.* Chicago: University of Chicago Press.

Wayne, J., Bogo, M., & Raskin, M. (2010). Field education as the signature pedagogy of social work education. *Journal of Social Work Education, 46*(3), 327–339.

Zull, J. E. (2002). *The art of changing the brain: Enriching teaching by exploring the biology of learning.* Sterling, VA: Stylus.

# 8

# Evaluation of Student Learning
*Marion Bogo*

As a competency-based model, the Educational Policy and Accreditation Standards (EPAS) specifies the outcomes students are expected to achieve; EPAS expresses these outcomes in terms of performance, or what students are able to *do* (Council on Social Work Education [CSWE], 2008). With this shift, social work education programs must pay more attention to the goals they wish to achieve and to multiple methods to assess students' learning. Field evaluations are a highly important part of assessment, and field directors can play an important role in adapting current evaluation methods and in developing new scales. Any field evaluation will need to be aligned with the EPAS (CSWE, 2008) standards and the program's mission, goals, and articulation of competencies.

Crucial information is gained from evaluating student learning in the field practicum. First, evaluation feedback provided to the student during the field practicum and at structured times throughout the semester is one of the most useful educational strategies to promote learning. Students receive ongoing and periodic information about their performance, information that can help them focus their efforts and seek out practice learning opportunities targeted to attaining specific goals. In this manner, formative feedback has a guiding effect. Second, summative or final evaluation, also referred to as educational outcomes assessment, determines a student's grade. This assessment is higher stake because it establishes whether the student will pass onto the next year or graduate into the profession. Third, aggregated data regarding all students' field performance provide the social work education program with information that indicates the degree to which the program is meeting its mission and goals, and the degree to which it contributes to quality assurance.

Because evaluation of learning is so important for individual students, the program, and the profession, social work educators have sought to articulate what is expected of students and to develop reliable, valid, and authentic methods of assessing learning and achieving competence. And, in common with other human service and health professions, social work educators recognize the complexities involved in this task. This chapter will review issues pertinent to evaluation of students' learning in the field practicum and provide examples of some attempts to address these challenges. Since the concept of competence frames evaluation in the field practicum, the first section of this chapter discusses competence in depth. The remainder of this chapter examines key issues related to assessment of students' competence and offers suggestions for both new and experienced field directors to implement evaluation.

## The Context of Field Education Evaluation

The CSWE is accountable to the American people to ensure that social work education programs graduate students who are able to carry out the core functions of the profession in a competent and ethical manner. Similar to accrediting bodies in related human service and health fields, EPAS (CSWE, 2008) makes use of a competency-based framework to guide the articulation of the school's mission and program goals, and to design learning and teaching activities to meet those competencies. A hallmark of competency-based education is that it begins with the end point—the program expresses the competencies as educational outcomes (i.e., what the program should produce in its graduates with respect to what they are able to do in the practice of social work). This focus and emphasis on competence—what graduates are able to *do*—means that evaluation of student learning and performance in field education is even more crucial than in previous accreditation frameworks. It also reflects the belief that professional programs are responsible for educating future practitioners in their profession's fundamental ways of thinking, performing, and acting with integrity (Shulman, 2005). Furthermore, EPAS (CSWE, 2008) designates field education as the signature pedagogy of social work, and recognizes the central role it plays in socializing students to social work practice and learning to integrate theory and practice.

It is important for field education leaders to have a sound understanding of the concept of competence including both definitions and critiques. Such an understanding provides the foundation for directing all aspects of the field program. Field directors must construct authentic, reliable, and valid evaluation methods of students' learning, and orient field instructors to this new perspective. The field program also provides guidance for the crucial gatekeeping role played by field education evaluation of students' competence and readiness to practice social work (Sowbel, 2011, 2012).

In the mid-1970s a number of social work educators, especially in undergraduate programs, provided competency-based frameworks for curriculum planning that would encompass both class and field (Arkava & Brennan, 1976; Baer & Frederico, 1978). In graduate programs many schools adopted a competency model, but this model applied only to learning in field education. Curriculum and learning objectives for university courses continued to be designed in traditional ways where learning was evaluated through the use of written essays or knowledge-based exams. The new focus on competency was in the interests of articulating what capable practitioners should be able to *do*. Moreover, articulating end goals in transparent and concrete ways could help adult learners become more active in identifying their learning goals and taking self-directed initiatives to meet them. The appeal of this new focus was that competency models could replace the ill-defined, broad, and vague practice dimensions that characterized most field evaluations at that time. Indeed, in two Delphi studies conducted ten years apart, field experts identified as the most important field education issues the difficulty in agreeing on field learning goals and the need for objective evaluation approaches (Raskin, 1983, 1994). Although individual programs made some progress in articulating competencies and methods to evaluate them, a national framework to organize field learning outcomes and to advance the profession did not exist until EPAS (CSWE, 2008).

## Competence

The concept of competence refers in general to a set of knowledge, skills, and attitudes or values that are evident in the behavior of professionals as they perform in the domains associated with their profession (Bogo, 2010; Kane, 1992). Specific competencies are then conceptualized as elements of competence that are interrelated, integrated, and performed at an acceptable level (Kaslow et al., 2004). The movement to develop competency models to guide professional educational programs became popular in the United Kingdom and Australia in the 1980s and was used by these countries' national governments to define occupational standards for a wide range of employment categories. The approach has been critiqued when it led to an analysis of work tasks that were then broken down into ever-growing lists of discrete, concrete, behavioral skills (Hackett, 2001; Kelly & Horder, 2001). These critics see such a view of practice as mechanistic, and believe that it ignores important aspects of professional practice. Specifically, professionals work in a way that is not linear or mechanistic. Rather, there is a holistic and organic nature to professional work where practitioners use knowledge in a thoughtful way, and are sensitive to the context in which service is delivered and the uniqueness of each client and situation (Cheetham & Chivers, 2005). The literature on professional practice recognizes the impact of practitioners' perceptions and subjective reactions to situations on their judgments, decisions, and actions (Eraut, 1994; Kane, 1992; Schön, 1983). The importance of emotional awareness, subjective understanding, and the capacity for self-reflection is a long-standing principle in social work (Fox, 2011; Ruch, 2007).

## Competency Models and Social Work

Prior to EPAS (CSWE, 2008), competence models in social work were developed in the pioneering work of the Strengthening Aging and Gerontological Education in Social Work Project supported by the Hartford Foundation (Damron-Rodriguez, Lawrance, Barnett, & Simmons, 2006); in the generic abilities offered by Gingerich, Kaye, and Bailey (1999); and in the holistic competence model of Bogo and colleagues (Bogo, 2010; Bogo et al., 2006). All models present competencies at a level that is not so abstract as to be vague or nebulous, nor so concrete as to be mechanistic. Finally, EPAS (CSWE, 2008, Educational Policy [EP] 2.1) reflects a complex model of competence with its articulation of ten core competencies and their forty-one related practice behaviors.

These core competencies are expected of graduates of both undergraduate and graduate programs. Each program is to identify advanced practice competencies for graduates of MSW programs specific to the concentration. A number of groups have taken the initiative to propose such competencies for practice with particular populations (see, e.g., in gerontology and in military social work), issues (e.g., for the prevention of substance use disorders), and method (e.g., clinical social work).

## Empirical Support

In a multiproject program of research, Bogo et al. (2006) elicited the practice wisdom of field instructors and identified implicit and explicit dimensions they drew on when describing student performance at various levels along a continuum. The first set of studies involved field instructors in micro or direct practice settings (Bogo et al., 2006). A holistic model of competence emerged that entailed two interrelated levels of competence. The first level is referred to as meta-competence and captures overarching qualities and abilities of a conceptual, interpersonal, and personal/professional nature. The second level refers to procedural competence, or observable behavioral skills.

Meta-competencies are of a higher order and affect the way students and practitioners engage as learners and with significant figures in the environment. This level of competence includes cognitive capacities such as the way practice is conceptualized, the active use of knowledge and values, the processing of information, bringing judgment to bear, and arriving at decisions regarding appropriate interventions for clients, communities, and organizations. Meta-competencies also include interpersonal dimensions that affect engagement with the field instructor, team members, and clients. Self-awareness, reflection, and self-regulation are aspects of personal meta-competence that affect our ability to carry out professional roles. The second level of competence, procedural competence, refers to skills and techniques associated with collaborative relationship building and maintenance, conducting assessments, offering interventions, and communicating professional information through verbal and written methods (Bogo, 2010; Bogo et al., 2006).

The second set of studies of field instructors' perceptions of student competence involved social workers in macro practice in community, organization, and policy field settings. The holistic model of competence was supported; when field instructors discussed students' performance they did so in a manner wherein they again identified qualities and abilities at two different but interrelated levels. The particular competencies differed from micro competencies in some dimensions. Meta-competencies included characteristics such as self-awareness, compassion, motivation, and commitment to social justice for students in macro practice. Procedural competencies included project management and presentation skills, and the ability to articulate and implement steps to attain goals (Regehr, Bogo, Donovan, Anstice, & Lim, 2012).

Emerging from these studies was the recognition that not all competencies are of equal importance. Rather, a hallmark of professional practitioners is their ability to differentially use skills based on a broader understanding of the context in which the skills are required and an understanding of the potential for multiple outcomes of any given intervention (Ericsson & Charness, 1994). This perspective recognizes the link between the cognitive processes involved in conceptualizing practice, including subjective perceptions and reactions, and the performance aspect of choosing and enacting skillful behavior. Therefore, when we ask field instructors to assess competence, it is likely that their judgments are not based solely on student behavior. As the field instructors in these studies identified, their evaluation of student competence includes their perception of the way students differentially use knowledge and professional self in practice.

In summary, complex models of competence must focus on performance of social workers—what they are able to do in practice. Practice behaviors are recognized as complex and as a demonstration of the practitioner's integration of the particular profession's knowledge, values, and skills. Competence most certainly involves social workers' ability to practice. It also involves their ability to examine, think critically, use the knowledge base, and use their own emotions and reactions gleaned from interactions with client systems. These latter elements involve focused attention to, and reflection on, internal cognitive or thought processes and subjective reactions. EPAS represents the development of a framework that captures these underlying and more-abstract dimensions (the ten competencies) as well as examples of concrete practice behaviors that illustrate the accompanying competence (CSWE, 2008).

In schools that have used a competency-based approach to field education and evaluation, field directors may need only to adapt their current field evaluation tools to accommodate the specific dimensions in EPAS (CSWE, 2008). In schools that have not used such an approach, field directors will need to be involved in defining practice behaviors and developing evaluation tools, issues discussed in the following sections. Since most social work practitioners generally do not think about their work in terms of competence, field directors can use orientation and training activities to provide insights into the competence framework as discussed in this chapter. It is also important to note that related helping and health professions, such as medicine (Accreditation Council for Graduate Medical Education, 2010; Epstein & Hundert, 2002), nursing (Scott Tilley, 2008), and psychology (Fouad et al., 2009; Kaslow et al., 2004), have also adopted competence models for education and evaluation.

The current challenge for all social work educators, including field directors, is to design evaluation methods and tools that accommodate the multifaceted levels of practice competence discussed thus far. Progress toward this goal will occur as we strive for methods and tools to assess students' learning that more closely align and link knowledge, cognitive and subjective reflection, and skill. This new framework for social work education provides an opportunity to define what social workers do in a more specific and transparent manner. As Kane (1992) observed, however, although it is important to attempt to clarify and understand the concept of competence, it is unrealistic to expect to eliminate the difficulties in evaluating it.

### Defining Competence

Social work programs are now engaged in designing a range of assessment tools to demonstrate that students have achieved the competencies set out by EPAS (CSWE, 2008). These tools are designed to reflect the mission and goals of the particular program. While the framework encourages commonality across programs, it also allows for tailoring to the specific characteristics of the program's context as expressed in its mission and goals. Educators have expressed the wish to share and not reinvent the wheel in the design of evaluation instruments. It is useful for educators to review others' tools. Replicating another school's assessment tool, however, deprives the program of using the competency framework to express its own unique character and objectives to identify additional competencies deemed important or that further specify practice behaviors that illustrate the competencies.

Social work educators need to consider a number of issues when defining competencies in field education. A first consideration is how to capture the generic and specific dimensions of practice. Students are assigned to do their practicum in a range of settings. Undergraduate and foundation-year master of social work (MSW) students are expected to have a generic field experience, and second-year MSW students are expected to be placed in a setting related to their specialization or concentration. Agencies, however, are specialized by virtue of their mandate and function. Programs must express competencies at a level that will be meaningful to the diverse settings accepting students. Moreover, both particular agencies and individual field instructors use various practice models and approaches. It is unlikely that unique practice procedures and intervention skills will all be specified in the competency framework of a particular school. The generic competencies and related practice behaviors, however, must be broad enough for individual field instructors to perceive the competencies involved in their practice and to translate the dimensions into the assignments they provide and the concepts and skills they teach students in the agency.

For example, the competency of engagement is presented in EP 2.1.10(a) with the practice behaviors of "substantively and affectively prepare for action with individuals and families, groups, organizations, and communities; use empathy and other interpersonal skills; and develop a mutually agreed-on focus of work and desired outcomes" (CSWE, 2008, p. 7).

Social work field instructors and their students will have different experiences in aiming to engage and build collaborative relationships that demonstrate this competency; their experiences are different largely because of the different settings in which their practicum occurs. Developing a working relationship and plan when practicing with clients who have asked for help in a community-based senior center that offers a range of in-home services and programs contrasts with the experience of a home visit to assess the risk of child safety due to a report to a child protection agency from a concerned day-care worker.

Field directors can identify more practice behaviors in their models and evaluation tools so that assessments include a range of setting-specific competencies. In the above example of child protection work, a practice behavior could refer to the student's ability to form a collaborative relationship while effectively using authority. This approach, however, might result in some settings stating that such a specific behavior is not relevant to their practice. It will also result in longer and longer lists of practice behaviors, and will increase the burden of evaluation for field instructors. Another approach is to use training for field instructors to illustrate how they can interpret generic competencies and practice behaviors to fit with the unique aspects of practice in their setting.

Ideally, schools' competency inventories and illustrative practice behaviors also emanate from an evidence-based approach and include complex behaviors identified in empirical work, which has demonstrated positive outcomes for clients and communities. Social work educators have become more active in developing evidence-based knowledge. Similar to educators in related health and human service professions, social work educators are expected to teach and evaluate students' competence in providing such practices. Educators do have a growing body of literature from which to construct competency models that are more textured. See, for example, the systematic reviews that identify effective practices at The Campbell Collaboration Web site (http://www.campbellcollaboration.org) and studies reported in the leading social work research journals. Cameron and Keenan (2010) reviewed the extensive literature on common factors that account for change and identify a set of practice strategies, such as providing a rationale for change, modeling, and feedback (p. 64). Field educators can quite easily include such specific skills in a list of practice behaviors, or use those skills as illustrations of effective interventions (CSWE, 2008, EP 2.1.10 [c]). Field directors should enlist faculty colleagues who are using such literature in their teaching and research to assist in identifying practice behaviors for inclusion in field evaluation.

A second issue regarding defining competencies relates to the process: how competencies and the related practice behaviors are defined, and who should be involved in defining them. Especially for programs that have used narrative descriptions in field evaluation, the move to competency-based education is a significant program change. It is wise to involve, from the outset, field instructors and agency leaders who will be instrumental in carrying out the new program approach. They can provide important insights and contributions as well as champion a competency-based approach. Members of the program's field advisory committee, field faculty and field staff, experienced field instructors, and teaching faculty can serve as a steering committee and begin the process of articulating practice behaviors using the framework of EPAS (CSWE, 2008) and relating them to the school's context, mission, and goals. The key question for field instructors to address is, What would the competencies and related practice behaviors look like in their settings with the populations they serve? Field directors could use such descriptors in different ways, for example as additional practice behaviors, or as illustrative examples in training field instructors and informing students of the content to be mastered in a particular program.

Once a program has developed a preliminary inventory of practice behaviors, the field director can involve any combination of field instructors, practitioners, educators, researchers, and service consumers and seek their response. Through a Delphi methodology, the school's unique model would emerge. The process of identifying practice behaviors is intellectually interesting because it forces the expression of concepts and values in grounded language. When representatives of the field community and the academic community work together on such a project, they build ownership of a shared vision of what is expected of the program's graduates.

Some useful examples of this process exist in social work. The California Social Work Education Center (CalSWEC) developed a set of competencies for child welfare with a consortium of twelve graduate schools of social work and fifty-eight county-level public social service departments (Clark, 2003). The Strengthening Aging and Gerontological Education in Social Work Project developed a competency framework for the Practicum Partnership Program (Damron-Rodriguez et al., 2006). As noted above, advanced competencies have been articulated for practice with particular populations.

The research team at the University of Toronto working on the Competency for Professional Practice Initiative used another approach to develop a competence model. The team conducted in-depth qualitative interviews with experienced field instructors. The team asked instructors to provide descriptions of students' competence on a range of dimensions distinguishing between exemplary, average, and problematic performance in clinical practice settings (Bogo et al., 2006) and in macro practice settings (Regehr et al., 2012). These narratives were analyzed, and six dimensions emerged for clinical practice: learning and growth, behavior in the organization, clinical relationships, conceptualizing practice, assessment and intervention, and professional communication. For macro practice, the dimensions were learning and growth, behavior in the organization and relationships, leadership, critical thinking, analysis, planning and implementation, professional communication, and values and ethics. For each dimension, the team extracted detailed descriptions of student performance.

In the following studies, another group of field instructors categorized students' behaviors, demonstrating high interrater agreement about the relative ranking of the behaviors (Bogo et al., 2004; Regehr, Bogo, Donovan, Lim, & Regehr, 2011; Regehr, Bogo, & Regehr, 2011). The field instructors categorized student performance into five decreasing levels: (5) exemplary, (4) ready to practice, (3) on the cusp, (2) needs more training, and (1) unsuitable for practice. Since the descriptors were provided in field instructors' language, they were authentic and represented the implicit and explicit constructs experienced instructors drew on when considering the components of expected competence of social work students. Vignettes of student performance and the respective rankings can be found at the University of Toronto home page (http://research.socialwork.utoronto.ca/hubpage/resources-2). The knowledge hub on building professional competence provides access to the vignette matching evaluation tool (Bogo, Regehr, Hughes,

Woodford, Power, & Regehr, 2006). This material can be useful in training field instructors to identify the underlying constructs and criteria used to evaluate students

In summary, a variety of approaches can be used to further elaborate the school's competency model generally, including to field education. Whereas EPAS (CSWE, 2008) provides the framework, the elaboration and specification of the practice behaviors can reflect the local context, mission, and goals of the program. When those instructors who will actually use the competency model for field instruction and evaluation are involved in its development, the model is more likely to be positively adopted. Given the availability of empirically based information about effective practice, competency models should incorporate this knowledge. Any effort to articulate competencies should be seen as iterative and ongoing. The resulting competency model will guide the design of evaluation tools that will then be used by field instructors, students, and field liaisons. Through use of the evaluation tool, the strengths, gaps, and problems will become apparent. In turn, this process will lead to refinement of the competency model—adding practice behaviors that are not included, deleting those that are repetitious, and clarifying those expressed in a manner that is too abstract or vague. As new knowledge and substantive issues regarding practice arise, they will be incorporated into an evolving and expanding competency model.

## Approaches and Issues in Evaluation of Students' Competence

"It seems reasonable to assume that the most valid evaluation of practice ability is the observation of students as they carry out social work practice roles and functions" (Bogo, 2010, p. 176). Since the essence of a competence approach is providing effective service, it behooves social work educators to find ways to observe students in their practice. Health professions' educators use simulations to evaluate student learning; this approach is now receiving attention in social work (Bogo, Regehr, Katz, Logie, & Mylopoulos, 2011; Bogo, Regehr, Logie, et al., 2011; Lu et al., 2011; Rawlings, 2012). All agree, however, that the authenticity provided through evaluation of performance in the practice or clinical setting is the gold standard for all professions.

As a result, field directors, in their leadership role, will want to encourage field instructors to use opportunities available in everyday practice to observe students in their interactions with clients, teams, community members, and on committees, as well as to structure periodic observations into the learning plan. In a competency model, as noted earlier, the emphasis is on evaluating the student's ability to perform the practice behaviors that demonstrate competence. Opportunities for observation include naturally occurring events, such as participation in a team meeting or coworking with a client system or group, as well as more-formal and more-structured events, such as observation of a practice interview or interaction, or review of a segment of an audio or video recording.

### Designing Evaluation Tools

A competency model guides the school's design of an evaluation tool, and a rating scale generally accompanies a competency approach. It is wise, from the outset, for a colleague who has expertise in scale design and testing to assist in considering issues in constructing the scale and testing its psychometric properties. Beyond clarity in expressing each item, some important measurement issues that need consideration are the number of items and the range of levels on the scale.

In small programs with few faculty resources, field directors may wish to collaborate with other local social work programs or with the regional consortium of field directors to develop an evaluation tool. Individual programs may still need to fine-tune such a generic tool to include practice behaviors they deem important, given their local context and particular mission. Assistance may also come from the teaching development center in the college or university. These centers are likely to have staff with experience in design of methods, and to have tools for outcomes assessment of student learning and evaluation of courses. Although these colleagues will not have social work content knowledge, they are experienced in educational outcomes assessment, a major trend in higher education in the United States today.

As discussed earlier, competence inventories with an ever-expanding list of practice behaviors risk characterizing practice as mechanistic. Such tools require the field instructor to deconstruct the student's practice in relation to a multitude of discrete behaviors, to remember instances of each behavior in question, and to assign it a rating. This process can take the instructor farther away from the authenticity and immediacy of her or his knowledge of the student's general performance ability. The challenge for field directors is to create tools with enough competency items to capture the essence of students' practice, defined in a way that is neither overly atomistic nor too general. Many tools have an item that captures a global rating of student performance, asking the instructor to rate the student's overall competence. The item may be worded as follows: "Based on your observation and knowledge of the student in this field setting, this student demonstrated competence at the level of. . . ." The instructor could then be given a choice of five or fewer ratings such as 5 excellent, 4 good, 3 needs more training, 2 poor, and 1 inferior. Brief descriptors for each of the ratings provide behavior anchors to guide the field instructors. In studies of medical students' performance on objective structured clinical examinations, researchers have found reasonable reliability and validity on such global ratings of clinical performance (Regehr, Freeman, Hodges, & Russell, 1999). Although such evidence regarding evaluation tools for social work students does not yet exist, it appears worthwhile to consider this finding from a related human service profession.

Given the above findings, it appears useful to include a narrative section in evaluation tools. A place for narrative comment can occur after each of the core competencies and/or at the end of the tool. The narrative section gives the field instructor the opportunity to comment on the student. A systematic analysis of such comments can yield important information about recurring issues and competencies that should be incorporated in future iterations of the evaluation tool.

Another issue of importance to consider in designing evaluation scales is the range of levels for each item and the definition of each level. For example, some scales have three, four, or five points on the scale with definitions related to the student meeting expectations: for example, (1) not yet met, (2) below expectations, (3) meets expectations, and (4) exceeds expectations. In such a scale, the field instructor must interpret what the term "expectations" actually means in order to rate the student. Such an approach is described where the competencies in the EPAS framework are listed with a scale to indicate the degree to which expectations have been met on each dimension (Petracchi & Zastrow, 2010). Levels can be more differentiated. For example, the former Baccalaureate Education Assessment Package (BEAP) was reorganized in 2013 and became the Social Work Education Assessment Project (SWEAP). The suite of assessment tools includes a Field Placement–Practicum Assessment Instrument that is related to the EPAS framework and consists of fifty-eight items scored on a 9-point scale, and a place for optional qualitative comments (see SWEAP home page, https://sweap.utah.edu/). Again, the field instructor must interpret what the items mean in actual practice.

Tools also exist where levels of performance on particular competencies are described in detail. For example, Regehr et al. (2011) describe the construction of an online evaluation tool. Working from the ranked vignettes of student performance (previously described), descriptors of actual student behavior were extracted for each of five levels of performance for each competence: (5) exemplary, (4) ready to practice, (3) on the cusp, (2) needs more training, and (1) unsuitable for practice. These researchers found that when field instructors were presented with numerical rankings for students, regardless of the type of scale used, they rated the majority of students at the highest end of the scale. Therefore, they constructed a new evaluation tool in an online format. Field instructors were presented with six competencies on the computer screen, with descriptive phrases about students for each of the competencies. These descriptors were extracted from the ranked vignettes and reflected field instructors' language. The descriptors were presented alphabetically with the numerical rating eliminated from the view of the evaluator. Students and field instructors completed the evaluation separately and selected "from the list of descriptive phrases those that best described the student using a pull down menu . . . an overall score for the student [was created] once all relevant phrases were selected for each dimension, and the evaluation was submitted" (p. 470). The computer program assigned a numerical value of 1 to 5 to each selected phrase "based on level of performance at which the phrase was an anchor. . . . A mean score was derived for each dimension and a final score was calculated as the unweighted average of the six-dimensional scores" (p. 470). An example of the computer screens in this tool is found in Regehr et al. (2011, p. 471).

In the summer of 2011 field and faculty members requested information about field evaluation instruments others were using with EPAS (CSWE, 2008) on the Baccalaureate Social Work Program Directors (BPD) Listserv. One response discussed the merits of using an instrument with an associated rubric commenting, "The rubric provides far greater specificity and more useful descriptors than a simple Likert-like rating scale" (Luciana, 2011, p. 206). Such tools enable field instructors to have a much more grounded understanding of what types of performance behaviors indicate a rating at a particular level. Concrete descriptors also assist students in understanding the rationale for a specific rating and in focusing further learning.

Over a short period each program will collect substantial numbers of completed evaluations. These tools can be examined for their factor structure, reliability, and validity, and results can inform further work on refining an evaluation scale. (For an example of an analysis of a competence scale see Bogo, Regehr, Hughes, Power, & Globerman, 2002.)

### Formative Evaluation

A consistent theme in the literature on field instruction is that students value and learn when they receive feedback about their performance (Fortune & Abramson, 1993; Knight, 2001). This form of information sharing is also referred to as formative evaluation. Field educators provide it to students in an ongoing manner; it contributes significantly to learning.

Characteristics of effective feedback have also been identified; those characteristics include attention to a number of factors (Abbott & Lyter, 1998; Bogo, 2010; Freeman, 1985):

1. It is important for field instructors to base feedback on the student's actual practice, rather than for them to rely only on written or oral reconstructions of what the student may have recalled. Recall is affected by memory and the tendency to distort and reconstruct what occurred. While written and oral communication of practice may be useful for examining student self-awareness, use of concepts, and assessment of practice situations, they are not preferred for assessing students' performance.

   Actual practice information can be obtained through direct observation, use of a one-way mirror, coworking, or review of segments of video or audio recordings. As discussed earlier, field directors can provide leadership to ensure that field instructors and students use these more-direct methods for teaching and learning. In orientation and training for new field instructors, field directors can demonstrate how to assist students to select specific segments of recordings, and to identify students' strengths and areas where they need assistance. Verbatim transcriptions of segments with written analysis of concepts, practice issues, and/or student skills can accompany recordings. Students' reflective analysis of actual practice can facilitate learning. That analysis also provides field instructors with access to the way in which students conceptualize their practice and use social work knowledge and values to understand situations and guide their interventions. Finally, reflections reveal the accuracy of student self-assessment of their skill levels. (For further discussion of this field instruction technique, see Bogo, 2010.)

2. Instructors should give feedback in a manner that is focused, specific, and related closely to the particular knowledge, skills, and attitudes in the competency framework. The more explicit the instructor can be in linking student performance with the outcomes of the competency model, the more likely it is that students will see the link between theory and practice. This is one important way in which a competency-based approach facilitates learning.

3. Feedback is most useful when the instructor offers it as close to the practice experience as possible, when the occurrence is still present in the student's awareness.

4. Instructors should frame feedback within a collaborative stance. The feedback should involve both the student and the field instructor in reflecting on a session, a segment of an interview, or a particular difficult interaction. Through encouraging students to identify their practice performance, field instructors assist in building students' ability to self-assess and set further learning objectives grounded in real experiences.

5. Students accept feedback from field instructors best when it is balanced, and when instructors specify both positive and critical aspects and behaviors in concrete terms so that students clearly understand what aspects of their performance need improvement.

In summary, field directors will need to train new field instructors and provide refresher sessions for experienced instructors to emphasize the importance of a competency model for using actual observations of what students can do in practice for teaching and for formative and summative evaluations. Such access to data about student performance goes beyond reviewing students' written notes or process recordings. Training sessions can involve groups of field instructors in reviewing samples of students' practice via video recordings, and discussion and rating of these samples using the school's new or revised evaluation scales. Such efforts aim to train instructors to achieve more-uniform interpretation of the rating scales.

In a study of the experiences of more than one hundred field instructors in giving feedback, some themes emerged; it is important for field directors to consider these themes when they provide training for field instructors (Bogo, Regehr, Power, & Regehr, 2007). A dominant theme was the expectation that students will receive and act on feedback in a variety of ways. Instructors identified students who are active and open learners, who, despite feeling initially thrown off by critical feedback, can use it to learn and improve their practice. Field instructors, understandably, find it rewarding to teach such students. Other students may struggle with the feedback, reject what the instructor offers, and ultimately use only some aspects. Instructors found this student response to be reasonable, and recognized a range of learning styles. Extremely challenging were students who utterly reject instructor feedback and are not open to considering other perspectives. These students may strenuously defend their position and/or become verbally aggressive with the instructor. Other difficult responses from students who do not agree occur when they become demoralized in the face of critical feedback, experiencing it as a blow to their self-concept and self-esteem. In such situations, students may then avoid and withdraw from supervision and hide their work.

When students cannot use feedback productively, and avoid or display negative attitudes toward learning, considerable tension and deterioration in the student–field instructor relationship can occur (Bogo et al., 2007). Examples were provided in the study where the relationship deteriorated, interactions became tense, and learning was severely compromised or halted. Field instructors shared situations where they remained committed to the student and attempted to continue to teach. The faculty field liaison was involved as well, which ushered in frequent meetings and reviews. When these approaches did not produce progress in learning, but the field placement continued until the end of the semester, the study described the experience as emotionally exhausting. Because little progress was occurring, the focus shifted to following policies and procedures to support a failing grade.

Given these findings, field directors can see the importance of training for students and field instructors not only about the importance of accessing practice data, but also about training to enhance their skills in giving, receiving, and using feedback. It appears that the great majority of field instructor and student dyads work well, and that students learn and achieve competence (Fortune & Kaye, 2002; Knight, 2001). When there are challenges in learning, it is imperative that the program provide educational support to these field instructor and student dyads. Field directors can design an early warning system to identify situations where additional input from the liaison can facilitate learning or implement gatekeeping procedures. Since resources for such efforts are needed, field directors may wish to reconsider the model of regular visits to all students in favor of greater efforts in situations where students might benefit from extra teaching and field instructors would welcome extra support. When field directors adopt new models such as this, they should document the procedures and related policies in a practicum manual and alert all students, field instructors, agency coordinators, and teaching faculty members of any changes.

## Summative Evaluation

Summative evaluation refers to final evaluation of students' performance at midterm or at the end of a practicum. It is associated with a grade or a pass/fail designation, and is used to determine whether, and under what circumstances, students can pass on to the next level of education or completion of the program. There are significant aspects of gatekeeping involved in such evaluation.

Ideally, summative evaluations are based on multiple and frequent observations of student performance in a range of practice roles and activities in the setting. This would include practice with different types of clients in micro settings and different types of work groups and projects in macro settings. Performance with team members, in field instruction sessions, and with student colleagues also provides important data. Written reports, notes, and records provide additional evidence of student capability, especially regarding cognitive processing and presentation skills, but are insufficient to provide data on which to base an assessment of performance.

Summative evaluations ideally are based on collating the impressions of a number of evaluators. Field instruction in social work has typically relied on the intense dyadic tutorial model of teaching and evaluating. Individual field instructors must use their judgment, based on the number of students they have seen and their own experiences and progress when they were students, to come to some fair assessment of the particular student. When students have been assigned to task instructors who provide teaching on a specific issue or modality, the field instructor should seek input from these instructors in preparing the final evaluation. When rotational models are used for field instruction, the evaluation consists of input from all field instructors who were involved in a particular student's practicum.

Where the student primarily worked with only one social worker, it is helpful to involve other field instructors or social workers in the setting in evaluation. This approach not only relieves the primary social worker from burden of evaluation, but also brings a richer range of experience and knowledge to consider the student's performance in relation to expected benchmarks. In settings with numerous students and field instructors, panels of field instructors can review and rate selections of each student's performance. Where there is only a sole field instructor, the faculty field liaison can also be involved in review and assessment.

### Training and Supporting Field Instructors in Evaluation

The authors' research team conducted a series of studies that designed and tested innovative evaluation tools. In each study, focus groups were always included to solicit field instructors' opinions about the experience of giving feedback and providing formative evaluation, as well as conducting the final evaluation (Bogo et al., 2007). It is important for field directors to use findings from these focus groups, which included more than one hundred participants, in designing training and support activities for field instructors in their role as evaluators.

A theme throughout these discussions was the tension field instructors experienced in balancing their education and evaluator role. The social workers were highly committed to practice principles of support, strength, and empowerment. They also valued adult education principles of active learning and mutuality between student and field instructor in structuring the learning experience. They aimed to create and maintain collaborative learning partnerships with students. When confronted with the authority and responsibility inherent in the evaluator role, however, they were struck with, and often uncomfortable with, moving into a more expert position that they perceived as hierarchical. When students accepted and agreed with their instructors' rating, the relationship progressed as before and instructors completed the evaluations smoothly. When students disagreed, field instructors reported a process of negotiation over ratings or grades. The previous collaboration and collegiality then became subject to the nuances of the power dynamic inherent in the instructor's role as evaluator.

When training field instructors to evaluate performance using a competency model, the emphasis is on outcomes: the degree to which a student is able to perform each competency and related practice behaviors at an expected level. Instructors may have difficulty with this focus. From their stance as social workers interested in promoting growth and development, the instructors perceive that the student has learned and progressed during the semester. Although a student may not reach the level of competence expected, many instructors wished to provide a higher rating, given that the student had made progress. Another issue relates to the agency context and the nature of assignments. Field instructors frequently excused less-than-expected student performance based on factors in the workplace such as an unsupportive interprofessional team, lack of resources, and complexities in client situations or projects assigned. Finally, social workers often blamed themselves and attributed some students' lack of achievement of competence to the inexperience of the field instructor, lack of time for intensive supervision, or to their own failure to address problems earlier in the practicum.

Social work programs differ in the degree to which the field office is involved in the actual evaluation of student learning and mastery of competence. Field instructor training seminars for new field instructors may include intense learning involving review of samples of students' actual work and practice rating using the program's evaluation tools. Faculty field liaison models vary from problem-solving, troubleshooting approaches, to approaches with regular visits and review of student practice. In the latter approaches, field liaisons may have the time to contribute to the evaluation based on their knowledge of the student's performance.

The issues presented throughout this chapter have implications for field instructor training. The key points for field directors to consider in using the EPAS competency model include the following:

- Competency models represent the core values, knowledge base, and attitudes of a profession. They also represent a signature pedagogy that socializes students by helping them integrate theory and practice, and to think, act, and behave in the ways of their particular profession.

- Competency models focus on performance—that is, what students are able to do in complex practice behaviors. These behaviors demonstrate the underlying professional foundation of knowledge, values, and skills. Some link between action and analysis or reflection can promote, learn, and aid in the evaluation of integration of theory and practice.

- The program expresses competency models at a level of generality so they can apply across the board to the many settings, populations, and practice approaches used in social work. Training efforts need to assist field instructors in interpreting broad competencies and practice behaviors in terms relevant to their context. Particular programs may add specific practice behaviors to further illustrate their unique approaches.

- A range of innovative approaches is available for field directors to use to train field instructors to evaluate student performance. One approach uses the discussion of descriptive vignettes to identify the underlying constructs field instructors use in evaluation. Groups of field instructors review samples of students' practice via video recordings and compare individual ratings to arrive at more uniform interpretation of the rating scales. Training for both students and field instructors can focus on best practices in giving, receiving, and using feedback.

In conclusion, when field directors orient and prepare field instructors to provide ongoing feedback and periodic and summative evaluation, they should attend to two interrelated factors: (1) the meaning of competency, the interpretation of practice behaviors, and the ratings of student performance; and (2) the process of providing feedback in a competency model and conducting formative and summative evaluations, and the impact of using a competency model on the field instructor. The review of salient issues connected to evaluation presented in this chapter can help field directors in orienting and training students and field instructors in these educational activities. The importance of evaluation of competence, and the challenges field instructors face in this role, warrant attention and support from schools of social work.

## Essential Readings

Abbott, A. A., & Lyter, S. C. (1998). The use of constructive criticism in field supervision. *Clinical Supervisor, 17*(2), 43–57.

Bogo, M., Regehr, C., Woodford, M., Hughes, J., Power, R., & Regehr, G. (2006). Beyond competencies: Field instructors' descriptions of student performance. *Journal of Social Work Education, 42*(3), 579–593.

Regehr, C., Bogo, M., & Regehr, G. (2011). The development of an online practice-based evaluation tool for social work. *Research on Social Work Practice, 21*(4), 469–475.

Sowbel, L. R. (2012). Gatekeeping: Why shouldn't we be ambivalent? *Journal of Social Work Education, 48*(1), 27–44.

## References

Abbott, A. A., & Lyter, S. C. (1998). The use of constructive criticism in field supervision. *Clinical Supervisor, 17*(2), 43–57.

Accreditation Council for Graduate Medical Education. (2010). *Outcome project: Common program requirements: General competencies.* Chicago: Author.

Arkava, M. L., & Brennan, E. C. (Eds.). (1976). *Competency-based education for social work: Evaluation and curriculum issues.* New York: Council on Social Work Education.

Baer, B. L., & Frederico, R. (1978). *Educating the baccalaureate social worker: Report of the undergraduate social work curriculum development project.* Cambridge, MA: Ballinger Publishing Company.

Bogo, M. (2010). *Achieving competence in social work through field education.* Toronto, ON: University of Toronto Press.

Bogo, M., Regehr, C., Hughes, J., Power, R., & Globerman, J. (2002). Evaluating a measure of student field performance in direct service: Testing reliability and validity of explicit criteria. *Journal of Social Work Education, 38*(3), 385–401.

Bogo, M., Regehr, C., Hughes, J., Woodford, M., Power, R., & Reghr, G. (2006). Vignette matching evaluation (VME) tool. Factor-Inwentash Faculty of Social Work, University of Toronto. Retrieved from http://www.socialwork .utoronto.ca/Assets/Social+Work+Digital+Assets/Research/Competency/ VME+Tool.pdf.

Bogo, M., Regehr, C., Katz, E., Logie, C., & Mylopoulos, M. (2011). Developing a tool for assessing student reflections on their practice. *Social Work Education, 30*(2), 186–194.

Bogo, M., Regehr, C., Logie, C., Katz, E., Mylopoulos, M., & Regehr, G. (2011). Adapting objective structured clinical examinations to assess social work students' performance and reflections. *Journal of Social Work Education, 47*(1), 5–18.

Bogo, M., Regehr, C., Power, R., Hughes, J., Woodford, M., & Regehr, G. (2004). Toward new approaches for evaluating student field performance: Tapping the implicit criteria used by experienced field instructors. *Journal of Social Work Education, 40*(3), 417–426.

Bogo, M., Regehr, C., Power, R., & Regehr, G. (2007). When values collide: Field instructors' experiences of providing feedback and evaluating competence. *Clinical Supervisor, 26*(1/2), 99–117.

Bogo, M., Regehr, C., Woodford, M., Hughes, J., Power, R., & Regehr, G. (2006). Beyond competencies: Field instructors' descriptions of student performance. *Journal of Social Work Education, 42*(3), 579–593.

Cameron, M., & Keenan, E. K. (2010). The common factors model: Implications for transtheoretical clinical social work practice. *Social Work, 55*(1), 63–73.

Cheetham, G., & Chivers, G. (2005). *Professions, competence and informal learning.* Cheltenham, UK: Edward Elgar.

Clark, S. (2003). The California collaboration: A competency-based child welfare curriculum project for master's social workers. *Journal of Human Behavior in the Social Environment, 7*(1/2), 135–157.

Council on Social Work Education (CSWE). (2008). *Educational policy and accreditation standards* (rev. March 27, 2010/updated August 2012). Alexandria, VA: Author. Retrieved from http://www.cswe.org/Accreditation/ 41865.aspx.

Damron-Rodriguez, J., Lawrance, F. P., Barnett, D., & Simmons, J. (2006). Developing geriatric social work competencies for field education. *Journal of Gerontological Social Work, 48*(1/2), 139–160.

Epstein, R. M., & Hundert, E. M. (2002). Defining and assessing professional competence. *Journal of the American Medical Association, 287*(2), 226–235.

Eraut, M. (1994). *Developing professional knowledge and competence.* London: Falmer Press.

Ericsson, K., & Charness, N. (1994). Expert performance: Its structure and acquisition. *American Psychologist, 49*(8), 725–747.

Fortune, A. E., & Abramson, J. S. (1993). Predictors of satisfaction with field practicum among social work students. *Clinical Supervisor, 11*(1), 95–110.

Fortune, A. E., & Kaye, L. (2002). Learning opportunities in field practica: Identifying skills and activities associated with MSW students' self-evaluation of performance and satisfaction. *Clinical Supervisor, 21*(1), 5–28.

Fouad, N. A., Hatcher, R. L., Hutchings, P. S., Collins, F. L., Jr., Grus, C. L., Kaslow, N. J., & Crossman, R. E. (2009). Competency benchmarks: A model for understanding and measuring competence in professional psychology across training levels. *Training and Education in Professional Psychology, 3*(4[Suppl.]), S5–S26.

Fox, R. (2011). *The use of self: The essence of professional education.* Chicago: Lyceum Books.

Freeman, E. (1985). The importance of feedback in clinical supervision: Implications for direct practice. *Clinical Supervisor, 3*(1), 5–26.

Gingerich, W. J., Kaye, K. M., & Bailey, D. (1999). Assessing quality in social work education: Focus on diversity. *Assessment and Evaluation in Higher Education, 24*(2), 119–129.

Hackett, S. (2001). Educating for competency and reflective practice: Fostering a conjoint approach in education and training. *Journal of Workplace Learning, 13*(3), 103–112.

Kane, M. T. (1992). The assessment of professional competence. *Evaluation and the Health Professions, 15*(2), 163–182.

Kaslow, N. J., Borden, K. A., Collins, F. L., Jr., Forrest, L., Illfelder-Kaye, J., Nelson, P. D., & Rallo, J. S. (2004). Competencies conference: Future directions in education and credentialing in professional psychology. *Journal of Clinical Psychology, 60*(7), 699–712.

Kelly, J., & Horder, W. (2001). The how and the why: Competences and holistic practice. *Social Work Education, 20*(6), 689–699.

Knight, C. (2001). The process of field instruction: BSW and MSW students' views of effective field supervision. *Journal of Social Work Education, 37*(2), 357–379.

Lu, Y. E., Ain, E., Chamorro, C., Chang, C., Feng, J. Y., Fong, R., & Yu, M. (2011). A new methodology for assessing social work practice: The adaptation of the objective structured clinical evaluation (SW-OSCE). *Social Work Education, 30*(2), 170–185.

Luciana, J. (2011). *Assessment rubric for field instructor evaluation.* Department of Social Work, Salve Regina University, Newport, RI. Retrieved from http://web.salve.edu/flipbooks/swk/index.html.

Petracchi, H. E., & Zastrow, C. (2010). Suggestions for utilizing the 2008 EPAS in CSWE-accredited baccalaureate and master's curriculums—reflections from the field, part 1: The explicit curriculum. *Journal of Teaching in Social Work, 30*(2), 125–146.

Raskin, M. (1983). A Delphi study in field instruction: Identification of issues and research priorities by experts. *Arete, 8*(2), 38–48.

Raskin, M. (1994). The Delphi study in field instruction revisited: Expert consensus on issues and research priorities. *Journal of Social Work Education, 30*(1), 75–89.

Rawlings, M. (2012). Assessing BSW student direct practice skill using standardized clients and self-efficacy theory. *Journal of Social Work Education, 48*(3), 553–576.

Regehr, C., Bogo, M., Donovan, K., Anstice, S., & Lim, A. (2012). Identifying student competencies in macro practice: Articulating the practice wisdom of field instructors. *Journal of Social Work Education, 48*(2), 307–319.

Regehr, C., Bogo, M., Donovan, K., Lim, A., & Regehr, G. (2011). Evaluating a Scale to Measure Student Competencies in Macro Social Work Practice. *Journal of Social Service Research, 38*(1), 100–109.

Regehr, C., Bogo, M., & Regehr, G. (2011). The development of an online practice-based evaluation tool for social work. *Research on Social Work Practice, 21*(4), 469–475.

Regehr, G., Freeman, R., Hodges, B., & Russell, L. (1999). Assessing the generalizability of OSCE measures across content domains. *Academic Medicine, 74*(12), 1320–1322.

Ruch, G. (2007). Reflective practice in contemporary child care social work: The role of containment. *British Journal of Social Work, 37*(4), 659–680.

Schön, D. (1983). *The reflective practitioner: How professionals think in action.* London: Temple Smith.

Scott Tilley, D. D. (2008). Competency in nursing: A concept analysis. *Journal of Continuing Education in Nursing, 39*(2), 58–64.

Shulman, L. S. (2005). Signature pedagogies in the professions. *Daedalus, 134*(3), 52–59.

Sowbel, L. R. (2011). Field note: Gatekeeping in field performance: Is grade inflation a given? *Journal of Social Work Education, 47,* 367–377.

Sowbel, L. R. (2012). Gatekeeping: Why shouldn't we be ambivalent. *Journal of Social Work Education, 48*(1), 27–44.

# PART III
## Critical Issues in Field Administration

The authors of the next three chapters examine overarching issues that permeate many of the field functions discussed in part II. These chapters illustrate the bind that field directors find themselves in when they support students' rights and educational goals while simultaneously screening those students for suitability for the profession; keep student information confidential while sharing it for educational and client safety purposes; and create practicum opportunities for students while minimizing associated risks. Gatekeeping, ethics, and safety are significant factors in field education. They affect all stakeholders and can adversely affect the school if something goes awry (e.g., student removal from a practice setting, mishandling of confidential information, or an injury or death in a placement). Part III stresses the importance of developing and reviewing program policies related to the content of these chapters.

In chapter 9, Gatekeeping, Ginny Terry Raymond and Lynda R. Sowbel analyze various points of gatekeeping when the field director is a key decision maker. These include development of criteria and policies for student admission, continuance, and termination from field. Ethics and accreditation compel all social work educators to take action if a student's behavior and competence are not congruent with academic and professional standards. Difficult gatekeeping decisions, however, are most often made by field educators. The authors encourage field directors to follow protocol and support students through due process before a dismissal from field. Sometimes administrators, wary of reputation, legal action, and extra work, do not support the field director's decisions.

Chapter 10, Legal, Ethical, and Pedagogical Issues, begins with two vignettes detailing answers to very important questions about confidentiality. Raymie H. Wayne's first question deals with what to do when a student reveals a criminal background. Wayne then addresses the dilemma that occurs when a faculty member reveals unsolicited information about a student's background. Many faculty and field directors do not know the details of legislation that affects actions related to confidentiality or how to apply those laws to field education. Wayne clearly explains and uses scenarios to illustrate the role in field education of the university legal counsel, the Family Educational Rights and Privacy Act, the American with Disabilities Act, and the National Association of Social Workers' (NASW) *Code of Ethics*. Chapters 9 and 10 supply concrete advice for designing or updating policies on student rights and gatekeeping.

Students are not immune from verbal and physical aggression while in their field practicums. Under the best conditions, all students and field instructors are well trained in safety and risk management. In chapter 11, Safety and Risk Management, Sharon C. Lyter describes the status of safety training. There is not sufficient research on best practices for harm reduction. There is also no mandate in the accreditation standards to ensure that this important preparation takes place in order to protect students, staff, and clients. In light of her research, Lyter recommends changes in the next iteration of the accreditation standards related to field and adds a practice behavior relevant to safety. The author guides field directors in educating students and field instructors about personal safety, necessary insurance, incident reporting, and management of risk factors.

Part III is intended to spark critical discourse among faculty, administrators, university legal counsel, field directors, field staff, and community practitioners. It is important to inform these stakeholders in order to stimulate deliberations that will lead to the formation, review, and revision of program field policies guided by research-based data. Existing policies are often reviewed by faculty only when they are tested by an incident that requires their implementation. Development or changes to program field policies in the critical areas of gatekeeping, ethics, and safety will not completely eliminate the chasm between the ideal of national standards (EPAS), and the reality of the day-to-day implementation of program policies that apply to student incidents that are complicated and individually nuanced. For example, without a specific reference to safety in the accreditation standards, a field director may become familiar with the requirements of the 2008 EPAS but will not have the guidance to train students and field instructors on safety issues and screen for agencies that have a safety plan in place. The authors, therefore, go beyond the program level and inform social work educators and those responsible for revision to the accreditation standards to the need for specific changes to national educational field policies. Recommendations by field scholars for national policy change provides field directors (new and seasoned) with role models on leadership in field education.

# 9

# Gatekeeping

*Ginny Terry Raymond and Lynda R. Sowbel*

The purpose of gatekeeping in social work education is twofold: (1) to promote quality services for the benefit and protection of clients, and (2) to promote the health and integrity of the profession by ensuring that those admitted to it are competent to practice. Social work educators have agreed that gatekeeping is an ethical responsibility (Leighninger, 2000)—a professional duty to ensure that graduates are "academically, behaviorally, and ethically" fit to practice social work (Cole & Lewis, 1993, p. 150). Though concerns about suitability for our profession have existed since its formative years, publications on the topic have been increasing in the past decade (Daehn Zellmer & Knothe, 2011; Gibbs & Blakely, 2000; Huff & Hodges, 2010; Raymond, 2000; Reynolds, 2004; Sowbel, 2011, 2012; Tam & Ming Kwok (2007); Urwin, Van Soest, & Kretzschmar, 2006; Wayne, 2004). Programs must spell out how they inform students of the suitability criteria they use to evaluate students' academic and professional performance, and must inform them of policies and procedures for grievance and for terminating students' enrollment in the social work program (Council on Social Work Education [CSWE], 2008, Accreditation Standards [AS], 3.2.7 & 3.2.8).

Field directors might reasonably assume that the classroom faculty are the primary gatekeepers for screening unsuitable students and will have done so well before such students are considered for field placement. They may assume that sufficient screening has taken place during the admission process or through assignment of grades in social work courses. The literature indicates, however, that program faculty view field instructors and the field director as the more likely source(s) for screening out unsuitable students (Gibbs, 1994; Sowbel, 2012). According to Watkinson and Chalmers (2008), "[T]he practice of professional and ethical conduct, and increased awareness of one's suitability and 'fit' with the profession will crystallize during the course of [the student's] field education or practicum experience" (p. 505).

This chapter provides an overview of gatekeeping functions, suitability of students for the profession, and challenges of gatekeeping, including the increased awareness and sensitivity to issues of gatekeeping for students with disabilities and those with criminal backgrounds. Given the imprecise and sometimes controversial issues of suitability, where two reasonable people can disagree, this chapter also provides suggestions for best practices.

## Admission to the Social Work Program

Social work programs set standards for admission and progression at both the bachelor of social work (BSW) and master of social work (MSW) levels (CSWE, 2008, AS B3.2.1 & M3.2.1). Before being admitted to a social work program, students must first meet university admission standards. Social work programs may set additional requirements, such as a higher GPA, letters of reference, an interview by faculty, and/or an essay that relates to the applicant's goals in the profession. The gatekeeping effectiveness of some of these admission requirements is questionable. For example, the applicant typically selects the person to write a reference, and the writer may choose not to mention concerns. Even when references include concerns, programs may not follow up.

It may not be feasible for large programs to interview all applicants. Some may interview an applicant only if concerns arise in the application process. Even when there are concerns subsequent to an interview, the final decision is often to afford the applicant an opportunity. The strengths perspective is a primary rationale to admit the student.

Some programs have minimal admission policies in order to keep student enrollment up so that the program is viable (Born & Carroll, 1988), a potential conflict to rigorous gatekeeping. Coleman, Collins, & Aikens (1995) found that, "while clearly defined admission policies and procedures uniformly and conscientiously applied may reduce the number of subsequent problematic situations that require attention and action, not all students deemed unsuitable to the profession are denied admission" (p. 267). Other faculty may not always share concerns about admitted students with the field director; these faculty may reasonably prioritize the values of giving students a fair chance to succeed and respecting students' privacy rights. Some fear legal action if students learn of the early sharing of information about them that could prejudice classroom instructors or field educators. One way to address such concerns is to inform prospective students in application materials, student handbooks, and field manuals of the program's policies and procedures related to sharing information.

## Gatekeeping in the Classroom

The classroom is the next point of gatekeeping. Cunningham (1982) found a correlation between GPA and performance in field; therefore, GPA is often used as a measure of classroom performance. Depending on the nature of the social work course and student enrollment, a classroom instructor may or may not have the opportunity to adequately evaluate a student's suitability for professional social work practice.

Typically, performance on exams and papers has the heaviest influence on final course grades. In required social work practice courses, however, expectations of learning outcomes and students' ability to perform essential practice skills at a passing level should be clearly stated in the syllabus. Students must have the opportunity to demonstrate competencies in class through role-play and other simulation techniques. The amount of time devoted to student demonstration of practice abilities can vary by instructor and is influenced by class size. Research is not conclusive as to whether the enactment of role-plays by students is adequate in determining how a person will perform in practice with actual clients (Miller & Koerin, 2001; Rawlings, 2007). Classroom instructors may assign passing grades to students about whom they have serious concerns, believing that field is the better place to evaluate practice skills and fit for the profession. Faculty, particularly those who are nontenured, fear receiving poor teaching evaluations from students unhappy with their grade.

As social work courses move increasingly online, faculty assessment of students' professional development will be even more of a challenge. Some problematic behaviors, such as high absenteeism, disruptive behavior, and late assignments, may be noticeable in the classroom or even in online courses, but, increasingly, certain problems might become apparent only during field placement (Lafrance, Gray, & Herbert, 2004). For example, avoidance or inability to communicate with clients, coworkers, or supervisors, or ignoring deadlines given for documentation or tasks may be indicative of issues not as easily recognized in the classroom.

## Gatekeeping in Admission to Field Education

Admission to field education is obtained by "only those students who have met the program's specified criteria for field education" (CSWE, 2008, AS 2.1.4, p. 9). Admission in many MSW programs and the submission of a field application allow the student to proceed directly to concurrent field placement without classroom instructors having had an opportunity to become familiar with the student. MSW programs with a block or delayed field model do not place students in field until after some period of time in classes. This timing allows for slightly more opportunity for gatekeeping prior to field placement.

Admission to field in BSW programs generally occurs after students have completed a specified number of social work courses. Increasing numbers of transfer students, however, also limit faculty contact with students before they are placed in the field. This still creates an important point for gatekeeping.

### Criminal Background

A student's criminal history poses challenges to admission policies; field directors work with faculty to make the difficult decisions when this issue arises. Requiring background checks on students and deciding what to do with the result has been controversial in social work education (Magen, Emerman, Scott, & Zeiger, 2000). In a study by Daehn Zellmer and Knothe (2011), 25 percent of BSW programs and 34 percent of MSW programs responding to their survey reported requiring applicants (to either the program or to field) to undergo a criminal background check. Raymond (2012) found that social work programs are increasingly requiring background checks on students at some point prior to, or at the point of, their consideration for field placement. Policy change by employers, field placement sites, and state licensure are the impetus for student criminal background checks. Field directors should seriously consider uniform requirements for background checks regardless of setting or student.

Depending on the background check required, it can sometimes take several weeks for the program to receive results. Allowing sufficient time to receive the report gives the field director time to review the reports and/or to place a student who has a criminal background, or for the program to engage in a review of the student and to counsel-out or refuse the student admission to field according to established program policies and procedures. Paying for the background checks is often the student's responsibility, similar to a lab fee. Most students have satisfactory background checks, but those few with a criminal history may pose difficulties in the placement process (Raymond, 2012).

The field director's response to a student with a criminal history is typically determined by the nature and timing of the crime(s) in the report(s). Offenses range from driving under the influence (DUI/DWI), to possession of an illegal drug, or a myriad of felony convictions. Some agencies will accept a student depending on how long ago the offense occurred and how many such reports are on the student's record. Typically, a student record that includes a violent crime is most problematic. Field directors should become knowledgeable about the policies of field agencies related to accepting students with criminal backgrounds. To best ensure due process for students, all materials for prospective and current students such as recruitment materials, the student handbook, application for field placement, and the field manual should include information about the program's required criminal background checks, including its nature, timing, and cost, and who bears that cost.

Some state social work licensure boards inquire about applicants' criminal history. In a 2009 survey of CSWE-accredited BSW and MSW programs in the United States, 63 percent and 75 percent, respectively, reported that an acceptable criminal background check is a contingency for state licensure (Daehn Zellmer & Knothe, 2011). The student should not learn this information only after completing the social work degree and applying to take a licensure exam. While students are in the program, state licensure board staff could speak to social work students to clarify the meaning of an acceptable criminal background. Having a criminal report does not automatically eliminate the possibility of progressing through the program, being allowed to take a licensure exam, or being hired as a social worker.

### Students with Psychiatric Disabilities and Communicative Disorders

Field directors have a responsibility to protect student's rights to access higher education. As such, they commit to the success of students with disabilities. Disability support programs in higher education are not currently individualized for students in professional programs, such as psychology, counseling, and social work. One of the imperatives of the Americans with Disabilities Act (ADA) of 1990 is that universities do not operate under stereotypical assumptions about specific disabilities. Different people with the same disability are unique individuals who may respond or function differently in various settings. With or without a disability, students may flourish in some field settings but not in others. Appropriate accommodations may make a difference for some students.

Gordon and Keiser (2000) found that students with psychiatric disabilities, learning disabilities, and attention deficit/hyperactivity disorder constitute the largest pool of students seeking accommodations in higher education. In the most recent report of the International Center for Disability Information (2000), mental illness or depression (15.3%) was almost as frequently reported among all master's degree students as were general health problems (15.4%). GlenMaye and Bolin (2007) indicate that students with attention deficit/hyperactivity disorder, in particular, were receiving increased attention in colleges and universities. Most recently, undergraduates and graduate students with high-functioning autism spectrum disorders, particularly those with Asperger's, have been seen in counseling and special support service centers in colleges and universities (Raymond, 2012). Such students have often received assistance from special education programs in elementary and high schools and have expectations for similar programs in higher education. Hallmarks of these disabilities are effects on the individual's communication and relationship-building skills, which are considered requisite skills of social workers and other helping professionals (Bogo, 1993; Knight, 2004).

Medications have significantly improved functioning for people with disabilities such as schizophrenia, and both medication and psychotherapy have been effective in reducing symptoms of depression. Especially challenging, however, are legal regulations related to episodic impairments. The Americans with Disabilities Act (ADA) Amendments Act of 2008 makes clear that if impairments in this category would substantially limit a major life activity when those impairments are active, they will be covered under ADA regulations even when they are latent or in remission.

Social work students are often reluctant to report psychiatric illnesses or communicative disorders to field directors. This may be true even if the disability support office sent letters to instructors on the student's behalf, asking for accommodations in classroom courses. Some students assume they will have no difficulties performing in field education. Others may have a variety of concerns, but may primarily fear not being given a field placement if they reveal their disability and, therefore, not being allowed to complete their degree and professional goals. Whatever the reason for not informing the field director of the student's disability, the resulting situation can present a challenge to the field director, who needs time to make the most appropriate arrangements for the student. The field director may learn about a student from other sources, or a prospective field instructor may discover the student's need for accommodations in a preplacement interview. Worse yet, the student may develop difficulties in the field placement.

It is therefore important for field directors to meet, weeks ahead of time, with all students who are planning to enroll in field placement. The field director will review the placement process, have students complete application forms, and emphasize the importance of indicating on the form any special needs, including accommodations. Reasonable accommodation instructions, however, must ultimately come from the official source on campus, not from the student.

When field directors are informed in advance by disability services of the reasonable accommodations needed, they are obliged to share this information with appropriate personnel at the prospective placement (field instructor and, perhaps, the agency administrator) only to the extent necessary to facilitate provision of accommodation. Field directors should not disclose medical or psychological details because those are legally protected confidential information. If agency personnel believe they cannot provide accommodations, the field director moves on to locate another placement. Stromwall (2002), however, suggests that agencies can be held legally responsible for discrimination if they reject a student solely because the student has a psychiatric or medical history. Stromwall stresses that the focus should be on current functioning and whether the student is following the prescribed treatment regime (p. 79).

### Delaying or Denying Entry into Field

Field directors in BSW and MSW programs occasionally decide that a student is not ready for field. An example of this might be a student who is frequently late or misses more time from classes than the attendance policy allows, without any explanation or effort to correct the behavior. This may become apparent in the screening process using the admission criteria, or in soliciting feedback from faculty. After careful consideration of such a situation, the field director and/or a committee may decide a student is not ready to enter the field practicum course. The field director must both protect the student from arbitrary or discriminatory decisions and serve as a gatekeeper protecting clients. A delayed placement can also occur if the student is turned down for placement by more than one field site. The decision to delay placement must be guided by clear written policies that indicate the number of times a student can be turned down by different agency sites before that student will not be offered another placement.

One gatekeeping strategy if a student's entry into field is postponed would be to advise students about resources, including career or professional counseling, that would help students develop the skills or insight needed. Often this decision to delay placement stipulates in writing what would be required for the student to progress in the program. It would specify a minimum time to achieve these requirements before the program would consider a new field application. If a student refuses remediation, or is unable to meet the remediation plan, the program will likely terminate that student for reasons of academic and professional performance. In addition, programs will stipulate their readmission policy and process, including a time frame.

Some programs, however, have a philosophy of guaranteeing admission to field. They purport that because the student's best occasion for demonstration of practice competencies is in field, they give the benefit of the doubt and the opportunity to enter even to those about whom there are serious concerns (Huff & Hodges, 2010; Madden, 2000; Watkinson & Chalmers, 2008). A question raised by this screening-in philosophy begs the question, Can anyone be a social worker?

## Gatekeeping during Field Education

Field directors will likely encounter students about whom there are serious concerns with regard to their competence and suitability during field placement and subsequently for the profession. Some directors may be concerned enough to question whether clients could be harmed by the student. It is imperative that policies and procedures are already in place and available to all students before such situations arise. Program faculty, field instructors, and the field director must be knowledgeable of, and have followed, these policies and procedures. The focus in the legal system is whether the program followed due process, or whether the program administered justice according to established policies and procedures of the program. A very small percentage of social work students, compared to students in other professions, are likely to fail out of the program (Gibbs, 1994; Sowbel, 2011).

Students are most likely to be terminated from the practice site by field instructors, who are also reluctant to fail students (Barlow & Coleman, 2003; Dudek, Marks, &

Regehr, 2005; Miller & Koerin, 2001). Gibbs (1994) found that 82 percent of field directors state that if students did not successfully complete their first field placement, they were given a second opportunity to complete a placement. These facts should be a wake-up call to social work educators. In field, students demonstrate competencies, and those who cannot practice in a competent and ethical manner are found to be not ready or unsuited for the profession.

Field directors create and enforce a structure and process that ensures scheduled and documented communication among the student, faculty liaison, and field instructor regarding the student's performance in field. Learning agreements and evaluations should contain expectations and clear benchmarks for passing or failing. There are defined remediation and dismissal procedures that include the right of students to due process, including the right to be clearly informed in writing of the problem(s) and what is expected regarding improvement, reasonable time to demonstrate competency, and the right to appeal. The liaison and/or field instructor should alert the field director early in the semester about student performance problems and any student who is in danger of failing.

### Field Liaison—Crucial Role in Gatekeeping

The field liaison has a crucial role in the process of a successful field placement and in gatekeeping. It is imperative that the field director stress the importance of early contact with the field instructor to answer any questions and to arrange a visit to the placement. The field liaison makes an initial introduction to open channels of communication, to encourage the field instructor and the student to contact the liaison if there are questions or if problems arise before the first scheduled liaison visit. Many liaisons do not make the initial contact to arrange a visit until perhaps midterm or later, with the rationale, "No news is good news."

The field instructor and student develop the learning contract; the student reviews that contract with the field liaison. During the placement, the liaison reviews areas of concern and utilizes the learning contract as a gatekeeping tool. There may still be sufficient time to address and satisfactorily resolve problems if discussed by midterm. If there are concerns about a student's ability to perform core competencies, the field director in conjunction with the field liaison must develop a written plan of remediation that clearly states behavioral expectations of the student and deadlines for the student to achieve those expectations. All parties sign the remediation plan (student, field instructor, liaison, and the field director).

The remediation plan might ask the student to read material related to the competency in question, observe experienced workers in the agency demonstrating the competency, practice the behavior or competency and receive feedback (the positive role of gatekeeping), and, ideally, develop competency in the required practice behaviors. The student should receive feedback and have the opportunity to respond, preferably in writing as well as orally. The timing of meetings of the parties should also be determined and included in the remediation plan. If the student is in danger of failing field education, the field director should notify that student in writing according to the due process requirements of the social work program and/or the educational institution.

Some students, especially the inexperienced, may be unsuitable for the profession at the time of their first field placement (Huff & Hodges, 2010; Lafrance et al., 2004; Rompf, Royse, & Dhooper, 1993). It may be necessary for an inexperienced student who arrives not ready, or a student who needs remediation for other reasons, to repeat the field placement in order to satisfactorily demonstrate the core competencies. Repeating the placement might be viewed as a crisis by the student and, perhaps, by the field instructor, field liaison, and field director. This option is appropriate if all parties agree that the student is capable of demonstrating the specified competencies. The remediation plan should state that repeating the placement does not guarantee passing it.

In each of these scenarios, the effectiveness of the remediation relates to the field liaison's timely communication with the field instructor. It is important for the liaison to follow protocol regarding contact and visits; if problems arise and a student is not informed of such problems and a remediation plan is not developed, then the student's right to due process may be violated. Earlier contact by the liaison could be helpful in resolving the situation or in finding a more suitable placement for the student. Even with early communication, however, deficiencies can become evident toward the end of a placement and the student might not pass field.

If the final assessment about the student's competence by the field instructor, liaison, and field director determines that a student is incapable of competent social work practice, and is unsuitable for the profession, then any of those might refer the student for a formal review by the program. Schools of social work must have a review policy, procedures, and a committee that could recommend that the student be dismissed from the program or that another remediation plan be developed. In all cases, the student should have a mechanism to appeal the decision.

### Ethical Violations during Field

Social work students should have reviewed the National Association of Social Workers (NASW) *Code of Ethics* prior to entering field education. Some programs require applicants to the professional program and/or field education to write an essay about the *Code*, and how it will affect their practice in field. Many programs require applicants to read and sign a document stating that they have read the NASW *Code of Ethics*, and that they will abide by it in their practice in field education. All field directors should consider instituting this practice, if it is not already in place.

If a student violates the *Code of Ethics* while in field, there may be grounds for dismissing the student from the program following a review under a program's established policy. Due process would include an assessment of whether the situation is primarily a learning experience; in that case, the program will allow the student to continue in a placement through a remediation process. Some ethical violations may not be appropriate for remediation; (e.g., if the student poses a threat to client safety or compromises agency licensure). Additionally, violations such as failure to report abuse, having an intimate relationship with a client, or committing a felony are typically not amenable to remediation, and the program would likely make a decision to dismiss the student from field and the social work program.

### Conflicting Educator Roles

The difficulties of gatekeeping are compounded by many factors, and field directors need to commit themselves to ongoing reflection and consultation. Concerns about the pitfalls of discriminating in some way against students, prioritizing a strengths perspective, and falling into the role of clinician/mentor versus educator/gatekeeper are common, especially for new field educators. Field instructors and field liaisons frequently find it uncomfortable to challenge students by providing negative feedback that might discourage them or affect the student–field instructor relationship. This can lead to unclear expectations and lack of awareness of areas or skills that students need to improve. Feature 9.1 illustrates one field director's struggles with the responsibilities of gatekeeping.

## Feature 9.1. A Gatekeeping Case Study

Years ago, I was working with a student who had a friendly demeanor, seemed highly motivated, and was an independent thinker. He liked to do assignments his own way (despite the resulting low grades). He had some writing issues, and sometimes did not seem to understand social work concepts. Although faculty members had given clear feedback, he insisted on handwriting a sixty-page paper instead of the ten-page document requested. He also missed more than a few days in the field for physical and emotional problems. Faculty wanted to try to help him achieve his goal to be a social worker. Though they spent many hours with him, and assigned him an experienced field instructor, problems of accepting feedback and complying with supervision prevailed. After a year and a half in the program he still could not meet the minimum expectations. When his noncompliance resulted in a serious ethical breach, the program failed the student in field. A meeting that included the student and field instructors was held. This process took time and all parties expressed their respective concerns. The student did not think the ethical breach was an issue; in the end the school of social work terminated him.

I can still remember the angst of having to tell him he could not continue. Perhaps another academic discipline might be more fitting. He cried, he yelled, he pleaded, and with each outburst I felt a bit more tired, more defeated. I asked myself what I usually ask when a student is not successful: Had we failed him? Had we been unable to find the individualized strategy for him? If we kept looking for strengths to overcome these problems, would they appear? Was he a person who fit that indefinable category of "unsuited"? The field instructor also felt exhausted, and even took a few years off from supervising students. I should have felt relief at the time and energy I would no longer have to spend on this student, but I did not. The ethical dilemma in this case was student self-determination versus protection of clients. In the end, the protection of clients took precedence.

Although these issues do not come up often and *most* programs give *most* students a second chance, educators must assume this unpleasant, unwanted task of gatekeeping. I tell myself that I have to feel content that I attempted every opportunity for remediation that all educators involved had spent enormous amounts of time supporting him and the field instructor and due process requirements were met. There are some people who may not be the suited to social work. Once everything has been done, student failures are proof of discernment within a process that is almost always difficult when social work educators try to protect clients and meet gatekeeping obligations.

I recently saw the student and it was truly amazing how happy he was, smiling, laughing with friends; life had gone on. Who knew back then that the concerns would disappear, but the contentment of knowing I had fulfilled my ethical duties would persist?

Lynda Sowbel, PhD, LCSW-C
Associate Professor and Director of Field Education
Department of Sociology and Social Work
Hood College

### Fear of Student Legal Challenges to Failure or Dismissal from Field

Many social work educators fear involvement in legal challenges if they fail a student or recommend dismissal from a professional school, which most often arises during field placement (Born & Carroll, 1988; Cole & Lewis, 1993; Gibbs, 1994). Such fear may lead to ignoring the problems and neglecting duty to the profession and to clients. These, in turn, are ethical violations.

Field directors, liaisons, and field instructors have legal and ethical responsibilities to the student and clients of the practice sites. Clients should know that the person assigned to them is a student in training, and should be informed of the contact information for the student's field instructor. The student should also tell them that the supervisor reads client records assigned to the student. Field instructors should be aware that they are responsible for the clients of their student. If the student's actions result in harm to the client, then the field instructor, by extension, is responsible for the incompetent or unprepared actions by the student that put the client at risk (Davenport, 1992; Kadushin, 1985). Given these ethical responsibilities and liabilities, field instructors must require students to keep adequate records in order to stay informed about students' actions and performance with clients. They must be able to recognize potential harm and ensure client well-being, while also allowing the student adequate autonomy (Zakutansky & Sirles, 1993).

In legal cases since the 1970s, courts have supported the academic decisions of faculty regarding student performance and suitability for the profession, *if due process was followed*. The U.S. Supreme Court has upheld the decision of lower courts that the dismissal of students from educational programs because of student behavior in classes or in internships was inconsistent with professional standards (*Board of Curators of the University of Missouri v. Horowitz*, 1978; *Regents of the University of Michigan v. Ewing, 1985; Richmond v. Fowlkes*, 2000).

These decisions have clarified that behaviors such as being chronically late or having poor interpersonal skills are academic matters. Courts have asserted that faculty in the discipline are the best judge of academic matters, not the courts. Attorneys for the plaintiff (students in the above cases) asserted that these are nonacademic matters and, therefore, cannot be reasons for dismissal of a student from a degree program. The attorneys also claimed that the degree program deprived the student of the Fourteenth Amendment right to "life, liberty, or property, without due process of law." The academic degree, they argue, is property that the student is being denied. Higher courts, however, have not upheld their arguments.

### Due Process Responsibilities of Field Director

In the Fourteenth Amendment, the phrase "without due process of law" should be the focus of a social work program and any field director in the process of reviewing a student for possible dismissal from the program. The university's legal staff should review the policies, and those policies should be readily available to all students, faculty, liaisons, and field instructors. These include timely and written expectations of, and warnings to, the student that also allow opportunity for improvement and demonstration by the student of acceptable professional behavior.

Orientation and training sessions for field instructors and field liaisons about their roles and responsibilities must stress mechanisms for due process in their work with students and performance evaluations. The field instructor in conjunction with the field liaison formally evaluates the student, preferably by midterm and again prior to completion of the placement. The field director reviews the learning contract form and procedures in these sessions, highlighting the importance of timely evaluation of students, identification of concerns, development of a written plan, and a signed agreement by all parties.

Assessment or review of the student's performance in field can and should occur at any point in the placement when the field instructor and/or liaison believes that the student is unable to accomplish the required practice behaviors, or is unsuited for the profession. They should consult with the field director and should conduct a review process, based on established policy and procedures.

## Conclusion

Legal history of protecting clients through gatekeeping is clearly on the side of leaving decisions in the hands of the faculty, who are considered the experts by the courts. The field director, following policies and procedures already in place, guides the remediation or termination process. Field directors must be constantly informed by the professional literature. They are ethically and professionally obligated to balance their responsibilities as educators of social work students and their gatekeeping responsibilities to the program, the profession, and the public. Professions are given autonomy by the public, but this authority is based on public trust that the profession regulates itself, including guarding the initial entrance gate to professional degree programs. Field directors effectively guard this gate following relevant, clear, widely disseminated policies and procedures that ensure due process for students. Despite the struggle that may be experienced, the difficulty of competing values or dilemmas, and the external pressures to do things the easy way, evidence-based gatekeeping must be actively engaged.

## Essential Readings

Americans with Disabilities Act of 1990, PL 101–336, 42d Cong., § 1201, § 2, 104 Stat. 328 (1991).

Sowbel, L. (2012). Gatekeeping: Why shouldn't we be ambivalent? *Journal of Social Work Education, 48*(1), 27–44.

Tam, D., & Ming Kwok, S. (2007). Controversy debate on gatekeeping in social work education. *International Journal of Learning, 14*(2), 195–204.

## References

Americans with Disabilities Act (ADA) Amendments Act of 2008, PL 110–325, 122 Stat. 3553 (2008).

Americans with Disabilities Act of 1990, PL 101–336, 42d Cong., § 1201, § 2, 104 Stat. 328 (1991).

Barlow, C., & Coleman, H. (2003). Suitability for practice guidelines for students: A survey of Canadian social work programmes. *Social Work Education, 22,* 151–164.

Board of Curators of the University of Missouri v. Horowitz, 435 U.S. 78 (1978).

Bogo, M. (1993). The student/field instructor relationship: The critical factor in field education. *Clinical Supervisor, 11*(2), 23–36.

Born, C. E., & Carroll, D. J. (1988). Ethics in admissions. *Journal of Social Work Education, 24,* 79–85.

Cole, B. S., & Lewis, R. G. (1993). Gatekeeping through termination of unsuitable social work students: Legal issues and guidelines. *Journal of Social Work Education, 29,* 150–160.

Coleman, H., Collins, D., & Aikens, D. (1995). The student-at-risk in the practicum. In G. Rogers (Ed.), *Social work field education: Views and visions.* Dubuque, IA, Kendall/Hunter.

Council on Social Work Education (CSWE). (2008). *Educational policy and accreditation standards* (rev. March 27, 2010/updated August 2012). Alexandria, VA: Author. Retrieved from http://www.cswe.org/Accreditation/41865.aspx.

Cunningham, M. (1982). Admissions variables and the prediction of success in an undergraduate fieldwork program. *Journal of Social Work Education, 18,* 27–34.

Daehn Zellmer, A., & Knothe, T. (2011). The use of criminal background checks in social work education. *Journal of Baccalaureate Social Work* (Summer), 17–33.

Davenport, D. S. (1992). Ethical and legal problems with client-centered supervision. *Counselor Education and Supervision, 31*(4), 227–231.

Dudek, N. L, Marks, M. B., & Regehr, G. (2005). Failure to fail: The perspective of clinical supervisors. *Academic Medicine, 80, 584–587.*

Gibbs, P. (1994). Screening mechanisms in BSW programs. *Journal of Social Work Education, 30,* 63–74.

Gibbs, P., & Blakely, E. (Eds.). (2000). *Gatekeeping in BSW programs.* New York: Columbia Press.

GlenMaye, L., & Bolin, B. (2007). Students with psychiatric disabilities: An exploratory study of program practices. *Journal of Social Work Education, 43*(1), 117–131.

Gordon, M., & Keiser, S. (Eds.). (2000). *Accommodations in higher education under the Americans with Disabilities Act (ADA): A no-nonsense guide for clinicians, educators, administrators, and lawyers.* DeWitt, NY: GSI Publications/Guilford Press.

Huff, M., & Hodges, J. (2010). A practical guide for developing effective technical standards in social work programs. *Journal of Baccalaureate Social Work, 15*(2), 17–30.

International Center for Disability Information. (2000). U.S. table 11: By disability type, the percent of graduate and professional students reporting disabilities, by type of degree program. West Virginia University. Retrieved from http://www.icdi.wvu.edu/disability/U.S%20Tables/US11.htm.

Kadushin, A. (1985). *Supervision in social work* (2nd ed.). New York: Columbia University Press.

Knight, C. (2004). Modeling professionalism and supervising interns. In M. J. Austin & K. H. Hopkins (Eds.), *Supervision as collaboration in the human services* (pp. 110–124). Thousand Oaks, CA: Sage.

Lafrance, J., Gray, E., & Herbert, M. (2004). Gate-keeping for professional social work practice. *Social Work Education, 23*(3), 325–340.

Leighninger, L. (2000). *Creating a new profession.* Alexandria, VA: Council on Social Work Education.

Madden, R. G. (2000). Creating a bridging environment: The screening-in process in BSW programs. In P. Gibbs & E. H. Blakely (Eds.), *Gatekeeping in BSW programs* (pp. 135–148). New York: Columbia University Press.

Magen, R., Emerman, J., Scott, N., & Zeiger, S. (2000). Should convicted felons be denied admissions to social work programs? *Journal of Social Work Education, 36*(3), 401–413.

Miller, J., & Koerin, B. (2001). Gatekeeping in the practicum: What field instructors need to know. *Clinical Supervisor, 20*, 1–18.

Rawlings, M. (2007). *Objective structured clinical exams fir assessment: Issues in design, reliability and validity.* Paper presented at the Annual Program Meeting of the Council on Social Work Education, San Francisco.

Raymond, G. T. (2000). Gatekeeping in field education. In P. Gibbs & E. H. Blakely (Eds.), *Gatekeeping in BSW programs* (pp. 107–134). New York: Columbia University Press.

Raymond, G. T. (2012). Should BSW programs require student background checks? Paper presented at Baccalaureate Program Directors in Social Work Conference, March 15, Portland, OR.

Regents of the University of Michigan v. Ewing, 474 U.S. 214 (1985).

Reynolds, L. (2004). Gatekeeping prior to point of entry. *Advances in Social Work, 5*(1), 18–31.

Richmond v. Fowlkes, 228 F.3d. 854 (8th Cir. 2000).

Rompf, E., Royse, D., & Dhooper, S. (1993). Anxiety preceding field work: What students worry about. *Journal of Teaching in Social Work, 7*, 81–95.

Sowbel, L. (2011). Gatekeeping in field performance: Is grade inflation a given? *Journal of Social Work Education, 47*(2, Spring/Summer), 367–377.

Sowbel, L. (2012). Gatekeeping: Why shouldn't we be ambivalent? *Journal of Social Work Education, 48*(1), 27–44.

Tam, D., & Ming Kwok, S. (2007). Controversy debate on gatekeeping in social work education. *International Journal of Learning, 14*(2), 195–204.

Stromwall, L. K. (2002). Is social work's door open to people recovering from psychiatric disabilities? *Social Work, 47*(1), 75–83.

Urwin, C., Van Soest, D., & Kretzschmar, J. (2006). Key principle for developing gatekeeping standards for working with student problems. *Journal of Teaching in Social Work, 26*(1/2), 163–180.

Watkinson, A., & Chalmers, D. (2008). Disability professional unsuitability and the profession of social work: A case study. *Social Work Education, 27*(5), 504–518.

Wayne, R. (2004). Legal guidelines for dismissing students because of poor performance in field. *Journal of Social Work Education,* (Fall), 403–414.

Zakutansky, T. J., & Sirles, E. A. (1993). Ethical and legal issues in field education: Shared responsibility and risk. *Journal of Social Work Education, 29,* 338–347.

# 10

# Legal, Ethical, and Pedagogical Issues

*Raymie H. Wayne*

### Scenario A: Student with a Drunk Driving Conviction and Field Education Paperwork

A student completes a series of forms used to assist the field education office in making appropriate placements. Her answer to a question on one of the forms indicates that she has a criminal record from a drunk driving conviction that took place more than twelve years ago. In a private meeting with the field director, she asks that the field director keep the information confidential. The student says that she already paid for her mistake and has been clean and sober ever since. Reminding her that a background check might reveal the conviction to potential placements, the field director encourages the student to be forthcoming about her history. The student requests a placement that does not conduct background checks and again asks for her disclosure to be kept confidential.

The field director wonders what to do. Roughly half of the program's placements require background checks. Would she be doing something unethical or illegal if she knowingly sent a student with a criminal history to a placement that does not require background checks? Does it matter if the student will be expected to transport clients? Is the field director violating the student's right to privacy if she informs potential field instructors of the student's criminal history status? What if the field director makes the disclosure only after the student is accepted at the placement?

## Scenario B: Casual Conversation about Childhood Trauma

> During a placement interview with the field director, a student makes statements that suggest a history of childhood trauma. After additional casual conversations, the field director makes a personal note not to place the student in a child protection setting. Though the student tells the field director that she can "handle anything," the field director worries that the student may be in the process of coming to terms with her own childhood experiences and may not be fully available to all clients. Later that day, the field director speaks to another faculty member who raises some questions about the student. The field director believes it is in the student's best interest for the faculty member to know some of the student's history but had not asked the student if she, the field director, had permission to make limited disclosures on the student's behalf. The conversation between the field director and the student flowed so casually, the field director wonders if the student is fully cognizant of the extent of her sharing.

What are the field director's legal and ethical obligations to the student? Is it assumed that the field director will treat what she learned as confidential? Or is it expected that faculty will use information to inform individual and collaborative assessments, so they can protect the vulnerable populations served by students, and serve as gatekeepers to the profession?

This chapter provides the tools that field directors need to address the questions posed above. Field directors must find the right balance between sharing information about students and honoring confidentiality concerns. The importance of sharing pertinent information about students is reviewed in light of ethical, pedagogical, and accreditation perspectives. Alternatively, federal law sets parameters about the type of information that can be shared and with whom it can be shared. This chapter dissects the federal law, in the context of social work ethical standards and best educational practices, so that field directors may draft sound privacy policies. The scenarios above are revisited in light of the information presented.

## The Value of Confidentiality and the Importance of Sharing Student Information

The National Association of Social Workers (NASW) *Code of Ethics* identifies confidentiality as a core value of the profession (NASW, 2008). The expectation of confidentiality is thought to facilitate the establishment of a trusting relationship and the honest disclosure of sensitive information (*Jaffee v. Redmond*, 1996). Yet in spite of the respect afforded to privacy and confidentiality, field instructors report they would like access to sensitive student information (Furness & Gilligan, 2004; Reeser & Wertkin, 1997). Open discussions among students, field instructors, and faculty liaisons is seen as essential for creating productive matches between the student and field instructor and for creating appropriate learning opportunities in the field (Zakutansky & Sirles, 1993). Theoretically, the more a field instructor knows about a student, the more he or she will be able to provide quality learning opportunities for the student and protection from poor practice for clients. Significantly, though the NASW *Code of Ethics* places a high value on confidentiality, it also makes protection of the client's interest the primary concern, thus the *Code* can be used as a tool to support both the protection and the disclosure of sensitive student information. To further complicate matters, federal law specifically regulates the sharing of student information.

Pedagogically, there are many reasons to support limited sharing of sensitive student information. Personal life experiences shape how we think and act as social workers (Furness & Gilligan, 2004), and incorporation of those experiences is a part of the professional use of self. As a part of developing one's repertoire of tools as a social worker, students must learn when and where it is all right, or even necessary, to share otherwise private information. Appropriate personal sharing can be regarded as an essential social work practice behavior. Furthermore, open communication about student strengths and challenges allows field instructors to address pertinent issues directly, creating a greater likelihood that clients are protected from harmful interactions with students. Furness and Gilligan (2004) found agreement among those who teach practice, placement coordinators, and students, that students must share relevant personal information, including information about past trauma, with the people responsible for teaching practice skills.

Students must master the art of appropriate sharing (Council on Social Work Education [CSWE], 2008). The first of the ten core competencies states that program graduates "[i]dentify as a professional social worker and conduct oneself accordingly" (CSWE, 2008, Educational Policy [EP], 2.1.1, p. 3); this competency serves as a good example of the incorporation of appropriate sharing into the foundation curriculum. Two of the practice behaviors used to measure the achievement of the first competency are to "practice personal reflection and self-correction to assure continual professional development" and "attend to professional roles and boundaries" (CSWE, 2008, EP 2.1.1, p. 3). Appropriate sharing that furthers social work practice goals must be mastered by social work students wishing to graduate with either a bachelor of social work (BSW) or master of social work (MSW).

An additional and related reason to share sensitive student information with potential and actual field instructors is the shortage of educationally appropriate field placements (J. Wayne, Bogo, & Raskin, 2006). Field agencies and instructors are under tremendous pressure to use resources wisely. Students who have problems in the field can take an extraordinary amount of a field instructor's time and emotional energy. The program's obligation to document problem behaviors in the field (R. Wayne, 2004) can add to time pressures experienced by field instructors and create fears of libel or slander accusations from a disgruntled student. Significantly, many agencies have policies about putting unflattering information about a student in writing. A field instructor who unknowingly accepted a difficult student may feel deceived if she learns that the program knew of the student's issues prior to the placement. Regardless of the timing of the program's knowledge, a difficult student placement can be further frustrated by a lack of information sharing, and can cause experienced field instructors to burn out, or agencies to discontinue serving as placement sites. Social work programs, now more than ever, need to nourish relationships with field instructors and practice settings by working openly and collaboratively to educate future social workers and to ensure quality client care.

## Federal Law and the Right to Educational Privacy

Since the 1970s students have had an explicit right to privacy. Policies and practices related to sharing or protecting student information are most directly governed by the Family Educational Rights and Privacy Act (FERPA), originally passed in 1974 as the Buckley Amendment (FERPA, 1974). FERPA applies to all educational institutions that receive federal funding from applicable programs, including Pell grants and federally guaranteed student loans. Several U.S. Supreme Court cases, congressional amendments, regulations by the Department of Education (DOE), and DOE advisory letters help educational institutions to interpret the purposefully vague legislation. FERPA governs policies and practices regarding the sharing of educational records and directory information among faculty, administrators, parents, and others who are involved in the student's education. FERPA governs institutional policies and practices, and not individual idiosyncratic practices. Given the emphasis on institutional policies rather than individual practices, it is essential that field education offices have established policies and procedures about sharing student information that are in compliance with the law.

FERPA is enforced by the Family Policy Compliance Office (FPCO) within the DOE. The FPCO investigates a school's policies and practices, and not specifics of a particular violation. As a rule, programs should have contracts with practice settings that specify how they will protect confidential student information. A field instructor who shares information about a student's progress in mastering the practice behaviors, in the practice setting with a coworker not involved in the student's education, is most likely violating FERPA. If a violation were reported, the FPCO would look to see if there were policies and practices in place to prevent and handle violations of the nature reported, rather than investigate to see if the specific violation occurred. After the FPCO's investigation of a complaint, it notifies the school of its findings, including its reasoning. If a problem is revealed, the FPCO will dictate specific conditions to resolve the complaint. The emphasis will be the correction of the specific policy problem. As indicated in the regulations, programs should have policies in place to handle individual FERPA violations, such as a five-year ban on working with any outside individual who has violated a confidentiality agreement (FERPA, 1974, 99.67[c]). If, however, an extreme pattern of violation exists, the FPCO may begin proceedings to eliminate federal funding.

The fear of losing federal funding and confusion over the language and intent of a specific FERPA provision are thought to have enabled the tragic killing of thirty-two students and faculty at Virginia Tech in 2007 (Chapman, 2009). Seung-Hui Cho, a student at Virginia Tech, had come to the attention of university personnel from several different departments due to his mental health issues, disciplinary problems, and suicidal ideation before he engaged in a shooting spree that took the lives of students and faculty, injured many others, and committed suicide. Investigations after the tragedy revealed that Virginia Tech administrators believed that they could not share, between and among departments, information regarding

Cho and his troubling behaviors. Additional nationwide follow-up, instigated by President George W. Bush, revealed that college and university administrators across the country were confused about how to correctly implement FERPA. In spite of the fact the FERPA did allow for private information to be disclosed in some circumstances, school officials across the country were found to lack an understanding of the type of circumstances that would qualify as an exception to the privacy mandate, and thus erred on the side of protecting confidentiality, fearful of the consequence of violating the law. Though these findings triggered a change to the FPCO's regulations, the substance of the law was left unchanged and confusion remains (Chapman, 2009). The Virginia Tech tragedy serves as an extreme example of why formal policies for sharing information within institutions are needed.

In spite of the need for formal policies about information sharing, there is little consistency among field education offices about policies for sharing and/or protecting such information (Reeser & Wertkin, 1997). A study by Miller and Koerin (1998) found that programs differ in how they handle student information. Some programs promise students that their information will be treated as confidential, while others explicitly say they will use and share the information as appropriate. Similarly, Reeser and Wertkin (1997) found that field liaisons, students, and field instructors within the same programs had different beliefs about the existence of information-sharing policies and the actual practices employed by colleagues in the program. It is likely that many field instructors, faculty liaisons, and students are not cognizant of the ethical and legal ties created by their working relationships and actions (Zakutansky & Sirles, 1993). The student's right to privacy, the profession's belief in the value of confidentiality, obligations to do no harm to clients, and complex organizational relationships create competing interests for the handling of sensitive student information (Reeser & Wertkin, 1997). The competing interests and mandates, in conjunction with the differing practices employed nationally, create confusion for field directors, faculty liaisons, and students who wish to share, or are asked to share, sensitive information about their past or present situations.

## Family Educational Rights and Privacy Act: Applied to Field Education Records and Practices

The analysis that follows will enable field directors to understand the legal and educational issues involved in creating privacy policies. When legal and ethical issues are present, Israel (2010) in his problem-solving model suggests first reviewing the legality of the action or inaction, and then engaging in an ethical analysis of the situation. Israel notes, as seen above, that ethical codes, which are not rank ordered, can be used to support opposing courses of action. The law, on the other hand, though not directive for every situation, will generally suggest a range of acceptable choices. Engaging in a legal analysis, followed by an ethical analysis, will generate a legally acceptable range of choices and ethical guidance for choosing among the options.

The pertinent aspects of FERPA dictate that institutions have policies regarding the protection and sharing of individual student educational records. In general terms, FERPA states that a student's educational records maintained by a school may be shared only with the consent of the student (or, in some cases, the student's parents or guardians). As is true with most laws, there are exceptions for various circumstances. In this case, an exception of primary interest to field directors is the circumstances that permit the sharing of educational records without the student's consent. FERPA allows records to be shared with "other school officials, including teachers, within the agency or institution whom the agency or institution has determined to have a legitimate educational interest" (FERPA, 1974, 99.31 [1][i][A]). There are other exceptions that allow educational records to be shared with agents outside the institution.

To correctly draft policies that are consistent with FERPA, the field director must think like a lawyer. Thinking like a lawyer requires breaking down each aspect of the legal dictate into bite-size pieces to ensure that each phrase is appropriately applied. In this case, the field director must determine which pieces of information qualify as part of an educational record, that is maintained by the institution, and who may qualify as having a legitimate educational interest within the scope of the regulations. Each of these questions is dissected below to help field directors identify all the factors they must consider in drafting useful, pedagogically appropriate, and FERPA-compliant policies regarding the sharing of student information with field instructors.

A field director must first consider what constitutes an educational record. Of particular interest to field directors are the application forms that students complete to assist the field office in appropriately matching students to field agencies and field instructors. Field placement applications may contain information about values and prior life experiences, reasons for wanting (or not wanting) a specific type of placement, criminal background, and challenges to the field placement antici-pated by the student. Scenario A above serves as an example of this type of disclo-sure. Also pertinent to this discussion are comments made by students during interviews with the field placement staff, as noted in Scenario B.

Educational records consist of "records, files, documents, and other materials which (i) contain information directly related to a student; and (ii) are maintained by an educational agency or institution or by a person acting for such agency or institution" (FERPA, 1974, 1232g[a][4][A]). Noticeably, the plain language of the statute defines educational records as information pertaining to a student, rather than specific types of academic data. Relying on the plain language of the statute, courts have interpreted the definition of educational records broadly. For example, the District Court for the Southern District of Ohio determined that disciplinary records were included under the heading educational records (*United States v. Miami University*, 2000). Whereas disciplinary records usually result from a viola-tion of university- or college-wide rules of conduct, educational records usually pertain to a student's successes and challenges in his or her studies (R. Wayne, 2004). Field directors, therefore, should take care to include disciplinary records in their policies regarding the sharing of student information. This is important: in other contexts, such as due process requirements for student dismissals, courts have made a strict distinction between disciplinary and academic processes (R. Wayne, 2004).

Both the FERPA legislation and DOE regulations exempt directory information, which includes name, address, telephone number, date and place of birth, honors and awards, dates of attendance, and other items from the educational record (FERPA, 1974, 1232g[a][5][A], 99.3[a]). Specifically, schools may disclose direc-tory information without a student's consent as long as the student had an oppor-tunity to opt out of the disclosure. Field directors are encouraged to become famil-iar with their institutions' policies on the disclosure of directory information. Likewise, field directors should be aware of symbols or notations used by their institutions to identify students who have indicated that they do not want their directory information shared. For example, some electronic information systems that manage student records and transcripts may include "FERPA Hold" next to students' names who have opted out of the sharing of their directory information.

Other DOE exclusions include notes kept only by the original author for the pur-poses of aiding memory and are not made available to another person (except for a temporary substitute) (FERPA, 1974, 99.3[b][1]). However, if a memory aid is revealed to, or accessed by, another person, including someone with a legitimate educational interest, the note no longer meets the exception criteria and becomes a part of the educational record. The memory aid exclusion is important, however, because it allows a mental health counselor or professor to withhold notes made for private use from a student requesting her file (Daggett & Huefner, 2001). Other exclusions include student health records, which are privileged through the Health Insurance Portability and Accountability Act of 1996 (HIPAA) and case law (see *Jaffee v. Redmond*, 1996); records collected after the student no longer attends the school; and grades on peer-graded papers before they are collected and recorded by a teacher (*Owasso Independent School District N. I-011 v. Falvo*, 2002, 34).

Based on the broad interpretations of educational records by both the DOE and the courts, it is safe to assume that all field records containing information directly related to a student, stored in the student's file or by the field office, qualify as an educational record. Field application forms, memos to the student about progress and concerns, learning contracts, and field evaluations all meet the criteria as an educational record maintained by the institution. The application information in Scenario A is thus protected by FERPA, and cannot be shared without student consent. FERPA does not, however, cover personal knowledge gained about a student through verbal interaction or direct observation, as is described in Scenario B. Students' interactions with faculty, both in and out of the classroom, can be freely shared with faculty and field instructors to help assess and correct problematic behaviors exhibited by students. If, however, observations are documented in a memo and placed in a student file, the memo becomes part of the educational record. As described in Scenario B, the memory aid was rather general and did not include specific data about the student or anything that was actually disclosed. In this case, the field director could share the information she gathered and observations she made during the placement interview.

Once it is determined that field education documents qualify as educational records, the next step is to discern who qualifies as a school official with a legitimate educational interest. This issue is more difficult than determining what qualifies as an educational record. This is especially true as applied to field instructors and even more difficult as applied to potential field instructors who may be considering offering a specific student a field placement, both of whom might claim a need to know about student challenges.

FERPA identifies two categories of people who may have a legitimate educational interest in receiving confidential information about students without the student's consent. The first category includes school officials and others within an institution who are determined to have a legitimate interest. Faculty in a social work program who share a concern about a specific student may freely discuss items in the student's educational record with each other. The second group of people who may gain access to educational records without the consent of the student includes contractors, volunteers, and others to whom the program has outsourced institutional services (FERPA, 1974, 99.31[a][1][i][B]). To qualify under the second category, the outside party must (1) perform an institutional service or function for which the agency or institution would otherwise use employees, (2) be under the direct control of the agency or institution with respect to the use and maintenance of educational records, and (3) follow FERPA rules regarding further disclosure (FERPA, 1974, 99.31[a][1][i][B][1]–[3]). A person need not be a paid employee to qualify as having a legitimate educational interest. Such people, however, must be informed of their obligations under FERPA to maintain confidentiality.

## Field Education Policy Recommendations

The relationships and responsibilities between and among field liaisons, field instructors, and students are complex and multifaceted (Zakutansky & Sirles, 1993). The findings from Reeser and Wertkin's (1997) survey of field liaisons and field instructors about access to information reinforced the uncertainty regarding field instructors' legal standing and status in social work programs. Regardless of the role and status of the field instructor, the CSWE has made the role of field education explicit. The 2008 EPAS states, "It is a basic precept of social work education that the two interrelated components of curriculum—classroom and field—are of equal importance within the curriculum, and each contributes to the development of the requisite competencies of professional practice (CSWE, 2008, EP 2.3, p. 8).

In spite of their integral role in social work education, field instructors do not, on the face of it, fit neatly into the FERPA legitimate interest categories. It is questionable if field instructors, as outside parties, meet the three criteria above. Social work supervision for field education is typically performed by non-university employees. University faculty occasionally offer supplemental supervision to students in a placement without a social worker on site, but it would be risky to argue that field instruction is a function for which the program would otherwise use employees. In making this argument, however, it would be useful to note that the 2008 EPAS places responsibility for the student's social work supervision on the program. Accreditation Standard (AS) 2.1.6 states, "for cases in which a field instructor does not hold a CSWE-accredited social work degree, the program assumes responsibility for reinforcing a social work perspective" (CSWE, 2008, p. 10).

Second, and perhaps most significantly, field instructors are not typically under the direct control of the school in which they serve. Alternatively, in most circumstances field instructors have direct supervision by, and accountability to, the agency for which they work. The third criterion, that outside agents abide by FERPA rules in relation to further disclosures, does not appear to pose a problem in this analysis. As noted below, the program and practice setting could execute a simple agreement outlining the field instructor's commitment to abide by FERPA.

One way to address the discrepancy between the educational functions of the field instructor and the explicit language of FERPA that dictates with whom records can be freely shared is to give field instructors faculty appointments. The faculty appointment would theoretically create a situation where field instructors are operating from within the academic institution when performing educational duties for the school. Given that most programs utilize formal contracts to delineate the relationship among the program, student, field instructor, and practice setting, it may not be too large a leap to identify the field instructor as teaching faculty. Offering library privileges and other similar low- or no-cost perks could further identify field instructors as members of the institution. It is recommended that students be made aware of the existence, nature, and depth of contracts between the academic institution and the field instructor or practice setting (Zakutansky & Sirles, 1993).

The agreements between the program and practice setting must clarify the field instructor's responsibility to abide by FERPA and to protect all records pertaining to the student's role as a learner. The field director should secure consent from the student so that field instructors may seek appropriate supervision from within the agency. Regardless of the information shared with the field instructor by the school, the field instructor can always share information about the student with program faculty (liaisons, administrators, and faculty). In fact, field instructors must be forthcoming with program faculty about student successes and challenges as a part of their mutual gatekeeping responsibilities (R. Wayne, 2004).

An alternative to arguing that field instructors are members of the program's faculty is to secure student consent to share information with potential and actual field instructors. In addition to being a legally safer way to proceed, securing student consent also honors the values of our profession. One way this could be accomplished is to include student consent on the field placement application. For example, an application could include language such as this: "By signing this form I certify that all information contained herein is accurate and complete to the best of my knowledge. So that my educational needs can best be met, I consent to the sharing of all information contained in my educational record, including that which is disclosed on this application, to be shared with potential or actual field instructors. This consent includes records and documents that would otherwise be protected under FERPA and applies to information currently in my educational record, as well as information that will be added during my tenure in the social work program."

To meet the criteria for informed consent, the waiving of FERPA rights must be voluntary. To be truly voluntary, students must be given options that do not include the waiving of their privacy rights. This means that the student should be told (and the form should indicate) that a placement will be available, though choices may be limited, even if the student does not sign the waiver. Students must also have the right to revoke the waiver "with respect to any actions occurring after the revocation" (FERPA, 1974, 99.12[c][3][i]).

Beginning the field placement process and relationship by identifying the scope of privacy and limits to confidentiality accomplishes several important goals. First, it models how to handle limits to confidentiality in practice, such as mandated reporting of child abuse. Obtaining the student's consent to share information honors the profession's commitment to confidentiality and self-determination. Significantly, Reeser and Wertkin (1997) found that a high percentage of surveyed field instructors, students, and faculty liaisons all believed that it is important to obtain the student's permission when sharing sensitive student information. The same survey found that 73 percent of students showed a willingness to file a grievance against the social work program if personal information was conveyed without their consent. Though FERPA does not create a private cause of action

(*Gonzaga University v. Doe*, 2002), the individual student may have other remedies created by school policies and/or state law. As Strom-Gottfried and Corcoran (1998) note, students should know how their information will be treated before they disclose any private information. The explicit sharing of information with field instructors may increase the legitimacy and authority of the field instructor as an educator in the eyes of the student (and the field instructor). Finally, a discussion of the need to share such information sends a clear message to the student about the importance of the information and the possible impact of the personal self in a professional relationship.

The legal analysis presented above supports obtaining student consent to share information as a requirement for that student to entering the field. The pedagogical and ethical analysis offered at the start of this chapter supports the same conclusion. The following policy guidelines and responses to the original scenarios will guide directors in successfully creating policies that allow for legal, ethical, and educationally sound disclosures.

## Policy Guidelines for Field Directors: Key Points

1. Field manuals must inform students of what comprises an educational record, who are the school officials with a legitimate educational interest, and the policies that guide what information may be shared with whom.

2. The agency–school contract and field manual should define field instructors as field faculty with the appropriate appointment and identify field instructors as having a legitimate educational interest in student records.

3. Field instructors should be required to sign a confidentiality statement saying that they are aware of and will abide by FERPA restrictions on sharing information about students.

4. The field application completed by the students should include consent to share student information with potential and actual field instructors.

5. If a field instructor were to violate the confidentiality provisions, the school should refrain from using that field instructor for five years (FERPA, 1974, 1232g[b][4][B]).

## Scenarios Revisited
### Scenario A: Student with a Drunk Driving Conviction and Field Education Paperwork

In Scenario A, a student disclosed a prior drunk driving conviction in her field application paperwork. If the field application contained the proper consent, the field director has several acceptable options. First, the field director should obtain more-specific information to determine if there exists any current risk to client safety or likely limits on field placement settings. Similarly, the field director should advise the student as to whether there is a foreseeable risk that the student may not be able to secure employment, work in specific settings, or obtain a required license. The field director should consider how much time has passed, the nature of the crime, the student's ownership of the situation, and reports of personal change. Next, the field director might determine that the information is more relevant for some types of placements than others. For example, it may be necessary to share the information with field instructors at placements where there is direct practice with vulnerable populations and less necessary at policy placements. The field director and the student can then decide together what type of placement to seek knowing the likelihood for the necessity of disclosure.

Scenario A concluded with the following questions:

> The field director wonders what to do. Roughly half of the program's placements require background checks. Would she be doing something unethical or illegal if she knowingly sent a student with a criminal history to a placement that does not require background checks? Does it matter if the student will be expected to transport clients? Is the field director violating the student's right to privacy if she informs potential field instructors of the student's criminal history status? What if the field director makes the disclosure only after the student is accepted at the placement?

Based on the legal, ethical, and pedagogical analyses above, it would be unwise for the field director to withhold the information from a potential practice setting or supervisor. Though it would be problematic to share the information with a potential field instructor without the student's consent, a proper consent on the field application would eliminate this concern. Even with the proper consent, the field director should consider disclosing the student's history only when the supervisor is considering offering the placement to the student. This would allow the student to make her own first impression at the practice setting, preserve some level of privacy, yet position the practice setting to make the final commitment from an informed perspective.

Field placements that involve activities or populations that directly relate to the student's prior challenges have a stronger need to know than those that do not. Therefore, a practice setting that would require the student to transport clients has a stronger right to know about a prior drunk driving conviction than a placement that does not include client transport. Similarly, the field instructor's interest in knowing about the student increases as the field instructor assumes the role of educator. A current field instructor has a stronger interest in knowing about a student than does a potential field instructor. Likewise, a supervisor that is about to accept a student has a stronger interest than one who is engaging in a preliminary interview.

A program that has followed the policy suggestions contained herein is well situated to share information with field instructors as the relationship between the student and practice setting solidifies.

### Scenario B: Casual Conversation about Childhood Trauma

In Scenario B, a student shared personal information about some childhood difficulties with the field director during the field placement interview. In this situation, the verbal exchange and personal note would not be entitled to FERPA protections. However, any notes the field director made for the file would become a part of the student's educational record. Similarly, if the field director thinks that the information belongs in the file, she should ask the student to make a note, or agree to words written by the field director on the application, so that there is no doubt in the student's mind what the program might share later. Regardless of whether the information is protected by FERPA, the field director is free to discuss the student and share sensitive student information with other faculty who have a legitimate educational interest in the student.

Scenario B concluded with the following questions:

> What are the field director's legal and ethical obligations to the student? Is it assumed that the field director will treat what she learned as confidential? Or is it expected that faculty will use information to inform individual and collaborative assessments, so they can protect the vulnerable populations served by students, and serve as gatekeepers to the profession?

In this case, the field director has a legal and ethical obligation to use the information gathered about the student to further the student's best interest and to fulfill the client protection and gatekeeping obligations entrusted to social work educators. When these demands conflict, the duty to protect the public from harm trumps the student's best interest. Field education policies and paperwork should ensure that the student has no expectation of confidentiality regarding information that she shares. All program materials should make explicit that the program will use information gained about students in collaborative assessments among faculty, including field faculty.

## Conclusion

This chapter reviewed the legal, ethical, and pedagogical considerations related to sharing sensitive student information with faculty colleagues, field instructors, and potential field instructors. The policy guidelines presented are consistent with federal law, best educational practices, and ethical standards. Field directors must find the right balance between sharing information about students and honoring confidentiality concerns. When drafting specific policies and when dealing with complicated cases, field directors are well advised to seek consultation and supervision from people with specialized knowledge, such as attorneys, administrators, program directors, and colleagues (Strom-Gottfried & Corcoran, 1998).

## Essential Readings

Family Educational Rights and Privacy Act (FERPA), 20 U.S.C. § 1232g; 34 C.F.R. pt 99. (1974).

Israel, A. B. (2010). *Using the law: Practical decision making in mental health.* Chicago: Lyceum Books.

Wayne, R. H. (2004). Legal guidelines for dismissing students because of poor performance in the field. *Journal of Social Work Education, 40*(3), 403–414.

## References

Chapman, K. (2009). A preventable tragedy at Virginia Tech: Why confusion over FERPA's provisions prevents schools from addressing student violence. *Boston University Public Interest Law Journal, 18*(2), 349–385.

Council on Social Work Education (CSWE). (2008). *Educational policy and accreditation standards* (rev. March 27, 2010/updated August 2012). Alexandria, VA: Author. Retrieved from http://www.cswe.org/Accreditation/41865.aspx.

Daggett, L. M., & Huefner, D. S. (2001). Recognizing schools' legitimate educational interests: Rethinking FERPA's approach to the confidentiality of student discipline and classroom records. *American University Law Review, 51*(1), 1–48.

Family Educational Rights and Privacy Act (FERPA), 20 U.S.C. § 1232g; 34 C.F.R. pt 99. (1974).

Furness, S., & Gilligan, P. (2004). Fit for purpose: Issues from practice placements, practice teaching and the assessment of students' practice. *Social Work Education, 23*(4), 465–479. doi:10.1080/0261547042000245053.

Gonzaga University v. Doe, 536 U.S. 273 (2002).

Health Insurance Portability and Accountability Act (HIPAA) of 1996, PL 104–191, 110 Stat. 1936 (1996).

Israel, A. B. (2010). *Using the law: Practical decision making in mental health.* Chicago: Lyceum Books.

Jaffee v. Redmond, 518 U.S. 1 (1996).

Miller, J., & Koerin, B. (1998). Can we assess suitability at admission? A review of MSW application procedures. *Journal of Social Work Education, 34*(3), 437–453.

National Association of Social Workers (NASW). (2008). *Code of ethics of the National Association of Social Workers.* Washington, DC: Author.

Owasso Independent School District No. I-011 v. Falvo, 534 U.S. 426 (2002).

Reeser, L., & Wertkin, R. A. (1997). Sharing sensitive student information with field instructors: Responses of students, liaisons, and field instructors. *Journal of Social Work Education, 33*(2), 347–362.

Strom-Gottfried, K., & Corcoran, K. (1998). Confronting ethical dilemmas in managed care: Guidelines for students and faculty. *Journal of Social Work Education, 34*(1), 109–119.

United States v. Miami University, 91 F. Supp. 2d 1132 (S.D. Ohio 2000).

Wayne, J., Bogo, M., & Raskin, M. (2006). The need for radical change in field education. *Journal of Social Work Education, 42*(1), 161–169.

Wayne, R. H. (2004). Legal guidelines for dismissing students because of poor performance in the field. *Journal of Social Work Education, 40*(3), 403–414.

Zakutansky, T. J., & Sirles, E. A. (1993). Ethical and legal issues in field education: Shared responsibility and risk. *Journal of Social Work Education, 29*(3), 338–347.

# 11

# Safety and Risk Management
*Sharon C. Lyter*

## Professional Leadership and Professional Ambivalence

Verbal and physical aggressions are realities in the social work profession. Students are at risk and receive inadequate protection against these risks. This chapter prepares field directors to educate students about personal safety issues and provides resources to social work programs for assessing and managing risk factors. It addresses institutional policies, liability, incident reporting, site-specific safety training, and ways to deal with traumatized victims.

One of the most controversial of all topics within field education is that of worker safety. In regional field director meetings across the country, directors grapple with this sensitive and divisive matter. Both social work client commitment and risks date back to the era of Jane Addams. The endurance of the profession's hallmark of social justice is celebrated, but the lack of comprehensive attention by the profession to worker safety is unfortunate.

According to a review of the research from the previous twenty years, more than twenty studies have chronicled acts of violence against social workers and insufficient safeguards (Criss, 2010). The national prevalence of worker exposure to client violence falls between 65 percent and 86 percent of workers. In a survey of National Association of Social Workers (NASW) members, Ringstad (2005) found that, over a career, 86 percent of social workers had been victimized by psychological aggression and 30 percent by physical assault during their careers. A survey of baccalaureate programs (Faria & Kendra, 2007) revealed that 26 percent of the programs had students who had experienced physical or verbal violence during the previous five-year period. Research from the United States and the United Kingdom (Dunkel, Ageson, & Ralph, 2000; Macdonald & Sirotich, 2001; Newhill, 2003; Shields & Kiser, 2003; Spencer & Munch, 2003) highlights the genuine pain, trauma, and costs that result from insufficient worker protections, including medical expenses, loss of productivity, physical disability, emotional trauma, and even death.

There is no longer any doubt that social work practitioners and practicum students face some risks to their own safety. At the same time, many agencies, institutions, and community organizations have been inconsistent and ambivalent with respect to safety. The title of an article from the *NASW News* (O'Neill, 2004) illustrates this ambivalence: "Tragedies Spark Worker-Safety Awareness: Many Think Client Violence 'Won't Happen Here.'"

Violence or threats of violence are common for social workers during their careers. But exactly how much risk is there? How much emphasis should be placed on risk reduction? Newhill (2003) provides some clarification: "Violence is what we call a *low-base-rate phenomenon*, meaning that in the range of all possible human behaviors, violence is a comparatively rare event" (p. 89; emphasis in original). There are sufficient data to project that lifetime risk is likely over 50 percent, although degree of immediate risk is unknown. The complexities of the data may partially account for the tendency of some professionals to ignore or minimize the matter.

The field director faces a dilemma. Should the director place emphasis on something that is rare in the scope of the daily work of thousands of social workers yet common across a career? Will students be frightened unnecessarily or not trust their clients? Indeed, is this not part of what we expect in social work? Clearly, the profession cannot entirely eliminate violence against workers, who have to accept a certain amount of personal risk, similar to other first responders such as police and firefighters. The critical difference is policy: police and firefighters are compelled to receive training to manage risk, whereas social workers are subject to inconsistent or nonexistent policies managing risk. Why should social workers be subject to unmanaged and often unnecessary risk? A profession that symbolizes principled positions and policies cannot continue to ignore this matter.

The remarks below and throughout the chapter exemplify social workers' ambivalence around safety issues. They were garnered by the author over fifteen years from regional field director consortium meetings, national and regional conferences, and discussions with faculty, field agency staff, and students. They provide powerful evidence of the controversy, emotion, and ambivalence associated with safety issues.

"My client bit me."

"My client spit in my eye."

"I had to have HIV testing after the client assaulted me."

"My parents think I'm foolish to go into a field like this. I won't make much money, and I will be in danger. But I love this work. What should I tell them?"

## Definition and Scope

For field directors, the program's definition of violence that is shared with students will frame the discussion for safety awareness. A broad definition will signal to students when violence is occurring. The following definitions serve as a guideline. According to Newhill (2003), violence includes actual and attempted physical harm to person and harm to property:

(a) intentional (not accidental) incidents of actual physical attacks, described as an incident in which an individual directly lays hands or a weapon on another individual with the intent to harm;

(b) attempted physical attacks, described as an incident in which an individual attempts to intentionally physically attack another individual but does not make actual physical contact;

(c) threats, described as a verbal threat to harm another individual or a deliberate threatening, physical gesture (including stalking) from one individual toward another; and

(d) property damage, described as an incident in which an individual intentionally damages another individual's personal property or property the individual was using at the time of the incident. (p. 17)

An expanded definition of violence against social workers is "intentional property damage, threats, verbal abuse, and attempted or actual physical harm against social workers or other service providers by individuals who are applicants, recipients, or former recipients of those services" (Beaver, 1999, as cited in Criss, 2010, p. 371). Ringstad (2005) adds psychological aggression to the definition: "[T]he term violence is interchangeable with physical and psychological assault. Psychological assault and psychological aggressions are, likewise, interchangeable" (p. 306).

## Professional Esteem, Shaming, and Underreporting

"Just be calm. If you are not calm, it's your own fault if something happens."

"Our commitment is to our clients—we need to be selfless."

"You should be caring about your clients, not yourself."

"Maybe your fears are really about biases against your clients."

"Your client threatened to kill you when you visit? Oh, I don't think that will really happen."

Do we deserve to be safe? Can we value our safety along with that of our clients? Social work has at times struggled with its professional self-concept and self-esteem. The profession's commitment to dignity and worth of the person has yet to be fully extended to the service providers themselves. Some suggest that failure to attend to harm reduction is emblematic of social worker selflessness.

The history of social work with regard to home visits gives some insight as to the image of the profession within the general population. In contrast to other helping professionals who make home visits, many social workers, particularly child protection workers, are charged with investigative functions (Lyter & Abbott, 2007). Consequently, some confusion is understandable: Is the worker there to provide services or to determine if a removal is warranted? Lack of clarity and negative public opinion can escalate worker vulnerability, worker anxiety, and professional self-doubt.

Students are socialized by faculty, faculty liaisons, field instructors, and other agency workers, integrating beliefs and practices of the professional culture. When the new worker or student has concerns about safety and seeks advice, what are supervisors' and colleagues' likely responses? Some will cause the worker to feel shame, chiding her for her fears, or will find a way to end the conversation, preferring to practice denial. Some will regale the novice with war stories that glorify their own bravado and fearless risk-taking. Finally, some experienced workers provide honest guidance that furthers the worker's skill set: that is the goal. An informed worker is the most effective worker. Proper instruction, bolstered by effective agency policy and practices, helps the frightened or avoidant worker to gain courage, the uninformed or naïve worker to gain commitment to safety and respect for personal well-being, and the irrationally bold worker to gain awareness of personal vulnerability and fallibility (Lyter & Abbott, 2007, p. 29).

Underreporting of incidents of violence is, for the most part, a product of shaming practices and lack of administration commitment to worker safety (Newhill, 2003). The cycle continues, with the newly socialized professionals expressing denial or guilt in sync with their superiors, failing to report incidents, and failing to teach their future trainees worker safety and proper reporting (Faria & Kendra, 2007).

### Student Vulnerability

"Sometimes I'm afraid to sit down in a client's home."

"I asked about safety issues at my placement. My field instructor seemed bothered by this. I found myself feeling ashamed for asking the question."

"Most of our clients are people of color. If I say I have some fears, it makes me sound racist."

"My agency wants me to use my own car to transport clients."

Students, indeed, are vulnerable. Similar to professional social workers, they are exposed during practicum to the usual risks, but it is probable that students are less prepared to respond than are those more senior in experience. In many instances, students take on roles similar to workers on staff, including making home visits alone. There is some indication that denial of vulnerability exists at the organizational level.

Students' fears can interfere with practice effectiveness and learning; students need to be protected through risk reduction (Dunkel et al., 2000). According to Faria and Kendra (2007), "[f]ailure to prepare students adequately to deal with the risks of social work practice is unacceptable" (p. 152). It is time that students are accorded the dignity of full disclosure so they have more control over their own experiences: "Students need to understand student rights" (Criss, 2010, p. 385).

Safety is not a topic that is comprehensively covered in schools of social work, and social workers are not typically prepared with adequate self-defense training, conflict resolution techniques, or resources to prevent violence. Social workers are expected to enter people's lives when those lives may be at their worst, solve seemingly intractable problems, help clients with life-threatening challenges, and work with people in their most vulnerable moments. Many of the required skills, however, the workers often learn on the job. This inconsistent approach is unacceptable and likely to result in continued assaults and tragedies, and to pose a barrier to the recruitment of future social workers who deem the profession too dangerous (Kelly, 2010).

## Taking Responsibility

"Don't open a can of worms. This will make our university liable for student safety. Let it go."

"Let's not scare away potential new recruits."

"New social workers should get their own training. This is not the school's job and not the agency's job."

Who has the obligation to address student safety in field: the student, the classroom instructor, field director, program director, field instructor, or agency director? Literature addresses the theme of responsibility and accountability to reduce risk. Examples of risk reduction include the need for administration to provide funding for lock systems, closed circuit television, and first aid for social workers in South Korea (Choong Rai & Soochan, 2009); risk reduction for social workers in rural Australia (Green, Gregory, & Mason, 2003); government documentation of violence against social workers in Great Britain (Miskelly, 2010); collaborations among community agencies, field faculty, students, and field instructors, with "schools of social work" taking a "leadership role in developing curriculum on risk reduction" in the United States (Dunkel et al., 2000, p. 15); and the need for universities in Canada to recognize the lack of "training and preparation to deal with client violence [in the] social work curriculum" (Macdonald & Sirotich, 2005, p. 779). Schools of social work must take a leadership role in developing curriculum on risk reduction and conducting research that tests the strategies of risk assessment, prevention, and intervention.

Ethics and legal liability are significant variables that may serve to urge reluctant or resistant entities to take notice. Ethical imperatives speak to the professional responsibility for "supervisors to educate and train their supervisees in areas relevant to practice as well as to assign cases within the area of supervisees' expertise" (Lyter & Abbott, 2007, p. 23), and for those supervisors to be competent in their areas of supervision. Those in authority are likely to acknowledge professional liability or professional malpractice that results in harm or potential harm to a client, striving to reduce "liability exposure of the agency and its board of directors, supervisor, social worker, social work school placing students, and social work student" (Lynch & Versen, 2003, p. 59). This reference to a hierarchy of responsibility includes the legal concept of vicarious liability, wherein the superior can be held responsible for acts of the subordinate.

Supervisors and educators may be held responsible for the actions of their students (Strom-Gottfried, 2000). According to Robb (2003–2004), "[C]ourt rulings consistently underscore the importance of providing adequate supervision. While no supervisor can eliminate vicarious risk, s/he can manage it by maintaining high professional standards. . . . Supervisors and field instructors have primary responsibility for knowing student caseloads and activities well enough to anticipate and prevent problems" (pp. 1–2). Lyter and Abbott (2007) indicate that supervisors are also responsible for the safety or well-being of workers.

If the *Code of Ethics* (NASW, 2008) and the law do not yet clearly compel attention to worker risk, perhaps worker retention is a motivator. With a large national sample (response rate of 49 percent of 10,000 social workers), a workforce retention study (Whitaker, Weismiller, & Clark, 2006) discovered that 44 percent of the social workers reported personal safety issues on the job, noting "A profession cannot successfully retain its workforce when issues of personal safety go unaddressed" (p. 35). Fields of practice were ranked as follows in terms of risk: criminal justice (67%), child welfare/family and addictions (both 52%), aging (32%), and higher education (13%) (p. 25).

Safety is a topic that can evoke considerable emotion and strong views on either side. One's perspective can be influenced by a value orientation that emphasizes blaming the worker and excusing the perpetrator of violence (Macdonald & Sirotich, 2005); by biases related to class or race, or fear of appearing biased (Dunkel et al., 2000); and/or by gender and authority disparities in exposure to violence, with positions that entail substantial direct client contact dominated by women and administrative roles dominated by men in "more protected management roles" (Macdonald & Sirotich, 2005, p. 778).

Over the previous decades the literature has placed more emphasis on raising consciousness about worker risk and less on pursuing evidence-based safe practices.

This scant progress on moving from exploration and inquiry to formal policies and practices has been a disappointment to many advocates who wish to see more progress. However, this is a realistic trajectory because change takes time. Strategies for safety are more likely to be based on practice wisdom than on empirical evidence. Future researchers need to rigorously study all aspects of the profession's ideology and value orientation that pertain to ambivalence toward worker/student safety. Strategies, policies, and procedures applicable to specific settings and populations also need research attention. Faria and Kendra (2007) recommend that research produce "comprehensive safety education content" (p. 151). This new research should reflect a transition from wisdom to the blending of wisdom with evidence.

While the profession improves safety research, Faria and Kendra (2007) recommend that social work programs assume more responsibility. The following is focused on bachelor of social work (BSW) education, but the recommendations apply equally to master of social work (MSW) programs:

> Those programs that do not teach safety education should implement a unit on the topic as soon as possible. Failure to prepare students adequately to deal with the risks of social work practice is unacceptable. Baccalaureate social work programs also should be knowledgeable about what safety education content is taught in field practicum. No program should rely on field practicum to teach safety education; programs have a responsibility to prepare students before entering the field experience. Programs should continually review what is taught in coursework and in field practicum and add content as necessary. Policies regarding student safety also should be developed and the reporting of client violence toward social work students should be strongly encouraged if not mandated. (p. 152)

### Taking Responsibility: Professional Organizations

**Role of the National Association of Social Workers and the Council on Social Work Education.** NASW's tradition of exercising moral courage could further promote worker safety. As evidenced by articles covering benchmark events from the previous decade, worker safety is recognized by the NASW Press. For example, O'Neill (2002) reported in the *NASW News* about a social worker slain by a client. In a *NASW News* article he observed, "Violence or threats of violence are reasonably common for social workers during their careers" (O'Neill, 2004). The NASW president recognized the "[u]rgency of social worker safety" in an *NASW News* editorial (Kelly, 2010). NASW supports the Teri Zenner Social Worker Safety Act; the NASW Center for Workforce has conducted research on worker safety. The NASW Web site (www.naswdc.org) has a resource page listing reports and materials related to safety. Clearly, NASW's acknowledgement of the weight of this issue is embodied in the establishment of its Memorial to Social Workers Who Lost Their Lives While Performing Social Work Duties.

Additional efforts are needed to codify the recognition by the professional organizations of the value of the worker and the worker's safety. The professional responsibilities expressed through ethical codes elevate commitment to the well-being of all persons. This author urges consideration of incorporation of language related to worker/student/staff safety into the NASW *Code of Ethics*. This could be accomplished in various ways, such as the addition of section (e) to 3.07 Administration: *"(e) Social work administrators should take reasonable steps to ensure that adequate agency or organizational resources are available to provide training and supervision to reduce risk to workers/students/staff in the work environment."*

The Educational Policy Accreditation Standards (EPAS) do not require that social work programs address safety issues (Council on Social Work Education [CSWE], 2008). "Because CSWE does not mandate safety training for students, educators may not believe there is a need to engage in formal curriculum building designed to prepare students" (Lyter & Abbott, 2007, p. 29). This leaves the responsibility to the discretion of individual programs, field agencies, or to no one. Innovative language in EPAS would help to propel the profession and those that govern educational policies to include worker safety. The following suggested changes, shown in italics, affect selection of field settings by the field director and a related practice behavior of a core competency that would be required of students:

> Accreditation Standard 2.1.5. Specifies policies, criteria, and procedures for selecting field settings *while ensuring that safety policies and procedures are in place to maximize the safety of staff, clients and students*; placing and monitoring students; maintaining field liaison contacts with field education settings; and evaluating student learning and field setting effectiveness congruent with the program's competencies. (p. 9)

"Education Policy 2.1.9. Respond to contexts that shape practice" (p. 6) would be amended to include a new related practice behavior: *recognize risks and dangers to workers and clients and participate in practices that protect both worker and client safety.*

**Role of Field Consortia.** Following is an example of one field director consortium's initiative to address risk awareness. The efforts by the Tri-State Consortium of Field Directors (based in Philadelphia) illustrate a path of change over a period of years. The process began in 1999 with a safety survey of approximately 201 field placement agencies in the region (Lyter & Martin, 2000). Only 18 percent of those agencies reported that they had a formal written agency safety policy. Clearly, the agencies were not fully prepared to provide direction to their workers or to students in training. In response to the finding, the consortium members collaborated in reviewing their own policies on student safety.

In 1999 social work educators at Rutgers University–Camden (located in a designated high-crime district), took the step of hosting a community safety forum in order to hear from stakeholders, share policy statements, and encourage collaborations. Eventually, the pursuit of safe practices was codified in the Rutgers University School of Social Work field manual, in a section titled "Student Safety in Field Practicum," with language pertaining to the agency's responsibilities to provide an orientation for personal safety (Pottick, 2012, pp. 27–28). Field directors who are facing considerable resistance to and animosity regarding acknowledgement of student safety issues should consider this example and follow through by identifying and convening the key stakeholders in order that the director not operate alone and without credible support.

In a follow-up study (Lyter, 2003) of the field directors of the eight schools participating in the Lyter and Martin survey (2000), about a third of the directors noted that violence had affected their own students during the previous year and three-fourths reported that students expressed safety concerns. In contrast to the earlier period of data collection, all directors reported progress in that all of their field settings had a safety policy, though many were informal. Seven of the eight schools began to include review of safety practices in the field practicum orientation.

Progress can be attributed to the consciousness raising provoked by the research initiative and actions subsequently taken by agencies and schools. Comprehensive change must be planned and needs to involve all stakeholders. Advocates need to understand that fundamental change occurs incrementally, especially in university environments.

Another factor that may have raised consciousness of risk is a series of tragic and high-profile incidents of violence in the United States over the past twenty years:

the massacre at Columbine High School in Littleton, Colorado, in 1999; the September 11, 2001, attacks in New York City, Pennsylvania, and Washington, DC; the Virginia Tech massacre in 2007; the shooting of social worker Gabe Zimmerman, community outreach director for U.S. Representative Gabrielle Giffords, in 2011; and the tragic Sandy Hook Elementary School shooting in 2012. These events have motivated higher security consciousness in schools.

### Taking Responsibility: Field Director Risk Reduction Strategies

"Why are we placing students in agencies that do not have safety policies?"

"I want to teach my students about safety, but how do you find balance on this tough topic?"

"My dean made it clear that I did not have 'permission' to discuss student safety."

"Let's not communicate our own fears to students."

Effective recognition of the need for risk management related to the social work practicum has been evolving for at least thirty years. It is understandable that change takes time, but the pace needs to accelerate and field is a crucial place to advance the process. The field director holds an influential position with entrée to both university and community decision makers to (1) develop and review field program safety policies, (2) advocate for organizational practices that protect both worker and client, and (3) include student safety content in the curriculum.

The field director needs to assess the readiness for change of the organizations in question, such as the university, department, and community agencies, and to be sensitive to resistance while simultaneously advocating for change. The field director, social work program, and community service providers should be resources to each other in assisting in the development of responsible policies and practices on worker and student safety. Education and research are often the most productive first steps. The first aim in terms of policy might be a statement in field education documents. For example,

### *Safety-Related Responsibilities of Host Agencies*

Violence against social workers cannot be eradicated, but in many cases it can be prevented and its impact can be lessened through agency-specific policies and practices. The Social Work Program trusts that host agencies will create safety plans that include prevention, intervention, and aftermath strategies and take steps to ensure the safety of students. It is expected that agencies provide safety plan training at the outset of the internship experience. (Kutztown University Department of Social Work, 2012, p. 9)

Another area of policy would be in selecting practice settings. Field directors should be cognizant of the agency's safety protocols and specifically request written information about whether the setting presents any unusual risks to students, and if safety training is provided as part of the student orientation. Practices for minimizing risk should include incident prevention, incident reporting, and trauma management. Occupational Safety and Health Administration (OSHA) recommendations include developing specific procedures for home visiting, use of the buddy system in working with high-risk clients, informing clients and employees that violence will not be tolerated, and requiring the reporting of all incidents of violence (OSHA, 2004). Field directors should ask agencies if safety technology such as beepers and cell phones are provided to workers, and, if they are, if the agency can provide them to students. Moreover, OSHA encourages the organizations to cultivate a relationship with "local police and state prosecutors" (OSHA, 2004, p. 15) and notify employees how to request police assistance or file charges and "help them to do so, if necessary" (OSHA, 2004, p. 16).

The field director can draw from existing resources in advocating for organizational practices and developing safety and risk management education. For example, Newhill (2003) provides a template for a syllabus on "Understanding and Managing Violence and Safety in Social Work Practice" that could be used to plan a semester-long course or to choose items to incorporate into modules (pp. 249–252). Some topics included are family and school violence, workplace violence, risk factors and assessment for violent behaviors, working with involuntary or resistant clients, and managing social work emotion and trauma. In 2004 OSHA published a report, *Guidelines for Preventing Workplace Violence for Health Care & Social Service Workers*. It gives advice to social workers and social services employers for establishing effective workplace violence prevention programs adapted to the practice setting. The Web site for the Massachusetts chapter of NASW has a well-developed resource outlining professional skills for safety and risk management, ideas for developing safety policy in agencies and schools of social work, and information for advocating for state and federal legislation on safety issues. NASW has updated *Guidelines for Social Worker Safety in the Workplace* (NASW,

2013). Of particular interest is the section on student safety in which NASW asserts that "schools of social work are responsible for ensuring that social work students are educated about concepts and techniques related to safety as well as supervised in safe environments" (p. 23). See figure 11.1 for suggested topics for safety training.

### Figure 11.1. Suggested Topics for Safety Training

**Risk Assessment and Potential for Violence**

High-risk practice settings (e.g., corrections, child protective services, mental health)
Characteristics/life experiences of people more likely to commit violent acts
Certain forms of mental illness associated with violent behavior
Physical signs that an attack is imminent
Self-awareness of feelings
What to look and listen for before entering a person's home
Encounters with illegal activities (e.g., drug dealing or prostitution)

**Safety Planning and Prevention**

Dressing appropriately
Maintaining a confident, secure demeanor
Where to sit when interacting with a client
Determining escape routes
Encountering people with weapons
Keeping supervisors informed of one's itinerary
Recognizing verbal acts of violence
What to bring or not bring to a home visit, such as money or a purse
When to request police escorts
Entering the room of an angry person
Ethical issues related to client violence
How to increase the client's sense of being in control
Protective equipment such as mace or cell phone
Car maintenance and safety
Entering a room when the person speaking cannot be seen
Legal issues related to client violence
What to do if one is a victim of violence (filing reports, dealing with physical and
    emotional aspects, etc.)
Places where weapons are likely to be kept
Training in nonviolent defense
Encountering biohazardous materials in health-care facilities or clients' homes

**Verbal de-escalation techniques**

How to behave with an angry client
Verbal de-escalation of client's rage

(Adapted from Faria & Kendra, 2007)

## Insurance Recommendations for Students in Practicum

Students are often confused about issues of liability and insurance. Some mistakenly believe that malpractice insurance will provide coverage should they be injured during practicum. Some students do not have personal health insurance and may not fully understand the impact of lack of coverage. Field directors should clarify what role insurance can and should have during the practicum experience. Malpractice liability insurance provides protection for the worker when professional negligence results in injury to the client. If the student is not covered by the agency or the university, the student can purchase malpractice liability coverage through NASW and other insurance carriers. A student's personal health insurance should provide reimbursement for the student if he or she is injured or suffers an illness, whether or not it is practicum related. Students are not employees and therefore are not covered by workers' compensation.

Perhaps the most controversial area of risk involving practicum students is that of transporting clients, particularly when the students are using their own vehicles. Transporting clients has risks. The client could distract the student from his driving; even a seemingly cooperative client can be unpredictable. What if the client is agitated and becomes violent, refuses to use the seat belt, and/or tries to open the door and jump out? What if the student is involved in a collision and someone is harmed? Who is liable? These situations are further complicated if the student is using a personal vehicle and personal insurance. As one student stated, "Everyone does it, so I am not comfortable making an issue of it." A review of field manuals online mentioned several approaches to this issue. Some universities prohibit the transport of clients by students, some allow it if the students provide evidence that their own automobile insurance carrier will provide coverage for this use, some allow it if the agency provides coverage, some allow students to drive agency-owned cars, and some make no reference to the topic. Students are at considerable risk if they use their own vehicles. Many students have basic coverage with minimal financial limits, increasing their exposure. If the insurance carrier considers driving clients to be a livery service, some states could deny a claim. Overall, it would be prudent for a student to have access to an agency vehicle that is covered under agency insurance.

## Incident Reporting and Trauma Management

Incident management is a zone where a collaborative relationship between agency and university is of critical importance. Field directors may become aware of situations in which a student is harmed in some manner but did not report the incident to the university (Lyter & Abbott, 1998). It is imprudent to place students in agencies that do not recognize the significance of incident prevention and incident response. The university–agency affiliation agreement and the field manual should include language that specifies the need for incident reporting and ongoing communication between agency and school.

Examples of incident report forms can be found through an online search and could be modified for individual schools. Typically, these instruments document violent incidents—threats or attacks—by clients toward students and are used to track data and revise policies. Both the agency and the university should follow any incident, paying attention both to the needs of the student—emotional needs, health, and welfare—and to policy review and potential revision.

These forms should include:

- Who (who was involved and should be notified, including the names of student, field instructor, and field liaison)

- When (specific date and time)

- Where (specific location)

- What and how (description by students and others of the incident)

- Actions and outcomes (e.g., injuries, hospitalization, damage to property, use of restraints, police action)

- Follow-up plan that includes debriefing and counseling as appropriate to address the impact on the student

- Follow-up plan for agency and school review and potential policy revisions

Trauma management is often an afterthought and may not be well-integrated into university or agency procedures. Comprehensive management begins with classroom education and extends through trauma care in the aftermath. Jayaratne, Croxton, and Mattison (2004) urge all BSW and MSW programs to understand the need to include measures to deal with the consequences of violence against social workers, including stress management. Dunkel et al. (2000) recommend early introduction of classroom units on risk reduction, both in order to inform and to address potential resistance to emotion-laden material. According to Criss (2010), "students need to understand student rights, including the right to refuse to proceed with a potentially dangerous encounter with a client" (p. 385).

Criss (2010) cautions that students need to take care in sharing scenarios of violence in field seminar, where some students may well be traumatized by the details of a story. Many field educators have experienced the challenge of finding the balance between communicating the dangers and taking care of students. Ultimately, it is the field director who is tasked to find the answers to such questions. What are the parameters for the determination of potential danger and for taking care in sharing scenarios of trauma in the classroom? The following two classroom risk reduction strategies address these questions.

The first strategy for risk reduction is under the umbrella of informed consent; proper framing of the prevalence of harm to workers in order to provide a context from which the learner can acknowledge the need to gain skills without unnecessary alarm. The student is informed of the risk potential but is provided with skills and knowledge. An informed-consent clause with a student could state, "Violence is . . . a low base-rate phenomenon, meaning that in the range of all possible human behaviors, violence is a comparatively rare event" (Newhill, 2003, p. 89). However, studies point to the likelihood that at some time in their career, most social workers will experience some client event that includes either a threat or act of violence, including verbal. Logic and data, of course, are superior to tactics that would instill unnecessary fear. Informing students of formal policies and strategies to reduce risk (Faria & Kendra, 2007; Ringstad, 2005) is likely to reassure and empower the learners.

The second strategy is supported by the theory of stress inoculation (SI), a method of exposing students to case scenarios of trauma over time. A cognitive-behavioral technique used in treating clients who have experienced trauma, SI is also valuable in preparing human services professionals for inevitable exposure to trauma in the field practicum and the workplace (Cunningham, 2004; Meichenbaum, 2003). Using SI and language associated with trauma helps to remove the taboo connotations of scenarios related to suicide, child maltreatment, partner violence, and incest, and to integrate self-care into the student's skill repertoire. Use of SI in a safe classroom environment encourages students to process the scenarios and normalize feelings, and to understand theory related to self-care and vicarious traumatization (Cunningham, 2004; Knight, 1999). The responsibility for risk reduction should not be that of the field office alone but ought to be a collaboration among all program components.

## Conclusion

The absence of attention to worker safety by the CSWE has served as an obstacle to educators who see the need to incorporate content on risk management and safety in the classroom. Without inclusion of the competencies and practice behaviors of the EPAS (CSWE, 2008), the classroom professor incorporates the content without articulated sanctions and supports. As such, the pedagogy has not yet benefitted fully from research that would shape curriculum. As more research is conducted, there will be more evidence about the effectiveness of classroom strategies.

Violence can affect social workers' emotional security, physical health, attitude toward their profession, and how they conduct themselves in their work (Newhill, 2003). The aftermath of an incident includes the potential for both trauma and skill development. If one is the target of violence, proper training and preparation serve to decrease negative outcomes. After an incident where a student is a victim of or witness to violence, it is essential that debriefing and support be provided not only by the agency, but also by field educators and faculty.

Failing to strive for risk reduction or to have an honest dialogue with students is both negligent and disrespectful. No student can be given a guarantee of absolute security. Exposure to risk is expected in social work, just as it is in other helping professions. Students are aware of harm and risk reduction strategies as those concepts apply to their clients, and can learn to use those same strategies for themselves. Students are capable and have the potential to manage complex decision making, given proper preparation and training. Every field director and university can strive to minimize risk and maximize safe practice through prevention, education, intervention, and follow-up. Once policies are deemed necessary and are fully instituted, programs can use empiricism to examine and refine best practices in social work safety and risk management.

## Essential Readings

Faria, G., & Kendra, M. (2007). Safety education: A study of undergraduate social work programs. *Journal of Baccalaureate Social Work, 12*(2), 141–153.

National Association of Social Workers (NASW). (2013). *Guidelines for social worker safety in the workplace.* Retrieved from http://www.socialworkers.org/practice/naswstandards/safetystandards2013.pdf.

Newhill, C. E. (2003). *Client violence in social work practice: Prevention, intervention and research.* New York: Guilford.

Occupational Safety and Health Administration (OSHA). (2004). U.S. Department of Labor. *Guidelines for preventing workplace violence for health care & social service workers,* OSHA 3148–01R 2004. Retrieved from http://www.osha.gov/Publications/osha3148.pdf.

## References

Choong Rai, N., & Soochan, C. (2009). Are social workers safe in their workplace?: South Korean managers' views. *Asia Pacific Journal of Social Work & Development, 19*(1), 39–49.

Council on Social Work Education (CSWE). (2008). *Educational policy and accreditation standards* (rev. March 27, 2010/updated August 2012). Alexandria, VA: Author. Retrieved from http://www.cswe.org/Accreditation/41865.aspx.

Criss, P. (2010). Effects of client violence on social work students: A national study. *Journal of Social Work Education, 46*(3), 371–390.

Cunningham, M. (2004). Teaching social workers about trauma: Reducing the risks of vicarious traumatization in the classroom. *Journal of Social Work Education, 40*(2), 305–317.

Dunkel, J., Ageson, A.-T., & Ralph, C. J. (2000). Encountering violence in field work: A risk reduction model. *Journal of Teaching in Social Work, 20*(3/4), 5–18.

Faria, G., & Kendra, M. (2007). Safety education: A study of undergraduate social work programs. *Journal of Baccalaureate Social Work, 12*(2), 141–153.

Green, R., Gregory, R., & Mason, R. (2003). It's no picnic: Personal and family safety for rural social workers. *Australian Social Work, 56*(2), 94–106. doi:10.1046/j.0312–407X.2003.00075.x.

Jayaratne, S., Croxton, T. A., & Mattison, D. (2004). A national survey of violence in the practice of social work. *Families in Society: Journal of Contemporary Social Services, 85*(4), 445–453.

Kelly, J. J. (2010, October). From the president: The urgency of social worker safety. *NASW News, 55*(9). Retrieved from www.naswdc.org/pubs/news/2010/10/social-worker-safety.asp.

Knight, C. (1999). The implications of BSW students' experiences with danger in the field practicum. *Journal of Baccalaureate Social Work, 4*, 133–149.

Kutztown University, Department of Social Work. (2012). *Field instructor manual.* Kurtztown, PA: Author.

Lynch, J. G., & Versen, G. R. (2003). Social work supervisor liability: Risk factors and strategies for risk reduction. *Administration in Social Work, 27*(2), 57–72.

Lyter, S. C. (2003). Safety survey of directors of field. Unpublished report.

Lyter, S. C., & Abbott, A. A. (1998). Safety survey of students enrolled in field practicum. Unpublished report.

Lyter, S. C., & Abbott, A. A. (2007). Home visits in a violent world. *Clinical Supervisor, 26*(1/2), 17–33.

Lyter, S. C., & Martin, M. (2000, February). Playing it safe: A survey addressing dangers in the field. Paper presented at Council on Social Work Education, Annual Program Meeting, New York.

Macdonald, G., & Sirotich, F. (2001). Reporting client violence. *Social Work, 46*, 102–114.

Macdonald, G., & Sirotich, F. (2005). Violence in the social work workplace: The Canadian experience. *International Social Work, 48*(6), 772–781. doi:10.1177/0020872805057087.

Meichenbaum, D. (2003). Stress inoculation training. In W. O'Donohue, J. E. Fisher, & S. C. Hays (Eds.), *Cognitive behavior therapy: Applying empirically supported techniques in your practice* (pp. 407–410). Hoboken, NJ: Wiley and Sons.

Miskelly, B. (2010). Social care staff need protection. *Community Care* (1845), 3.

National Association of Social Workers (NASW). (2008). *Code of ethics of the National Association of Social Workers.* Washington, DC: Author.

National Association of Social Workers (NASW). (2013). *Guidelines for social worker safety in the workplace.* Retrieved from http://www.socialworkers.org/practice/naswstandards/safetystandards2013.pdf.

Newhill, C. E. (2003). *Client violence in social work practice: Prevention, intervention and research.* New York: Guilford.

Occupational Safety and Health Administration (OSHA). (2004). U.S. Department of Labor. *Guidelines for preventing workplace violence for health care & social service workers,* OSHA 3148–01R 2004. Retrieved from http://www.osha.gov/Publications/osha3148.pdf.

O'Neill, J. V. (2002, May). Practitioner is slain by a client. *NASW News, 47*(5). Retrieved from http://www.socialworkers.org/pubs/news/2002/05/slain.asp.

O'Neill, J. V. (2004, April). Tragedies spark worker-safety awareness: Many think client violence "won't happen here." *NASW News, 49*(4). Retrieved from https://www.socialworkers.org/pubs/news/2004/04/tragedies2.asp?back=yes.

Pottick, K. (2012). Rutgers School of Social Work MSW field manual 2012–14 (rev. June 2012). Retrieved from http://socialwork.rutgers.edu/Current/Field.aspx.

Ringstad, R. (2005). Conflict in the workplace: Social workers as victims and perpetrators. *Social Work, 50*(4), 305–313.

Robb, M. (2003–2004). Supervisor beware: Reducing your exposure to vicarious liability. *Practice Pointers,* a service of The NASW Insurance Trust, Washington, DC. Retrieved from http://www.naswassurance.org/pdf/PP_Vicarious_Liability.pdf.

Shields, G., & Kiser, J. (2003). Violence and aggression directed toward human services workers: An exploratory study. *Families in Society, 84*(1), 13–20.

Spencer, P. C., & Munch, S. (2003). Client violence toward social workers: The role of management in community mental health programs. *Social Work, 48*(4), 532–544.

Strom-Gottfried, K. (2000). Ethical vulnerability in social work education: An analysis of NASW complaints. *Journal of Social Work Education, 36*(2), 241–252.

Whitaker, T., Weismiller, T., & Clark, E. (2006). *Assuring the sufficiency of a front-line workforce: A national study of licensed social workers. Executive summary.* Washington, DC: National Association of Social Workers.

# PART IV
# Sustaining Field Directors and Field Programs

The final part of this book emphasizes leadership: preparing for participation in regional and national field education committees, creating a vision for the use of technology to facilitate the myriad of field processes, and, more immediately, influencing the culture of schools of social work. Chapter 12, Professional Development, by Martha L. Ellison, Sandra Posada, and Lisa Richardson, offers recommendations for thriving and succeeding in an environment where the academic and administrative nature of the field director's position is unique. Mentorship, research, continuing education, and practicing self-care are ways to sustain field directors. The authors provide guidance on how to balance field responsibilities, scholarship, and promotion and tenure. Readers will be oriented to field education professional networks including the Council on Social Work Education, the Baccalaureate Program Directors, the North American Network of Field Educators and Directors, and regional consortia.

Field directors are in charge of managing and interpreting vast amounts of data. The questions on the use of technology are no longer if, but how and what and when. Chapter 13, Advancing Field Education through Technology, delves into the multifaceted ways that field directors use technology to organize and archive information, place students, facilitate communication, conduct evaluations, and train field instructors. Author Sheila R. Dennis reviews popular and specialized software and connects them to their applicability to an array of field functions. She writes to a wide audience and considers the range of technology literacy among field educators. The swift pace of change in technology makes any discussion on the topic a moving target. Nonetheless, Dennis captures the essential functions of the field office and introduces possibilities for improvement using existing tools. The use of technology in administration and education brings with it foreseen and unforeseen ethical challenges, such as confidentiality and user competency.

The book concludes with an analysis of leadership attributes and management skills intended to bolster the capacity of field directors to influence organizational change. In chapter 14, Leadership and Management, Michael J. Holosko and Jeffrey Skinner familiarize the readers with their five core leadership attributes: having and implementing a vision, influencing others to act, collaborating, problem-solving, and creating positive change. They provide examples of how these attributes relate to various field director roles. Highlighting the elevated role of field education in the current educational standards, the authors stress the importance of field directors moving beyond management to assume leadership.

The chapters on professional development, technology, and leadership and management conclude the book, but all need to be incorporated into the professional life of a field director from the first day on the job. The journey through these chapters brings the reader to a juncture in the path of directing a field program. For a field director to remain active, creative, and productive in the field position, the pathway to sustainability draws on networking, and attainment of skills not yet perfected, such as management and technology. A field program that incorporates up-to-date technology, supported by resources from administrators, may lead to a more cost-effective program. The path without a mentor or lack of opportunities for self-care, or the unavailability of resources to engage in scholarship and conference attendance paves the way for a short-term career as a field director. Attention by administrators to the field directors' time, position status, salary, and committee assignments can contribute to the field director staying on that path for the long term. It is in the best interest of deans and directors to find ways to retain productive and effective field directors.

# 12

# Professional Development

*Martha L. Ellison, Sandra Posada, and*
*Lisa Richardson*

The field director is a skilled practitioner across the spectrum of social work practice. Policy, advocacy, direct practice, leadership, technology, ethics, and administrative skills are all embodied in the field director's role. Professional development is addressed in the core competencies as a component of professional social work identity. Social workers "commit themselves to the profession's enhancement and to their own professional conduct and growth" and "engage in career-long learning" (Council on Social Work Education [CSWE], 2008, Educational Policy [EP] 2.1.1., p. 3). The social work profession's *Code of Ethics* identifies competence as one of six core values and outlines steps to remain competent, current, and proficient in practice (National Association of Social Workers [NASW], 2008).

This chapter focuses on professional development for new and established field directors. The authors outline strategies for developing and carrying out a professional development plan, beginning with the articulation of job responsibilities and evaluation criteria and the establishment of professional goals. They consider the challenges of multiple roles and functions and the impact of career-stage. Finally, they discuss the need to balance performance with self-care for long-term effectiveness. It is possible to carry out the complex responsibilities of a field director, create a professional development plan, and perform self-care activities.

### Know Thyself—Defining the Field Director Position, Role, and Expectations

The position of field director is by nature a hybrid role, bridging responsibilities for both administration and pedagogy (Buck, Bradley, Robb, & Kirzner, 2012; Hawthorne & Holtzman, 1991). The essential question of whether the position is administrative or educational is mirrored by the range and variety of position designations. Job classifications, contract lengths, promotion possibilities, and retention criteria vary widely from institution to institution (Dalton, Stevens, &

Maas-Brady, 2011; Ellison, Fogel, Moore, & Johnson, 2008; Hawthorne & Holtzman, 1991; Lyter, 2012.) Field directors may hold tenure-track appointments or nontenured faculty contracts, or may serve in nonfaculty, administrative positions.

With the variety of position types, an essential first step in professional development is to define the field director's position, role, and expectations. Faculty and administrators may not always understand the skill set that must be present for a field director to adequately perform the job (Hawthorne & Holtzman, 1991; Lyter, 2012). As a starting point, field directors should consult an existing position description or create a description for the role of field director. Field directors should clearly articulate evaluation expectations, and they should understand those expectations. Some field directors may have expectations for the traditional triumvirate of teaching, scholarship, and service. Others may be designated as non-tenure, ranked; or clinical faculty, where evaluation and retention criteria may mirror that of tenured faculty without a publication requirement. Field directors in nonfaculty staff positions may receive annual performance reviews based on their job descriptions. The position type and contract designation will determine the frequency of reviews, criteria, and supporting materials required. Field directors should consult with deans and promotion and tenure committees to clarify the expectations related to the position, and how administrative duties relate to tenure, promotion, and retention requirements.

## Professional Development Agenda and Activities

With a clear sense of the position and evaluation expectations, the field director can establish goals, create an agenda for professional development, and embark on a series of professional development activities. As noted in the NASW Practice and Professional Development statement, "Professional development is a self-directed process, which requires social workers to assume responsibility for the growth of their own professional knowledge base. Regardless of career stage, social workers are ethically required to keep informed of current research, theory, and techniques that guide social work practice to better serve clients and constituents" (NASW, 2013, para. 1).

### Networking

The professional development of the field director is significantly enhanced through networking. National organizations and regional consortia provide valuable support for field directors, offering resources for best practices, innovation, and problem-solving; they also offer opportunities for field directors to influence policy and practice, accreditation standards, and the future of field education. By creating "a 'community of practice' in social work field education" (Drolet, 2012, p. 2), field directors can both give and receive relevant knowledge, technical expertise, and support.

A first step in professional development is for the field director to become a member of one or two social work education organizations: the CSWE, the accrediting body for both graduate and undergraduate social work programs; and the Baccalaureate Program Directors (BPD), the membership association representing the interests of undergraduate education and practice in social work. Through membership in the CSWE and/or the BPD, field directors will have access to a variety of resources and opportunities that will support their ethical responsibilities to engage in professional growth.

Within the CSWE and the BPD field directors can become involved in professional activities through commissions, councils, and committees. In the CSWE, the Council on Field Education is under the auspices of the Commission on Educational Policy. During 2011–2012 there were twenty members representing the ten CSWE regions (Posada & McFall, 2012). The Council on Field Education has established a field director Listserv, the Field Directors Development Institute at the Annual Program Meeting, and a transparent nomination process.

The BPD Field Education Committee is a standing committee that was established in 2002 (J. Bradley, personal communication, July 24, 2011). The committee delivers a BPD preconference training for new field directors that provides an overview of field program management. In addition, the committee meets quarterly to discuss field education issues, support research initiatives, and plan conference trainings.

The North American Network of Field Education Directors (NANFED) is a third membership organization, which has led the effort to coordinate regional field consortia. Some twenty-one field consortia exist throughout the United States and represent approximately 262 bachelor of social work (BSW) or master of social work (MSW) programs. Field consortia are organized by state or region, and differ in organizational structure and operations. Some consortia provide continuing education opportunities for faculty, students, and field instructors, while others provide opportunities for field directors to share information and collaborate on regional field concerns.

Field directors can further network through the BPD Listserv and the CSWE field director's Listserv. These vehicles provide an avenue for social work educators and field directors to post questions and seek information from colleagues.

### Conferences and Continuing Education

Both the CSWE and the BPD hold annual conferences, providing several days of presentations on social work education that include training for field directors, roundtable discussions, general plenary sessions, board-sponsored sessions, and poster presentations. Field directors should advocate for professional development funds with their universities to attend the CSWE Annual Program Meeting and the BPD conference on a regular basis in order to stay abreast of field education and accreditation standards.

A professional development plan should include membership in the NASW and participation in its regional and national continuing education events, including Webinars and podcasts from the NASW Professional Education and Training Center. Field directors can engage in continuing education in an area of specialization related to the mission of the respective BSW or MSW program, advanced credentials, or specialized licenses. Additionally, the administrative demands on the field directors may lead them to seek continuing education in supervision or an advanced degree in education, social work, business, law, or leadership. The authors encourage field directors to apply for scholarships in the Summer Leadership Program for Higher Education Resource Service and/or Harvard Institute of Higher Education. The CSWE also has a Commission on Professional Development and the CSWE Leadership Institute.

## Teaching, Scholarship, Service, and Administration

For many field directors the professional development agenda will be dominated by the evaluation framework of teaching, scholarship, and service. As noted in Accreditation Standard [AS] 3.3.5 (CSWE, 2008, p. 13), "Faculty demonstrate ongoing professional development as teachers, scholars and practitioners through dissemination of research and scholarship, exchanges with external constituencies such as practitioners and agencies, and through other professionally relevant creative activities that support the achievement of institutional priorities and the program's mission and goals." The relative importance of teaching, scholarship, and service varies between institutions (Green, 2008). Field directors also perform administrative duties in fulfillment of the responsibility for overall management of the field education program. The following section suggests possibilities for locating field director activities under the four headings, while enhancing the field education program.

### Teaching

Many field directors will teach either the integrative field seminar or other courses of the curriculum. Field directors who teach courses avail themselves of faculty development opportunities, including training on teaching methods, syllabus and curriculum development, and emerging areas of content delivery (e.g., online learning). They utilize the institution's standard process for evaluation of teaching, including student course evaluations. They also might consider additional forms of evaluation, such as peer observation or mid-semester feedback from students. Field directors who serve as liaisons can document the teaching of both the student and the field instructor during agency visits. These strategies will help to build evidence of a commitment to professional growth and teaching effectiveness.

Many other aspects of the field director's duties can be included in the "teaching" category, including oversight of the field education curriculum, development and revision of course policies and objectives, assessment of student learning, and development of course bibliographies. Field directors influence student learning and professional development through each step of the field placement process and the practicum experience. The gatekeeping function, for example, provides oversight for student retention in areas related to professional behavior and learning in the field. Other teaching functions include academic advising, linking students to fellowships and grants, and educating faculty who serve as field liaisons.

A significant area of teaching comes through the training of agency-based field instructors. This effort to foster the capacity of field instructors to teach and evaluate is a unique and significant aspect of the field director's role. Field directors use the available research on field instructor training and curricula, as well as best practices in adult learning, to give evidence to the breadth and depth of their teaching portfolios.

Documentation of teaching should reflect these responsibilities, including work with field instructors, field liaisons, and students relative to the orientation and training provided. To accomplish this documentation, field directors should develop a template of a syllabus for orientations and trainings. Field directors should also document the curriculum for preplacement workshops, field placement fairs, and safety training that are provided to students. They can use an evaluation instrument, distributed after each presentation or training session, to evaluate effectiveness in teaching. The field education manual, outlining the objectives and framework of field education under the stewardship of the field director, serves as documentation as well.

### Scholarship

Green (2008) noted that deans and directors believed that scholarship was salient in the academy (p. 125). Field directors should set their professional development agenda with a thorough understanding of the expectations for job performance and evaluation, including clear expectations for both the amount and type of scholarship.

The field director's pivotal position in the academy, between the program and the professional community (Hawthorne & Holtzman, 1991, p. 320), creates unique opportunities for research. Lyter (2012) stated that field directors, deans, and program directors agreed on "the need for field directors and field education to be involved in some way with pursuing research" (p. 183). Lyter also noted that "a role in research initiatives has the potential to advance knowledge and status of the field director and advance the state of the art of field education in line with the concept of signature pedagogy" (Lyter, 2012, p. 182).

An advantage of being involved in field education is that there are many areas that still require exploration. Areas for research include assessment of student learning, student professional behavior and development, field education pedagogy (including the use of seminars and distance learning), supervision and field instruction, assessment of practice, and the structure and scope of the field director's role. Drolet (2012) stated that the impact of research and evaluation "plays an important role in improving learning practices and outcomes for students, in supporting student learners, and in enhancing quality placements" (p. 3). Scholarship in field education will not only advance the field director's professional development, but also will contribute to the field program's quality.

In many schools the role of field director is a lone position. Partnering with colleagues in one's own department or initiating interdisciplinary collaborations can enhance the research agenda. The professional networks (CSWE, BPD, NASW,

NANFED, regional consortia, Listserv, or a mentor), are additional resources to identify research areas and collaborate on scholarship across geographic regions. Research in conjunction with local agencies based on service needs empowers practitioners in the research process and enhances services in the community. The field director is in a unique position to assess service gaps and participate in "community-based action research" (Drolet, 2012, p. 3). Serving as a committee member and adviser to student research exemplifies the field director's role as a scholar.

In many institutions the pursuit of grants is recognized as scholarship. The federal Title IV-E grant, to improve services in child welfare, can bring resources and benefits to the program, students, and community. Grants may offer opportunities to strengthen or create new partnerships with area agencies. They may result from emerging social and political factors, such as changing demographics, health-care reform, and changes in the delivery of health care, such as an emphasis on integrated care and prevention. When the field director obtains grants, the result is enhanced visibility and demonstrated research skill; at the same time, grants also enhance the program's responsiveness to community needs and emerging areas of practice.

Field directors should consider ways to both conduct and disseminate scholarship. Dissemination can emanate from peer-reviewed articles, publications, poster sessions, paper presentations, social work practice, consultation, and workshops. The recent launch of the open source *Field Educator Journal*, from Simmons College has raised the profile of field education research, offering an accessible source of research to inform practice, and to provide opportunities for publication. Field directors may be able to access faculty writing groups to help develop, shape, and support their efforts to publish (Rooney, Rodenborg, Marrs Fuchsel, Fisher, & Vang, 2012). Finally, field directors can enhance their own skills by reviewing abstracts for professional conferences.

### Service

The field director's service agenda should include activities that benefit the institution, the social work profession, and the community. Institutional service on interdisciplinary committees, strategically chosen, puts the field director in contact with colleagues that share similar interests such as admissions, ethics, globalization, service learning, and student practicums. The contacts that field directors have with community agencies offer opportunities to serve on committees, and to conduct training and workshops. Community service also keeps field directors informed about the context of practice in which they are preparing students. From this vantage point, field directors can create opportunities for deeper and more-creative involvement of field students in helping to identify community strengths and address community problems.

Effort toward professional development is frequently self-initiated and requires keen advocacy skills; it also offers opportunities for visibility and leadership. Serving on committees with BPD, CSWE, or NANFED, or becoming a CSWE site visitor for reaffirmation of accreditation gives national visibility to the institution and field director. Election as a coordinator of a field consortium or assuming a position with NASW demonstrates leadership skills.

### Administration

In some schools administration may be recognized as a fourth area of the evaluation process. In schools where this is not the case, field directors may translate some of these responsibilities into the teaching/scholarship/service framework.

Administrative activities that serve the success of the social work program include agency recruitment (development of relationships with community partners, negotiating contracts, managing placement data), organizing the policies and procedures for the field placement process, and managing events (e.g., field instructor appreciation events). Some leadership activities are supervising and evaluating administrative staff; leading the field faculty team, including liaison evaluations; representing field education to new and prospective students and university administrators; and coordinating the field advisory council. Field directors have a critical role in the stewardship of the "signature pedagogy" (CSWE, 2008, EP 2.3, p. 8) and in the accreditation and reaffirmation process. Their role in planning and implementing change in the field program, in accordance with new research and emerging areas of practice, helps to ensure that social work programs "respond to contexts that shape practice" (CSWE, 2008, EP 2.1.9, p. 6).

### Professional Development and Career Stages of Tenure and Promotion

The career trajectory for all tenure-track faculty can be divided into at least three career stages: early, middle, and late. The professional development needs of faculty differ according to their career stage, as does their focus and activities. Knowledge of these differences will be helpful for field directors planning an academic developmental path. Feature 12.1 presents a personal reflection by a veteran field director on balancing the pressures of obtaining tenure, administering a large field program, and having a personal life.

**Feature 12.1. What I Should Have Known about Professional Development When I Became a Field Director**

I joined the faculty on the very same day students arrived for orientation. There I stood with some sense of competence since I had substantial experience as a social worker, both as a practitioner and an administrator. I also had some sense of trepidation as the students were told I was the new field director, and they immediately began to swarm around me, needing answers to their questions about their placements. I thought I knew what would be expected of me as a tenure track faculty. Would I be able to balance the administrative role of director of field and earn my tenure in the specified time frame?

The first few weeks were actually frightening, as students were quite demanding; I found myself working a minimum of ten hours a day. How was I going to publish, attend meetings, and discuss components of the curriculum as if I were an expert? I needed more time to digest the understanding of what CSWE standards required of field. My experiences as a student and as a field instructor were very different from what I was experiencing. I was advised to maintain my research day, but there were mandatory or important meetings held on that day. Time was in short supply. In addition, I had a young child at home and an elderly mother who had recently come to live with me. Selecting Friday as my research day, I believed, would give me time to work on projects over the weekend if the need arose.

Having time for teaching, directing field, and scholarship can be overwhelming. My advice: use your time effectively! Do not feel like a failure if you face these demands. A major part of developing a stress-free work environment is controlling your time to complete a project. Having too much on your plate is a stress creator and, based on the competing priorities, can leave you overwhelmed and unproductive. For a tenure-track person, this is not good.

What could I have done to make the transition to academia smoother and to fully understand my role as director of field education? First, meet with other academicians and field directors to get a realistic idea of what to expect. Second, find a mentor! Written materials guided me on how to do field but advice from others can provide practical help on handling the crises that cropped up in field education, such as placement disruptions and student emergencies. A mentor might also have advice on working with faculty liaisons that had a different philosophy about field procedures and policies than I had.

There are prescriptive tasks that tenure-track faculty must complete to achieve tenure. Universities and schools have processes and expectations that these faculty members need to achieve. Be sure that you understand how to achieve these expectations, such as excellence in teaching, research (identify an area of expertise), publications, conference presentations, and grants. Attending conferences and other opportunities are essential in your development as a scholar and field director. Finally, learn self-care: without it nothing else really matters.

Ruby M. Gourdine, DSW
Professor
School of Social Work
Howard University

## Tenure/Promotion: The Early-Career Field Director

A significant focus of the early-career faculty is related to learning the ropes of the institution and gaining the "knowledge and skills pertaining to teaching, research, professional attitudes and habits, interpersonal skills, and professional knowledge about higher education" (Gillespie & Robertson, 2010, p. 366), along with meeting tenure and/or promotion criteria. With regard to promotion and tenure, most institutions place more emphasis on the quality of instruction and scholarship than they do on service (Buller, 2010, p. 58). Buller suggests to "choose one truly significant area of service each year until you are granted tenure, and use the remaining time to enhance the quality of your teaching and to complete additional works of scholarship" (p. 58). Identifying and developing a research agenda is an important component of a professional development plan in career advancement, regardless whether the institution has a research or teaching emphasis. For recent graduates from doctoral programs, the dissertation can help focus a research and publication agenda.

### Post Tenure: The Mid-Career and Late-Career Field Director

The mid-career stage is a time when the probationary period has ended and faculty assume more leadership, administrative, and service duties, and learn to effectively deal with the time pressures that come from taking on these additional duties. Other tasks for mid-career faculty are "staying interested, staying alive, and staying engaged. . . . It's difficult to do after 20 years" (Baldwin, DeZure, Shaw, & Moretto, 2008, p. 52).

Faculty members who have achieved tenure can reorder their priorities by "moving from a framework in which teaching and research are their first priorities to a framework in which research and service are their first priorities" (Buller, 2010, p. 67). Mid-career faculty can take on more responsibilities to serve on committees, and can be more discerning about which committees to serve on, and which research to pursue. Seeking a nomination to serve the BPD Field Committee or the CSWE Field Council may be appropriate at this time. This may also be a time to experiment with different field models or ways of delivering field education.

The late-career stage is defined as the period when faculty are ten to twelve years away from retirement. The tasks for faculty in this stage are similar to those at the mid-career stage with the inclusion of retirement planning (Gillespie & Robertson, 2010). Mid-career/late-career faculty can give back to social work education and practice by assuming leadership roles in professional organizations. Leadership opportunities can be found through the CSWE Commission on Professional Developments or that commission's Leadership Development Institute. Mid-career and/or late-career faculty members may consider becoming a Fulbright scholar, which can provide an opportunity to examine field education internationally. The CSWE Katherine A. Kendall Institute for International Social Work Education strives to prepare educators through its programs and initiatives. The CSWE Center for Diversity and Social & Economic Justice and the Gero-Ed Center provide opportunities to influence social work education and practice. Mid-career/late-career faculty have much to offer to field education and are positioned to put their years of experience to good use, while continuing to learn and grow.

## Mentoring

The importance of identifying and developing a mentoring relationship throughout one's career cannot be overstressed for professional development. Mentoring is beneficial to mentor, mentee, and the institution, a win-win-win situation (Johnson, 2007). During each stage of career development, field directors can seek a mentor to further a professional development plan.

Many field directors assume the position with little to no experience in academia (Dalton et al., 2011; Hunter & Ford, 2010). According to a national study of the mentoring of field directors, 70 percent of nonmentored field directors learn their jobs through trial and error; mentoring can be a means to learn the field director's job without relying solely on trial and error (Ellison & Raskin, 2010). Furthermore, mentoring can provide field directors with much needed support as they strive to perform their jobs.

The overall benefits of mentoring are increased faculty productivity and satisfaction; improved performance in teaching, research, and publication; and socialization in the academy (Frongia, 1995; Johnson, 2007; Wilson, Valentine, & Pereira, 2002). As Mullen and Kennedy (2007) indicate, "mentoring and collegiality can go a long way to support tenure-earning faculty in understanding their complex environments and in adjusting and experiencing success more quickly" (para. 2). Furthermore, many mentees relate that mentoring helps them achieve their professional goals and provides them with emotional support and encouragement (Ellison et al., 2008; Ellison & Raskin, 2010; Wilson et al., 2002). Sixty-seven percent of informally mentored field directors reported achieving their professional goals as a result of having a mentor. These field directors also reported high satisfaction with their mentoring (Ellison & Raskin, 2010).

Even though satisfaction was high, mentored field directors indicated that they did not receive services of joint publications, presentations, and research with their mentor. It will be incumbent on the mentee to make her or his needs known to the mentor and to be prepared to develop multiple mentoring relationships. While there can be some disadvantages in mentoring relationships, problems are somewhat rare and mentoring has been found to be beneficial to the mentee (Johnson, 2007).

The field director's role as a leader in social work education creates opportunities to provide mentoring, as well as to receive it. They carry responsibility for the success of students, field instructors, and field liaisons, and can offer critical support to constituents in each of these groups. Since fewer than a third of field directors provide mentoring, this is an unmet need (Ellison & Raskin, 2010). Mid-career and late-career field directors can become mentors to others who are just starting their academic careers. Field directors can model active engagement in scholarship and be a resource on best practices and emerging trends.

## Self-Care

In order to sustain role effectiveness, an important component of a field director's professional development agenda is self-care. It is almost universally known that social workers enter the profession to help or care for others. Social workers are experts at "other-care" (Skovholt & Trotter-Mathison, 2011, p. 249.) Field directors have mastered other-care in daily responsibilities and tasks, care that is purposeful, efficient, and effective. The challenge is for workers to apply this expertise and skill in other-care to self-care.

NASW's attention to self-care has been ongoing and consistent. The NASW policy statement on Professional Self-Care and Social Work defines professional self-care as "a core essential component to social work practice [reflecting] a choice and commitment to become actively involved in maintaining one's effectiveness" (NASW, 2012, p. 268). A lack of self-care may lead to compassion fatigue, stress, and burnout (Blosser, Cadet, & Downs, 2010; Lloyd, King, & Chenoweth, 2002; Schwartz, Tiamiyu, & Dwyer, 2007). The NASW Membership Workforce Study examined workplace stress and found that participants identified lack of time (31%) and heavy workloads (25%) as the major contributors to workplace stress (Whitaker & Arrington, 2008, p. 2). Field directors must work with many constituencies: students, faculty, program directors, field instructors, field advisory boards, CSWE, BPD, regional field consortia, the university, office of disabilities, legal counsel, and the community. The collective experiences of field directors may be similar to that of practitioners. "We learned that it was not the clients themselves who are causing the major portion of the stress, but the work environment itself" (Dale, 2008, p. 1).

A self-care plan is as critical as a professional development plan (Berg-Weger & Birkenmaier, 2011). Skovholt's Practitioner Professional Resiliency and Self-Care Inventory is one instrument that can guide the development of a plan (Skovholt & Trotter-Mathison, 2011). Another tool is the Self-Care Assessment Worksheet, developed by Saakvitne and Perlman, that measures one's degree of self-care activities and strategies (Alkema, Linton, & Davies, 2008).

For the sake of one's physical and mental health, field directors must take care of themselves in order to take care of others. A plan is proactive that contributes to job satisfaction and success, and it can be a means to diminish stress and prevent burnout (Cox & Steiner, 2013; Lloyd et al., 2002). Feature 12.2 addresses the everyday process of cognitive reframing.

---

**Feature 12.2. Self-Care for a Field Director**

Self-care is now widely recognized as an important remedy for the stress encountered in social work. Until recently, however, self-care has been only superficially understood. In *Self-Care in Social Work: A Guide for Practitioners, Supervisors and Administrators* (Cox & Steiner, 2013), the authors argue that true self-care goes beyond adding a healthy activity to an already packed schedule. It involves reflecting on our thinking in relation to self, colleagues, clients/consumers, and the work setting. Professionals are sometimes burdened by pessimistic or irrational thinking that saps energy and contributes to feelings of being overwhelmed. Making a cognitive shift can lighten the load and be emotionally uplifting. Below are common beliefs that result in stress and overload for field directors.

*I must ensure that my students have a successful placement.* It can be tempting for field directors to believe that they have the ultimate responsibility for ensuring student success in the field. Consequently, it is disappointing when a placement fails. In many cases, a failed placement yields valuable benefits. It provides constructive feedback to students about their behavior on the job. It helps students recognize an area of practice that is not a good fit for them, and helps agencies learn what to look for in future practicum students. Directors carry out an important gatekeeping function when they identify students who should not continue in the field or should not continue without more time and experience.

*I must ensure that my students receive quality supervision in their field setting.* The quality of supervision by agency field instructors will vary no matter what the field director does to support best practices with regard to agency-based supervision. When students' needs are not met through supervision, a valuable opportunity is provided for them to voice their needs to their field instructor. This experience may also drive home the reality that one person cannot meet all the needs for training, vicarious learning, and emotional support. Students can learn the value of finding mentors and collegial support in the workplace.

*My colleagues (faculty) should work as hard as I do to identify and counsel students who are struggling.* When students are in crisis or struggling with life challenges and emotional stress, it can manifest most quickly in their practicum. Field directors may be the first to know, as field instructors or faculty liaisons may call it to their attention. The director may wonder why faculty members are not paying attention to and addressing idiosyncrasies in student behavior. Often, however, students are able to sustain academic efforts even when in the midst of emotional crisis. These issues may not rise to the surface in an academically oriented course. Field directors might seek help from student advisers or program directors when students are in crisis versus taking it all on themselves. Cognitive shifts can also be helpful in coping with other challenges unique to the role, such as when field directors are faced with diminishing placements, poor attendance at field orientations, or an inadequate number of faculty liaisons. At times these challenges may seem like insurmountable barriers. To counteract this focus on limitations, field directors might appreciate every small step taken toward improving field education at their school.

Kathy Cox, PhD, LCSW
Associate Professor
School of Social Work
California State University, Chico

## Conclusion

The complexity and centrality of the field director's role heighten the importance of professional development for field directors. The field director's long-established "pivotal position" between social work education and the practice community (Hawthorne & Holtzman, 1991, p. 320), combined with the recent designation of field education as the signature pedagogy of social work education (CSWE, 2008,

EP 2.3), amplify the importance of the field director. Through careful attention and articulation of job duties (spanning education and administration) and clarity of evaluation expectations, field directors can initiate a professional development plan. They build on existing strengths and then move on to identify areas for growth. The agenda should reflect the priorities of their particular institutional context and outline activities that both build and demonstrate skill. The use of relationships, including professional networks and mentoring, is a central resource for the professional development process. As part of a comprehensive professional development agenda, field directors should identify avenues for self-care leading to long-term role success.

## Essential Resources

BPD-L Listserv. http://www.bpdonline.org/BPD_Prod/BPDWCMWEB/ Resources/List_Serv.aspx.

CSWE Council on Field Education (COFE). http://www.cswe.org/About/ governance/CommissionsCouncils/15533/15538.aspx.

CSWE field directors Listserv. http://www.cswe.org/cms/15538.aspx.

North American Network of Field Educators and Directors (NANFED). http://nanfed.com/.

The Field Educator. Simmons School of Social Work. Boston. http://fieldeducator .simmons.edu/about/. Open Access (Free) Journal. http://fieldeducator.sim-mons.edu/about/.

## Essential Readings

Buck, P. W., Bradley, J., Robb, L., & Kirzner, R. S. (2012). Complex and competing demands in field education: A qualitative study of field directors' experiences. *Field Scholar*, 2(2). Retrieved from http://fieldeducator.simmons.edu/article/ complex-and-competing-demands-in-field-education/#more-1094.

Cox, K., & Steiner, S. (2013). *Self-care in social work: A guide for practitioners, supervisors, administrators.* Washington, DC: NASW Press.

Lyter, S. (2012). Potential of field education as signature pedagogy: The field director role. *Journal of Social Work Education*, 48(1), 179–188.

# References

Alkema, K., Linton, J. M., & Davies, R. (2008). A study of the relationship between self-care, compassion satisfaction, compassion fatigue, and burnout among hospice professionals. *Journal of Social Work in End-of-Life & Palliative Care, 4*(2), 101–119.

Baldwin, R. G., DeZure, D., Shaw, A., & Moretto., K. (2008). Mapping the terrain of mid-career faculty at a research university: Implications for faculty and academic leaders. *Change, 40*(5), 46–55.

Berg-Weger, M., & Birkenmaier, J. (2011). *The practicum companion for social work: Integrating class and field work* (3rd ed.). Boston: Allyn and Bacon.

Blosser, J., Cadet, D., & Downs, L. (2010). Factors that influence retention and professional development of social workers. *Administration in Social Work, 34*(2), 168–177.

Buck, P. W., Bradley, J., Robb, L., & Kirzner, R. S. (2012). Complex and competing demands in field education: A qualitative study of field directors' experiences. *Field Scholar, 2*(2). Retrieved from http://fieldeducator.simmons.edu/article/complex-and-competing-demands-in-field-education/#more-1094.

Buller, J. L. (2010). *The essential college professor A practical guide to an academic career.* San Francisco: Jossey-Bass.

Council on Social Work Education (CSWE). (2008). *Educational policy and accreditation standards* (rev. March 27, 2010/updated August 2012). Alexandria, VA: Author. Retrieved from http://www.cswe.org/Accreditation/41865.aspx.

Cox, K., & Steiner, S. (2013). *Self-care in social work: A guide for practitioners, supervisors, administrators.* Washington, DC: NASW Press.

Dale, M. (2008). The profession must prioritize self-care. *NASW News 53*(10). Retrieved from https://www.socialworkers.org/pubs/news/2008/11/default.asp.

Dalton, B., Stevens, L., & Maas-Brady, J. (2011). "How do you do it?" MSW field director survey. *Advances in Social Work, 12*(2), 276–288.

Drolet, J. (2012). Statement of teaching philosophy: My role as field education coordinator. *Social Work Education: The International Journal, 31*, 1–4.

Ellison, M. L., Fogel, S., Moore, W., & Johnson, A. (2008, October). *What's the status of faculty mentoring in BSW programs?: An exploratory study.* Paper presentation at Baccalaureate Program Directors Annual Conference, Destin, FL.

Ellison, M. L., & Raskin, M. (2010, March). Mentoring of field directors: A national study. Paper presentation at the Baccalaureate Program Directors Annual Conference, Atlanta, GA.

Frongia, T. (1995). Active mentorship in scholarly publishing: Why, what, who, how. In J. M. Moxley & L. T. Lenker (Eds.), *The politics and processes of scholarship* (pp. 217–230). Westport, CT: Greenwood Press.

Gillespie, K. J., & Robertson, D. L. (Eds.). (2010). *A guide to faculty development* (2nd ed.). San Francisco: Jossey-Bass.

Green, R. G. (2008). Tenure and promotion decisions: The relative importance of teaching, scholarship and service. *Journal of Social Work Education, 44*(2), 117–127.

Hawthorne, L., & Holtzman, R. F. (1991). Directors of field education: Critical role dilemmas. In D. Schneck, B. Grossman, & U. Glassman (Eds.), *Field education in social work: Contemporary issues and trends* (pp. 320–328). Dubuque, IA: Kendall/Hunt.

Hunter, C. A., & Ford, K. A. (2010). Discomfort with a false dichotomy: Field directors' dilemma with micro-macro placements. *Journal of Baccalaureate Social Work, 15*(1), 15–29.

Johnson, W. B. (2007). *On being a mentor: A guide for higher education faculty.* New York: Lawrence Erbaum Associates.

Lloyd, C., King, R., & Chenoweth, L. (2002). Social work, stress and burnout: A review. *Journal of Mental Health, 11*(3), 225–265.

Lyter, S. (2012). Potential of field education as signature pedagogy: The field director role. *Journal of Social Work Education, 48*(1), 179–188.

Mullen, C., & Kennedy, C. (2007, May 23). *It takes a village to raise new faculty: Implementing triangular mentoring relationships.* Connexions, Houston, TX. Retrieved from http://cnx.org/content/m14546/1.2/.

National Association of Social Workers (NASW). (2008). *Code of ethics of the National Association of Social Workers.* Washington, DC: NASW Press.

National Association of Social Workers (NASW). (2012). *Social work speaks: National association of social workers policy statements 2012–2014* (9th ed.). Professional self-care and social work. Washington, DC: NASW Press.

National Association of Social Workers (NASW). (2013). *Practice & professional development.* Retrieved from http://www.socialworkers.org/pdev/default.asp.

Posada, S., & McFall, J. (2012). *2010–2011 Annual update council on field education.* 2012 annual report for the Council on Social Work Education. Alexandria, VA: Author. Retrieved from http://www.cswe.org/File.aspx?id=65081.

Rooney, R., Rodenborg, N., Marrs Fuchsel, C., Fisher, C., & Vang, P. (2012, November). *Social work faculty writing groups: How to encourage and support productivity.* Panel presentation at the Council on Social Work Education Annual Program Meeting, Washington, DC.

Schwartz, R. H., Tiamiyu, M. F., & Dwyer, D. J. (2007). Social workers hope and perceived burnout: the effects of age, years in practice, and setting. *Administration in Social Work, 31*(4), 159–180.

Skovholt, T. M., & Trotter-Mathison, M. (2011). *The resilient practitioner: Burnout prevention and self-care strategies for counselors, therapists, teachers, and health professions* (2nd ed.). New York: Routledge.

Whitaker, T., & Arrington, P. (2008). *Professional development: NASW membership workforce study.* Washington, DC: National Association of Social Workers. Retrieved from http://workforce.socialworkers.org/studies/ProfDev.pdf.

Wilson, P. P., Valentine, D., & Pereira, A. (2002). Perceptions of new social work faculty about mentoring experiences. *Journal of Social Work Education, 38*(2), 317–333.

# 13

# Advancing Field Education through Technology

*Sheila R. Dennis*

Technology is transforming all spheres of social life. Ubiquitously interwoven in all levels of societal functioning, technology is reengineering the way we communicate, create communities, conduct business, and approach education. By shifting how we conceptualize instructional design, delivery, and the learning context, technology is revolutionizing pedagogy, and social work education is no exception. Programs have, at varying levels, integrated technology into every aspect of the curriculum, including that of field education (Coe Regan & Freddolino, 2008). As technology's incursion into social work education continues to influence approaches to teaching, learning, and social work practice, field education will also need to continually reconfigure in order to infuse technological innovation. This chapter will illuminate approaches to the integration of technology in functions central to field education.

To guide social work educators in their persistent quest to design and deliver field education, the chapter provides a general overview of the ways technology is presently shaping the architecture of social work field education, including a glossary of terms (figure 13.1). The areas to be addressed include a contextual perspective, field education administration, and digital knowledge and resources. The chapter will also promote considerations and criteria for assessing the viability of technology for a program's unique field education needs. Finally, a forecast of future technological trends stretches our collective vision into new frontiers.

## Technology and Field Education: A Contextual Perspective

A myriad of social, political, and economic forces converge to amplify the call for technological advancement in field education delivery. The near universality of cyber communication among both adults and children is transforming the way students learn (Greenhow, Robelia, & Hughes, 2009) and how clients seek and receive

**Figure 13.1. Glossary of Terms**

Asynchronous: Online learning that takes place at different locations and outside the constraints of time

Cloud computing: The storing and sharing of information on remote servers that users can access through the Internet

Course management software (CMS), also referred to as learning management software (LMS): Online medium used to manage and enhance course instruction and delivery

Digital native: Someone whose life has been fully immersed in digital technologies and for whom digital devices are naturally interwoven in all spheres of life

Encryption: Encoding information so that it is unintelligible to those not authorized for its use

Information communication technology (ICT): An umbrella term that includes any technological device and application used to handle information and facilitate communication

Net generation: Demographic cohort that has not known life without the Internet

Open source: Nonproprietary software based on an initiative to freely share and revise openly available software code as long as revisions are consistent with the Open Source Initiative

Synchronous: Online learning that takes place at a distant location of other learners and instructors but at the same time

support services (Menon & Rubin, 2011; Mishna, Bogo, Root, Sawyer, & Khoury-Kassabri, 2012). From a socioeconomic perspective, institutions of higher education are pressed by market forces to lower costs and promote accessibility (Anderson, Boyles, & Rainie, 2012). In just one decade, the Internet has shifted from being mostly a content-based resource to a dynamic social living space that encapsulates almost all spheres of both formal and informal daily activities (Lankshear & Knobel, 2006). It is estimated that by 2014 nearly 90 percent of all people in the United States will be connected to robust, high-speed Internet systems (Greenhow et al., 2009). This unprecedented advancement of technology is yielding a new context for social work field education.

According to Holloway, Black, Hoffman, and Pierce (n.d.), a recalibration in focus in social work education from content- to competency-based learning has heightened the attention to context that manifests in three primary ways: program, student learning, and practice. With the focus on demonstration of competency rather than on requisite content, contextual features influencing individual programs in these three dimensions are now integral to formulating a program's unique curriculum. There is more elasticity for responding to contextual characteristics—that is, how a program integrates technology to support curricular needs. Consequently, as the digital age continues to stretch our conceptualization of context for curriculum delivery, social work education is now more agile in how it can respond both collectively and locally. One significant paradigm shift occurring is instructional design and delivery through virtual learning and distance education.

Many social work programs are using various levels of distance education to support their program and institutional missions (Drisko, 2010), a trend that is expected to increase in the future (Vernon, Vakalahi, Pierce, Pittman-Munke, & Adkins, 2009). Distance education programs often are established to promote accessibility of social work education, particularly in rural areas or in states where few social work programs exist (Vernon et al., 2009). Although not an exhaustive account, the Council on Social Work Education (CSWE) lists twenty-three (four bachelor of social work [BSW] and nineteen master of social work [MSW]) accredited distance programs on their Web site (CSWE, n.d.). Birkenmaier et alia (2005) cite literature evidencing the application of distance learning and Internet technology in nearly all areas of undergraduate and graduate social work curricula since the late 1990s. With the growing occurrence of distance education and online programs, there is a swelling emphasis on field education to incorporate strategies to accommodate geographical distances in field education delivery. A search of the social work literature reveals almost no discussion about the impact of distance education on field education delivery. Despite the growing emphasis on technology in social work education and practice, field education has lagged historically behind other areas of the social work curriculum in its integration of Internet-based technology (Birkenmaier et al., 2005; Finn & Marson, 2001).

As the context becomes more digitized, the world becomes more interconnected. In this global environment, boundaries for education and social work practice are fading. New technologies are catalyzing innovative ways of pedagogy and practice that are more inclusive of international influences and cultures (Altbach, Reisberg, & Rumbley, 2009). For field education, technological advancements inject opportunity and vision to cultivate and support international field placements (Panos, 2005).

Finally, technology continues to permeate social work practice. As cyber technology becomes increasingly pervasive in our world, there are compounding demands for online social work services. Preparing students for emerging technology-based practice trends is critical. Furthermore, the practice domain persists in its complexity and economic constraints (Maidment, 2006). Strategies to support students and field instructors are needed and include integrating theory, practice, and technology to provide a more efficient and supportive field education delivery structure.

## Advancing Field Education Administration through Information and Communication Technology

While much of the technological emphasis is on the explicit aspects of the social work field curriculum, technology use also enhances the implicit components that support the delivery and effectiveness of field education. In the 2005 standards for technology, both the National Association of Social Workers (NASW) and Association of Social Work Boards (ASWB) implore social workers to utilize technology for program administration (NASW & ASWB, 2005). *Information and communication technology* (ICT) continues to evolve in ways that allow for more efficient and more robust administrative strategies to compile, store, manage, and retrieve student data. With the compounding attention to student and program assessment, there is a greater impetus for generating field reports of student assessment data. The CSWE (2008) states in Educational Policy [EP] 4.0, "Assessment is an integral component of competency-based education. To evaluate the extent to which the competencies have been met, a system of assessment is central to this model of education. Data from assessment continuously inform and promote change in the explicit and implicit curriculum to enhance attainment of program competencies" (p. 16).

Additionally, the Council on Higher Education Accreditation, from which the CSWE derives its authority to accredit social work programs, now requires that accredited programs publicize program assessment outcomes at regular intervals. Consequently, the CSWE mandates that assessment outcomes appear on program Web sites and that they be updated every two years (CSWE, 2008, Accreditation Standard 4.0.4). With the CSWE requirement that field education yield assessment of the students' demonstration of competency (CSWE, 2008, EP 2.3), it is imperative that assessment data and outcomes deriving from the field practicum are managed and articulated. ICT technology is essential not only for compiling and accessing student data for evaluation purposes, but also for risk management.

Navigating legal concerns is a component of field coordination and involves risk management of records and information (Lemieux, 2004). Business models for risk management typically indicate that 5 to 20 percent of an information technology

(IT) budget is dedicated to risk management (Swartz, 2003, as cited in Lemieux, 2004). Ensuring security of student information through proper electronic data storage, and maintaining, facilitating, and integrating risk management agreements (i.e., memorandum of understanding, student acknowledgement of risk) are essential field education functions. Overall, there are mounting calls for more-sophisticated ICT systems that can aptly integrate and manage data to support growing administrative demands placed on field educators.

Social work programs use a spectrum of technology-based strategies to manage data and coordinate placements. Some field educators still rely heavily on traditional telecommunication devices, such as phone, email, Listserv, facsimile machines, and conventional document-creation software, such as Excel and Word through Microsoft Office Suite software. There is a growing momentum toward using internship management software in field education to assist with placing students, as well as managing learning agreements, field evaluations, and field-related data. Some programs use Internet-based applications to facilitate the matching process between student and agency by offering placement descriptions that students can review online (see figure 13.2). The Internet interface provides a space where students and field instructors can retrieve and upload required documents and evaluations, eliminating the transmission of paper and allowing field liaisons and field directors to have easy access. Postage is eliminated and the use of paper is greatly reduced. Data are integrated and more accessible for analyses and reports. Social work programs utilizing field placement software have approached this supportive technology in different ways.

**Figure 13.2. Using Technology to Assist the Field Placement Process**

| | | |
|---|---|---|
| Provides portal for student and field instructor information submission and retrieval | Facilitates agency and student matching process | Supports data gathering, storage, and integration |
| Reduces field staff/faculty time needed to input and upload student information | Saves money on copying and postage | |

Typically, social work programs will use proprietary or *open source* software systems (see figure 13.3). Some programs, such as the School of Social Work at University of Maryland–Baltimore, have chosen to work with their university IT to build a software program tailored to their individual program's needs. Some programs have chosen to purchase proprietary software packages. See, for example, Intern Placement Tracking (IPT) by Alcea Software (home page, http://www.alceasoftware.com/alcea/overview.html) which organizes and tracks field information. Other programs have sought open source software packages that are part of the Open Source Initiative. This initiative encompasses software codes that are intended to be freely shared (Simonson, Smaldino, Albright, & Zvacek, 2009); the codes include the ability for the user to modify the program to meet individual program needs and to lower maintenance and upgrading costs. While open source programs are accessible to the public, they typically require hiring a software consultant to fashion the open source software to suit unique programmatic needs. Choosing a software system option is contingent on a social work program's infrastructure, resources, and administrative needs.

Project management is another area of field administration that is including new ICT. The prolific growth of the Internet has spawned free project management options that were inconceivable a few years ago. There is a shift occurring with project management transitioning from a desktop approach to Internet-based

**Figure 13.3. Considerations for Choosing Proprietary vs. Open Source Software**

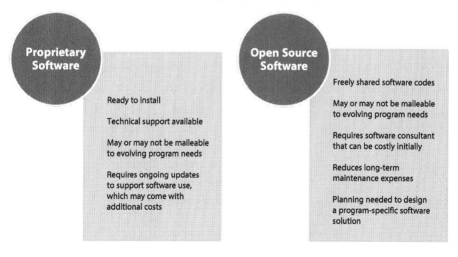

Proprietary Software

Ready to install

Technical support available

May or may not be malleable to evolving program needs

Requires ongoing updates to support software use, which may come with additional costs

Open Source Software

Freely shared software codes

May or may not be malleable to evolving program needs

Requires software consultant that can be costly initially

Reduces long-term maintenance expenses

Planning needed to design a program-specific software solution applications (Greenhow et al., 2009). Web sites such as Google Drive offer opportunities for anyone to collaborate on documents, presentations, and spreadsheets from remote locations and to store work through an Internet address that is accessible anywhere there is a computer and Internet available. Various Web sites provide visually interactive applications to assist with scheduling meetings amongst numerous people. Finally, more-sophisticated and more-affordable options for videoconferencing offer ways to connect social work programs with multiple campus sites for meetings and other activities.

Vulnerable to loss and theft, portable storage devices may soon be eclipsed by online options for data storage, or *cloud computing*, including those that are available at no charge through Web sites, such as Dropbox (see figure 13.4). Cloud services store data in an off-site server, protecting information from corruption, disaster, and hardware malfunction and are accessible anywhere there is an Internet connection. Because of confidentiality and security concerns, student data should not be stored in off-site servers unless sanctioned by a program's institutional setting. Additionally, system compatibility and Internet connectivity are essential to mobile project management technology.

### Field Instructor Training and Student Orientations

Technology used to support field instruction training and student orientations is becoming increasingly multimodal. While ICT offers creative options to support and orient field instructors and students, the telephone and email are still vital tools for ensuring that pertinent information is delivered. Promoting remote accessibility, Webinars—a real-time, online presentation medium—provide field

**Figure 13.4. Examples of Project Management Technology for Field Education**

| Project Management Technology | Administrative Function |
| --- | --- |
| Google Drive | Space for collaboration on documents, presentations, spreadsheets, and survey creation |
| | Forms allowing invitation and response management accessible from different locations through Internet site |
| Doodle | Internet site to facilitate scheduling events and meetings |
| Skype, Adobe Connect, iChat, Google+ Hangouts | Internet-based videoconferencing |
| iCloud, Dropbox, Google Drive | Cloud computing data storage through the Internet, accessible through a Web-based interface |

instructors and students access to training and orientations through a Web site link, reducing the need for travel, and saving time and expense. The School of Social Work, University of North Dakota, with an established distance education program, provides Web-based orientations and training to field instructors by utilizing Adobe Connect, a Web conferencing platform. With Internet connection and a computer equipped with audiovisual capacity, field instructors can virtually attend a training or orientation and provide text-based questions in real time to the presenter, allowing for a two-way interactive session (C. Schneweis, personal communication, July 26, 2012). Other modes incorporate the traditional Microsoft PowerPoint presentation with audio-only streaming, or a prerecorded video-streamed one-way presentation that participants can view asynchronously.

### Using Technology to Facilitate Field Instruction

Online and mobile technologies provide creative ways to execute the role of the field liaison. As videoconferencing has become more accessible and cost-effective, online field supervision and advising is increasing in viability. There are now free Web sites that offer this computer-mediated capability. Basic hardware, including a computer, Webcam, and broadband Internet, can facilitate an audio and visual two-way, real-time interaction. For geographically separated placements, video-conferencing promotes accessibility and flexibility, and also lowers social work program costs by reducing travel for field liaisons (McAdams & Wyatt, 2010). The advent of online supervision options also expands options for field placements (Watson, 2003, as cited in Chapman, Baker, Nassar-McMillan, & Gerler, 2011).

Enhanced videoconferencing functionalities and accessibility foster new possibilities for international learning opportunities (Aguirre & Mitschke, 2011). Panos (2005) outlines how videoconferencing can assist with coordinating and supervising international field placements. With as few as 40 percent of international field placements having available on-site social work field supervision that meets CSWE requirements (Panos, Panos, Cox, Roby, & Matheson, 2002), videoconferencing offers mechanisms for additional university support. Panos (2005) refers to the increased transmission of emotional support, including understanding, empathy, and using Internet-based modalities as "emotional bandwidth" (p. 839).

While online supervision offers many benefits, questions and challenges remain (see figure 13.5). Panos et al. (2002) exhort social work educators to be mindful of nascent ethical guidelines for online supervision. For international placements,

**Figure 13.5.  Considerations for Online Practicum Supervision**

| | | |
|---|---|---|
| Choice | While online supervision is in a formative state, students should have choice of face-to-face supervision. | Chapman et al. (2011); Nelson, Nichter, & Henriksen (2010) |
| Access | Student and field instructor should have sufficient access to the adequate technology required for *asynchronous* and *synchronous* supervisory needs. | Chapman et al. (2011); Nelson et al. (2010) |
| Competency | Students and field instructors for online supervision should be prepared for online supervision through field training and orientation. | Chapman et al. (2011) |
| | Field directors should consider students' and field instructors' technological proficiency when using online supervision. | Chapman et al. (2011); Nelson et al. (2010); Vaccaro & Lambie (2007) |
| Quality | Quality of and consistent access to technology and Internet connection affect online supervision. | Panos et al. (2002) |
| | Supervisors located at a distance are unavailable to respond in person to a crisis, potentially affecting the stability of the placement and client care. | McAdams & Wyatt (2010); Vaccaro & Lambie (2007) |
| | The lack of human connection could impede professional bonding between field instructor and student. | Olson et al. (2002) as cited in Nelson et al. (2010) |
| | Online supervision quality should be equal to that of face-to-face supervision. | Panos et al. (2002) |
| | There should be a back-up plan should technology problems affect supervision. | Nelson et al. (2010); Vaccaro & Lambie (2007) |
| | Educators and supervisors must maintain measures to ensure quality evaluation of student competence. | Vaccaro & Lambie (2007) |
| Security | Users should ensure encryption transmissions for security of supervisory information. | Shaw & Shaw (2006), as cited in Vaccaro & Lambie (2007) |
| Confidentiality | Field educators must ensure confidentiality of both students and information about clients during telecommunication sessions. | McAdams & Wyatt (2010); Panos et al. (2002); Vaccarro & Lambie (2007) |
| | The client's informed consent protocol should include acknowledgement that online supervision could result in unauthorized access of client information. | Vaccaro & Lambie (2007) |

attention to ethical boundaries is especially critical as students interface with cultural differences, and in countries where ethics might be different (Panos et al., 2002). Online supervision could pose disadvantages, including the lack of a sense of supervisory connection. The perception of supervisory attachment could be lessened by challenges with demonstrating empathy through an audio or video medium rather than face to face (Olson, Russell, & White, 2002).

Field liaisons will need to ensure security and confidentiality by assessing the privacy of the supervisory session before confidential information is shared (Olson et al., 2002; Panos et al., 2002). *Encryption* of the online supervisory interaction is essential. In addition, students should have the opportunity to acknowledge potential challenges to online supervision (Olson et al., 2002). Finally, faculty workload concerns arise as technology could promote efficiency, which has the potential of translating into increased field liaison assignments. Overall, there remains a dearth of research exploring the efficacy of online field supervision both from a programmatic and a student's experiential perspective. Despite the burgeoning use of both asynchronous and synchronous online supervision in social work and other helping professions, there is scant attention in the literature to this integral pedagogical component. This phenomenon needs closer examination as it becomes a more established field education practice.

### Tools to Enhance Field Education Learning and Assessment

Technology can also provide tools to enhance learning with field instruction and in the integrative seminar. While students value direct observation of their practice skills (Bogo, 2010); demands on field instructor time in agency settings can make this type of valued supervisory experience prohibitive. Technology through the use of video- and audiotaping assists with capturing students' practice experiences. It also allows for feedback based on direct observation rather than on text-based process recordings that can lose critical data through the transcription process (Bogo, 2010). The emergence of more portable and mobile devices could be a conduit for this central evaluative function.

Since their entry in March 2010, mobile tablets have quickly captured society's attention (Rossing, Miller, Cecil, & Stamper, 2012), and there are efforts to explore how these tablets can galvanize field education (Galyean & Dennis, 2012). Through content mapping applications, e.g., Popplet, mobile tablets offer creative ways to formulate ecomaps that users can share digitally with others. Mobile tablets could provide creative ways to engage students and future clients. The size and mobility of these tablets offer ways to capture process recordings through recording apps and bookmark segments of the process recording (Galyean & Dennis, 2012). Newer mobile tablet versions are equipped with more advanced video capacities that could also help facilitate videotaping of client sessions for additional assessment and supervisory feedback.

With the emphasis on competency assessment in field education, strategic ways to reenvision evaluation tools are emerging. E-portfolios have become a way for students to electronically compile learning artifacts from the field practicum that then transform into a composite picture of the student's proficiency. With more-sophisticated survey tools emerging, there are now ways that field evaluation tools can be implemented in electronic versions, tailored to reflect unique program needs. Benefits include the absence of copying, transferring documents, and data extraction. Through the use of survey software, such as Qualtrics, online field evaluations are available to students, field instructors, and field liaisons through a Web site link. Field instructors and students enter assessment scores into an online document that then automatically integrates the individual student assessment data and aggregates student cohort data, making it expeditiously available for program evaluation purposes. Some software functionalities allow for students to monitor their own progress throughout the placement through graphs that are automatically generated from field instructor and student assessments. Despite the appeal of these online assessment tools, challenges persist with having the human and technological resources for users to develop, learn to use, and sustain these innovations. Additionally, faculty buy-in is essential with facilitating the cultural conversion that includes supporting partner agency participation in online evaluation tools.

### Designing and Delivering Online Integrative Seminars

Internet technology is transforming the manner in which field seminars are delivered. The advent of *course management software* (CMS), interchangeably referred to as *learning management software* (LMS), has made a significant impact on instructional delivery and design. Since the early 2000s CMS has ushered in a new era of online course instruction by providing an organizational structure mechanism for communication, document transmission, and course content delivery (Aguirre & Mitschke, 2011). The interactive technology of CMS also has the capability of facilitating active learning spaces and a social presence (Waterhouse, 2005) through both asynchronous and synchronous delivery methods.

Online and blended seminar courses offer many benefits. Aguirre and Mitschke (2011) suggest that a hybrid model infusing CMS into a face-to-face course improves learner satisfaction and concurrently bolsters students' technology skills. For blended courses, students are able to post materials for review prior to a seminar session, saving time and promoting more reflective discussions. The various functionalities offered through CMS are optimal for reflective writing. (See figure 13.6 for common functionalities available through CMS.) Given the intensity of the practicum environment, the online discussions may provide asynchronous peer support and feedback throughout the practicum experience (Maidment, 2006). Some field courses may choose to promote student connectivity through social media sites. For example, field directors and/or field liaisons could generate a field seminar Facebook page where students can communicate and collaborate. Field directors must address parameters to ensure confidentiality and professionalism; these are discussed later in the chapter.

To further enhance CMS functionalities in delivering online or blended field seminars, proprietary options are beginning to emerge. One example is the E-Field Program, that offers an interactive comprehensive Web site designed to facilitate field practicum communication, paperwork and data collection for assessment. A distinctive functionality of E-Field is that it has been formulated to interweave the CSWE competencies throughout the learning activities and promotes an active learning space specifically designed for field seminars (Matich-Maroney, 2013). Many social work programs have employed the E-field software. The cost to social work programs is minimal, given that students purchase the E-Field Program, similar to how they purchase a textbook. Programs with minimal technology budgets might find this option appealing while others might weigh the additional cost to the student as burdensome when students are already encumbered with significant tuition costs.

Another option for delivering synchronous, online field seminars is through interactive videoconferencing software systems, such as Adobe Connect. These types of systems provide a platform for synchronous, two-way, online seminars with students who log on wherever they are located. Hardware equipment requirements are minimal: a computer, Internet connection, Webcam, and a headset. Access to

**Figure 13.6.  Course Management Software Functions to Support Online Integrative Seminars**

| Common CMS Functions | Purpose | Potential Benefits to Online Field Seminars |
|---|---|---|
| Gradebook | Provides ongoing posting of student's assessment scores. | Students can monitor course progress; grades can be exported to an excel spreadsheet or to information management systems. |
| Resources | Repository for course-related resources. | There is space for uploading course materials, including journal articles, practice resources, Web site and video links, and presentation documents. |
| Assignments | Contains assignment descriptions and mechanisms for submission | Students can access remotely quizzes and tests. |
| Podcasts | Three- to five-minute topical summary, usually in audio format. | Conveys the most important points or a summary of content covered. |
| Wikis | Allows students to cocreate documents by synchronizing access and concurrently inserting ideas. | Provides a tool for collaboration. |
| Announcement Board | Mechanism to communicate course announcements to students. | Communication source ensures students are informed of any essential and/or emergent information pertaining to the course. |
| Syllabus | Holds digital version of syllabus for student access throughout course. | Provides accessible copy to students at any time throughout the course. |
| Blog | Web log on which an individual student can post an ongoing thread. | Fosters individual reflections on which a field liaison or field instructor could offer feedback. |
| Discussion Forum | Provides multiple student access to a discussion thread that usually addresses one identified topic. | Promotes student interaction, reflective thinking, and peer feedback; provides field liaison or field instructor with access to students' challenges in field setting. |
| Email/Messaging | Electronic communication mechanism through course site. | Facilitates seminar-specific information; typically allows option to be linked to university email system. |

these types of videostreaming resources may depend on the IT resources of a given institution. Adobe Connect typically requires a university/college subscription, which sets limits on which computer can be used, and consequently planning is required to ensure adequate student access to these types of cyber seminar options.

**Knowing the Learners**

As contextual forces create an environment fertile for the further development of online field seminar options, it is important to understand potential attitudes that surround online learning. A report from the Pew Research Center found that only 29 percent of the public perceives online courses as being equal in value when compared with face-to-face classroom courses (Hampton, Goulet, Rainie, & Purcell, 2011). The study also found that enrollment in online courses at colleges and universities has grown at a faster rate than overall enrollments (21% growth in online enrollment versus 1.2% increase in postsecondary education enrollment), however. Indeed, there are conflicting expectations on social work educators as they plan for the future with online field seminar offerings. Students expect and desire distant and online learning options, but they prefer to learn via face-to-face interactions (Simonson et al., 2009).

Skill level among students varies. For some students, commonly referred to as *digital natives* or the *net generation*, multimedia environments that promote interaction, collaboration, and connection are optimal (Berk, 2010). Other students not exposed or given access to the same level of technology may need additional assistance. Regardless, field educators conducting seminars will need to assess students' technology skill and comfort level at the start of the seminar session (Rossing et al., 2012). Educators should be careful not to assume that increased comfort level translates into critical thinking acumen with technology (Rossing et al., 2012). All levels of students will need guidance in utilizing new technologies employed for field instruction.

## Digital Knowledge and Resources to Enhance Field Education

ICT is also affecting how information and knowledge is stored and acquired for application in field education. Within the past decade, the digitization of information has revolutionized all facets of library and information sciences. Most universities now have some method for users to remotely connect to the library, increasing the portability and accessibility of resources for students while in their field placements. Online journal databases and e-books (electronic books) allow students to access resources to support their fieldwork without entering the library building; citation software, such as Endnote and Refworks, assists students with organizing and citing online journal sources. Librarians have evolved into experts in navigating the intricate and vast world of digital information networks and provide assistance through virtual methods such as instant messaging, further promoting students' remote access to library resources from remote field placement locations. With the anticipated increase in distance education, field education will likely grow in its demand for information and scholarship portability.

Electronic applications to various sources of knowledge also increase accessibility and transportability of knowledge. Various knowledge sources, including journal publishers, provide personal digital assistant (known as a PDA) applications that allow for access to scholarship available on mobile devices, including cellular phones and mobile tablets (e.g., the iPad). Users can use these applications to link with many university library holdings through synchronization with their PDAs. Furthermore, staying connected or sharing resource information can occur with a touch on a screen through links to social media sites such as Facebook, LinkedIn, and Twitter. WorldCat, an international digitized interlibrary system, assists students with locating materials and submitting requests for interlibrary loans. Even textbooks are digitized, a trend which shows no signs of abating (Taylor, Parker, Lenhart, & Patten, 2011).

For field education, this kind of remote accessibility and portability further supports geographical separation of students. Students in placements that do not allow access to the physical library setting can remain connected to necessary resources throughout their field practicum. As distance education becomes more common, the digitization of resources promotes universal library access. Panos (2005) found that students in international placements reported not having adequate resources to guide field work. Having remote access to university libraries could have significant benefits for students in international placements where scholarly and practice resources are limited.

For all of the databases and software mentioned, there is the issue of connectivity and hardware to support the emerging technologies. Compatibility with software and hardware must be discerned because newer software does not always work with older equipment. Agency firewalls may prevent user access to certain types of digitized knowledge sources. Moreover, technical and librarian support needed to ensure the reliability of the technology over time is a cost factor and workload issue for social work programs to consider.

## Challenges and Considerations

The pervasive presence of technology and cyber communication in social work education and practice has practical, clinical, ethical, and legal implications (Congress, 2002; Mishna, Bogo, et al., 2012). Cyber technologies affect professional relationships (Mishna, Bogo, et al., 2012), and students will need support and guidance in navigating these emerging challenges. It is essential for social work educators and practitioners to develop competence in critically analyzing how to apply ethical frameworks to newly developed technologies (Blaschke, Freddolino, & Mullen, 2009), since many forecast an unceasing demand for online social work services and communication (Menon & Rubin, 2011) as well as a continued expansion of the social networking landscape (Hampton et al., 2011).

As field education incorporates technologies, educators also have an ethical responsibility for ensuring the confidentiality and security of student and client information, adhering to the Family Educational Rights and Privacy Act (FERPA) and the Health Insurance Portability and Accountability Act of 1996 (HIPAA) (Congress, 2002). The NASW and ASWB (2005) have also established standards for social workers' use of technology. While these standards do not explicitly identify parameters with social media, they do establish an imperative that social workers adapt practice protocols to ensure ethical practice.

The proliferation of social media and the public display of personal thoughts and information require field educators to be responsive to arising ethical concerns. Students placed at community agencies need guidance with appropriate communication and boundaries while posting personal information on social media sites. Field education units are responding with technology-related policy statements that are now incorporated into field manuals and communicated directly to field instructors and students at orientations (see figure 13.7). These statements should be framed in a way that First Amendment rights, allowing free speech and expression, are not violated. These statements should avoid language outlining potential disciplinary action. Most ethical violations and disparaging remarks that might occur with student use of social media will be covered under program and field policies addressing student conduct in the student handbook and field manual.

**Figure 13.7. An Example of a Technology Statement**

**Use of Technology in the Field**

The Internet has created the ability for students and social workers to communicate and share information quickly and to reach millions of people easily. Participating in social networking and other similar Internet opportunities can support a student's personal expression, enable individual social workers to have a professional presence online, foster collegiality and camaraderie within the profession, and provide the opportunity to widely advocate for social policies. Social networks, blogs, and other forms of communication online also create new challenges to the social worker–client relationship. Students should weigh a number of considerations when maintaining an online presence:

1. Students should be cognizant of standards of client privacy and confidentiality that must be maintained in all environments, including online, and must refrain from posting identifiable client information online.
2. When using the Internet for social networking, students should use privacy settings to safeguard personal information and content to the extent possible, but should realize that privacy settings are not absolute and that, once on the Internet, content is likely to be there permanently. Students should routinely monitor their own Internet presence to ensure that the personal and professional information on their own sites and, to the extent possible, content posted about them by others, is accurate and appropriate.
3. If they interact with clients on the Internet, students must maintain appropriate boundaries of the social worker–client relationship in accordance with professional ethical guidelines, just as they would in any other context.
   a. To maintain appropriate professional boundaries, students should consider separating personal and professional content online.
   b. When students see content posted by colleagues that might be unprofessional, they have a responsibility to bring that content to the attention of the individual so he or she can remove it and/or take other appropriate actions. If the behavior significantly violates professional norms and the individual does not take appropriate action to resolve the situation, the student should report the matter to appropriate authorities.
   c. Students must recognize that actions and content posted online may negatively affect their reputations among clients and colleagues, may have consequences for their social work careers, and can undermine public trust in the social work profession.

*Source*: Indiana University School of Social Work, Bachelor of Social Work Program Student Handbook (2011, pp. 32–33).

## Assessing the Viability of Technological Integration

While there exists an undeniable consensus that some level of technology is inseparable from field education, a techonology planning team, that includes the field director, needs to carefully assess what technology will benefit a program. Given the level of resource investment and constant state of flux that characterizes technology, having an analytical framework by which to guide decisions for planning and implementing new technological strategies is critical.

Beaulaurier (2005, p. 156) sets forth a planning model that involves four primary stages: assessment, planning, implementation, and maintenance (see figure 13.8). The following analytical framework builds on Beaulaurier's initial work with a planning model for ICT integration in social work education. The integration of technology in field education requires a team approach. Stakeholders should carefully assess the need and employ a multidimensional approach to the planning process. This planning team should also have the ability to affect an organizational structure in a way that inspires a vision, should the decision be made to adopt new technology (Simonson et al., 2009).

**Figure 13.8. A Process Guide for Integrating New Technology**

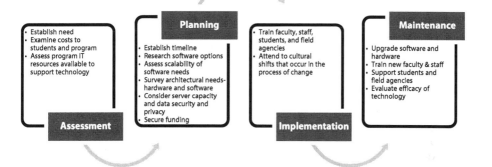

### Assessment

According to Beaulaurier (2005), a primary task of the assessment stage involves exploring student and faculty access. It is essential for the planning team to discern what a reasonable equipment requirement is for students, given the surge in tuition costs. Also imperative during the assessment process is a careful examination of the administrative or learning needs the ICT is intended to address. This component of the assessment process is critical because, once developed, software may not be malleable to accommodate new functions. Surveying the current IT infrastructure, including IT support, server capacity, and existing hardware is essential in the assessment process to understand what ICT proposals are viable.

Finally, an important task for the team is to critically analyze whether the technology will be a vehicle for the intended benefits. This should be done during the assessment stage to ensure that the technology does not unintentionally serve as a deterrent toward the intended goals for its integration (Beaulaurier, 2005). It is imperative for the team to examine short- and long-term budgetary requirements for integrating technology. Much time can be spent formulating a plan that is abruptly stalled by a shortfall of funds, or launching new technology only to encounter a flagging success due to deficiency of funds available to sustain its long-term implementation.

### Planning

Upon establishing the scope of the technological need, the team should create a timeline for planning and implementing the project. With a guiding timeline in place, a careful review of available hardware and software options is an important next step in the planning process. Numerous open source options exist that can reduce ongoing maintenance costs over time. Software consultant fees, however, can be significant. When reviewing software options, scalability should be considered, which includes evaluating if a software package can accommodate growth and evolve with the needs identified for field education. A scan of the technological architecture is essential to ensure that the proposed software packages are compatible with different operating systems used by students, field agencies, and the social work program. It is also critical to consider server capacity, data security, and privacy issues. Purchasing new hardware requires thoughtful planning, as hardware becomes obsolete in approximately three years (Beaulaurier, 2005). Purchasing hardware prematurely could result in a shortened compatibility timeframe for emerging software. With a lucid assessment and plan, the final step in the planning stage is to secure needed funding for hardware, software, and ongoing maintenance.

### Implementation

Once the plan has been established and the software needs identified, the next step is to purchase and implement the software. Faculty, staff, students, and field agencies will need support and training with learning the new technology functions. Depending on the scale of the change, a cultural shift may occur that requires additional time and attention.

### Maintenance

The final stage of maintenance entails upgrading software and hardware as needed and training new users of the technology over the course of its implementation. New faculty and staff need an initial orientation to the use of the program's technology. Field instructors, students, and field agencies must keep abreast of the changing technology utilized by the field program. The technology team institutes regular training and support for new faculty, staff, field agencies, and students. Assessing the efficacy of the technology occurs over time and is an iterative process (Beaulaurier, 2005). Evaluation must be ongoing as to the usefulness of the software and its support of administrative and learning goals.

### Support of Technology

Consistent institutional support is needed for students and faculty unprepared for Internet and digital technologies in teaching and learning (Corbel & Valdes-Cobell, 2007, as cited in Rossing et al., 2012). User-friendly technical support is also needed to support students, field instructors, and field faculty in maintaining and accessing ICT for effective, technologically enhanced field education delivery (Maidment, 2006).

Faculty support and attitude affect technology application. Drisko (2010) asserts that faculty's efforts with integrating technology into teaching remains undetermined as either teaching and/or scholarship for promotion and tenure, which could further enervate faculty's commitment to launching new supportive technology for field education. As field directors consider enhanced technology to support field education, they should include field faculty in the deliberation and the training. Much of the success of new technology rests on the instructor, therefore support for field faculty is essential (Rossing et al., 2012).

### The Future of Technology in Field Education: New Frontiers

Historically, the emergence of technologies has birthed new global paradigms that also penetrate higher education (Rajasingham, 2007). In his classic work *The Structure of Scientific Revolutions*, Thomas Kuhn (1962) observes that "when paradigms change, the world itself changes with them" (p. 110). As technologies insert new ideas and global perspectives into higher education (Rajasingham, 2007) and social work practice (Mishna, Bogo, et al., 2012), the zeitgeist of social work education is also shifting.

There is a growing sense that the context for higher education and social work education will change, perhaps significantly, in the near future (Vernon et al., 2009). In a nonrandomized study with technology experts, the majority surveyed believes that higher education will undergo extreme changes by 2020 (Anderson et al., 2012). Respondents anticipated that changes will include a mass retooling driven by distance and online learning capabilities and higher education's need to be more economically competitive. The forecasted changes were also predicated on a transitioning societal view toward learning, compelled by the significant shifts in mobility, instant accessibility, and Internet-based computing.

Most of the youth today have digitized lives (Berk, 2010). They do not know life without email, cell phones, text messaging, Twitter, or Facebook. Many are accustomed to mastering multiple technical devices and naturally interweaving them in their everyday lives (Ahmedani, Harold, Fitton, & Shifflet Gibson, 2011; Berk, 2010). Research using mobile tablets as a learning device suggests that students desire constant accessibility to information and flexibility with the process. As there is a growing emphasis on mobility and accessibility, mobile devices, with the capability of wireless connection and synchronization, could provide opportunities for collaborative learning that aspires to multiple learning styles in field seminars (Rossing et al., 2012). With the ease of information exchange, field directors will need to further educate students on professional boundaries and ethical considerations, particularly with ensuring confidentiality with client and agency information.

Administratively, field education will encounter shifts as well. Anderson and Rainie (2010), synthesizing the views of numerous experts, predict that by 2020 cloud computing will encompass most of our document production and data management rather than through a desktop, or at least more of a hybrid approach than what presently exists. Our collaborative work will occur mostly through cyberspace-based applications accessed through networked devices. This transition will propel mobile connectivity through smartphones and other Internet devices. Some project that mobile tablets will surpass desktops by 2015, as society increasingly seeks wireless capabilities (International Data Consortium, 2011). Overall, field educators will need to become more technologically literate if they are to guide and engage future students whose lives are saturated by a digital existence.

Developing innovative field practicum opportunities that correspond with the emerging cyber communication context will be central to advancing student skills in the digital age. Early indications of this type of approach are emerging. Mishna, Levine, Bogo, and Van Wert (2012) created a pilot cyber practicum opportunity for

MSW students to serve undergraduate students at a college counseling center. The pilot project highlights the need to prepare students for a practice context that is characterized by a growing interest in online technologies. Not only is there a need for more opportunities for students to grow in cyber practice skills, but there is also a need for more information and research about how cyber counseling is provided (Menon & Rubin, 2011) and how to educationally prepare social workers for this emerging modality of service provision.

Virtual reality persists as an emerging technology that could also penetrate field education in the future. Rajasingham (2007) outlines technological capabilities that seem otherworldly, such as a HyperClass (HC), but that are already occurring in formative ways. HC blends real and virtual realities into a conventional classroom space. The technology would allow for 3D images to be integrated into a real physical classroom setting and would entail the synchronous interaction of physically real objects with virtual objects. Through this virtual connection, real and unreal objects share a space. These HC spaces would allow for interaction with virtual classmates anywhere in the world. While almost unimaginable in the present, HyperWorld spaces could revolutionize field instructor training opportunities, field supervision, and synchronous field seminars.

The immensity of technological expansion in social life is a catalyst for both creative opportunities and substantive challenges. This chapter has captured some of the most essential adaptive responses field education is making to attend to the technological epoch. Most of the advances are predicated on the expansion of a more comprehensive broadband infrastructure. For some countries and rural areas, that infrastructure is still in a formative stage. Still, as our digital world continues to arise, field education will evolve to shape social workers for the future of social work practice.

## Essential Readings

Coe Regan, J. R., & Freddolino, P. P. (Eds.). (2008). *Integrating technology into the social work curriculum.* Alexandria, VA: Council on Social Work Education Press.

National Association of Social Workers (NASW) and Association of Social Work Boards (ASWB). (2005). *NASW & ASWB standards for technology and social work practice.* Washington, DC: NASW.

Simonson, M., Smaldino, S., Albright, M., & Zvacek, S. (2009). *Teaching and learning at a distance: Foundations of distance education* (4th ed.). Boston: Pearson.

## References

Aguirre, R. T. P., & Mitschke, D. B. (2011). Enhancing learning and learner satisfaction through the use of WebCT in social work education. *Social Work Education, 30*(7), 847–860.

Ahmedani, B. K., Harold, R. D., Fitton, V. A., & Shifflet Gibson, E. D. (2011). What adolescents can tell us: Technology and the future of social work education. *Social Work Education, 30*(7), 830–846.

Altbach, P. G., Reisberg, L., & Rumbley, L. E. (2009). *Trends in global higher education: Tracking an academic revolution.* Report prepared for the UNESCO [United Nations Educational, Scientific and Cultural Organization] 2009 World Conference on Higher Education. Retrieved from http://graduate institute.ch/webdav/site/developpement/shared/developpement/cours/E759/Altbach,%20Reisberg,%20Rumbley%20Tracking%20an%20Academic%20Revolution,%20UNESCO%202009.pdf.

Anderson, J., Boyles, J. L., & Rainie, L. (2012). *The future of higher education.* Washington, DC: Pew Research Center's Internet & American Life Project. Retrieved from http://www.pewinternet.org/Reports/2012/Future-of-Higher-Education.aspx.

Anderson, J., & Rainie, L. (2010). *The future of cloud computing.* Washington, DC: Pew Research Center's Internet & American Life Project. Retrieved from http://www.pewinternet.org/Reports/2010/The-future-of-cloud-computing.aspx.

Beaulaurier, R. L. (2005). Integrating computer content into social work curricula: A model for planning. *Journal of Teaching in Social Work, 25*(1/2), 153–171.

Berk, R. A. (2010). How do you leverage the latest technologies, including Web 2.0 tools, in your classroom? *International Journal of Technology in Teaching and Learning, 6*(1), 1–13.

Birkenmaier, J., Wernet, S., Berg-Weger, M., Wilson, R. J., Banks, R., Olliges, R., & Delicath, T. (2005). Weaving a web: The use of internet technology in field education. *Journal of Teaching in Social Work, 25*(1/2), 3–19.

Blaschke, C. M., Freddolino, P., & Mullen, E. E. (2009). Ageing and technology: A review of the research literature. *British Journal of Social Work, 39*(4), 641–656. doi:10.1093/bjsw/bcp025.

Bogo, M. (2010). *Achieving competence in social work through field education.* Toronto, ON: University of Toronto Press.

Chapman, R. A., Baker, S. B., Nassar-McMillan, S. C., & Gerler, E. R. (2011). Cybersupervision: Further examination of synchronous and asynchronous modalities in counseling practicum supervision. *Counselor Education and Supervision, 50*(5), 298–313.

Coe Regan, J. R., & Freddolino, P. P. (Eds.). (2008). *Integrating technology into the social work curriculum.* Alexandria, VA: Council on Social Work Education Press.

Congress, E. P. (2002). Social work ethics for educators: Navigating ethical change in the classroom and in the field. *Journal of Teaching in Social Work, 22*(1/2), 151–166. doi:10.1300/J067v22n01_10.

Council on Social Work Education (CSWE). (2008). *Educational policy and accreditation standards* (rev. March 27, 2010/updated August 2012). Alexandria, VA: Author. Retrieved from http://www.cswe.org/Accreditation/41865.aspx.

Council on Social Work Education (CSWE). (n.d.). *Distance education.* Alexandria, VA: Author. Retrieved from http://www.cswe.org/Accreditation/Information/DistanceEducation.aspx.

Drisko, J. (2010). Technology in social work education. In J. W. Anastas (Ed.), *Teaching in social work: An educator's guide to theory and practice* (pp. 115–150). Chichester, NY: Columbia University Press.

Finn, J., & Marson, S. (2001). Social work programs' use of the world wide web by social work programs to facilitate field instruction. *Advances in Social Work, 2*(1), 26–37.

Galyean, E., & Dennis, S. (2012, March). I have an app for that! Utilizing the iPad in field education. Presentation at the Baccalaureate Program Directors Annual Conference, Portland, OR.

Greenhow, C., Robelia, B., & Hughes, J. E. (2009). Learning, teaching, and scholarship in a digital age. *Educational Researcher, 38*(4), 246–259. doi:10.3102/0013189X09336671.

Hampton, K. N., Goulet, L. S., Rainie, L., & Purcell, K. (2011). *Social networking sites and our lives.* Washington, DC: Pew Research Center's Internet & American Life Project. Retrieved from http://www.pewinternet.org/~/media/Files/Reports/2011/PIP%20-%20Social%20networking%20sites%20and%20our%20lives.pdf.

Holloway, S., Black, P., Hoffman, K., & Pierce, D. (n.d.). *Some considerations of the import of the 2008 EPAS for curriculum design.* Alexandria, VA: Council on Social Work Education. Retrieved from http://www.cswe.org/file.aspx?id=31578.

Indiana University. (2011). Bachelor of Social Work Program student handbook (2012–2014) BSW. Retrieved from http://socialwork.iu.edu/files/documents/bsw_student_handbook/BSW%20Handbook%202012-2014%20Final.pdf.

International Data Consortium. (2011). IDC: More mobile internet users than wireline users in the U.S. by 2015 [Press release]. Retrieved from http://www.infodocket.com/2011/09/12/idc-more-mobile-internet-users-than-wireline-users-in-the-u-s-by-2015/.

Kuhn, T. S. (1962). *The structure of scientific revolutions.* Chicago: University of Chicago Press.

Lankshear, C., & Knobel, M. (2006). *New literacies: Everyday practices and classroom learning* (2nd ed.). Maidenhead, UK: Open University Press.

Lemieux, V. L. (2004). *Managing risks for records and information.* Lenexa, KS: ARMA International.

Matich-Maroney, J. (2013). *E-field program: A competency-based system for the social work practicum.* New York: Pearson.

Maidment, J. (2006). Using on-line delivery to support students during practicum placements. *Australian Social Work, 59*(1), 47–55. doi:10.1080/03124070500449770.

McAdams, C. R., & Wyatt, K. L. (2010). The regulation of technology-assisted distance counseling and supervision in the United States: An analysis of current extent, trends, and implications. *Counselor Education and Supervision, 49*(3), 179–192.

Menon, G. M., & Rubin, M. (2011). A survey of online practitioners: Implications for education and practice. *Journal of Technology in Human Services, 29*(2), 133–141. doi:10.1080/15228835.2011.595262.

Mishna, F., Bogo, M., Root, J., Sawyer, J., & Khoury-Kassabri, M. (2012). "It just crept in": The digital age and implications for social work practice. *Clinical Social Work Journal, 40*(3), 277–286. doi:10.1007/s10615–012–0383–4.

Mishna, F., Levine, D., Bogo, M., & Van Wert, M. (2012). Cyber counseling: An innovative field education pilot project. *Social Work Education: The International Journal, iFirst Article,* 1–9. doi:10.1080/02615479.2012.685066.

National Association of Social Workers (NASW) and Association of Social Work Boards (ASWB). (2005). *NASW & ASWB standards for technology and social work practice.* Washington, DC: NASW.

Nelson, J. A., Nichter, M., & Henriksen, R. (2010). *On-line supervision and face-to-face supervision in the counseling internship: An exploratory study of similarities and differences.* Retrieved from http://counselingoutfitters.com/vistas/vistas10/Article_46.pdf.

Olson, M. M., Russell, C. S., & White, M. B. (2002). Technological implications for clinical supervision and practice. *Clinical Supervisor, 20*(2), 201–215.

Panos, P. T. (2005). A model for using videoconferencing technology to support international social work field practicum students. *International Social Work, 48*(6), 834–841.

Panos, P. T., Panos, A., Cox, S. E., Roby, J. L., & Matheson, K. W. (2002). Ethical issues concerning the use of videoconferencing to supervise international social work field practicum students. *Journal of Social Work Education, 38*(3), 421–437.

Rajasingham, L. (2007). Perspectives on 21st century e-learning in higher education. In L. Tomei (Ed.), *Integrating information and communication technologies into the classroom* (pp. 289–306). Hershey, PA: Information Science Publishing.

Rossing, J. P., Miller, W. M., Cecil, A. K., & Stamper, S. E. (2012). iLearning: The future of higher education? Student perceptions on learning with mobile tablets. *Journal of the Scholarship of Teaching and Learning, 12*(2), 1–26.

Simonson, M., Smaldino, S., Albright, M., & Zvacek, S. (2009). *Teaching and learning at a distance: Foundations of distance education* (4th ed.). Boston: Pearson.

Taylor, P., Parker, K., Lenhart, A., & Patten, E. (2011). *The digital revolution and higher education.* Washington, DC: Pew Internet & American Life Project.

Vaccaro, N., & Lambie, G. W. (2007). Computer-based counselor-in-training supervision: Ethical and practical implications for counselor educators and supervisors. *Counselor Education and Supervision, 47*(1), 46–57.

Vernon, R., Vakalahi, H., Pierce, D., Pittman-Munke, P., & Adkins, L. F. (2009). Distance education programs in social work: Current and emerging trends. *Journal of Social Work Education, 45*(2), 263–276.

Waterhouse, S. (2005). *The power of eLearning: The essential guide for teaching in the digital age.* Boston: Pearson.

# 14

# Leadership and Management
*Michael J. Holosko and Jeffrey Skinner*

The Educational Policy and Accreditation Standards (EPAS) of the Council on Social Work Education (CSWE, 2008) have reconfigured social work education in many ways. Among the more significant are (a) the transformation of knowledge, values, and skills into competencies; (b) the requirement for articulated and measureable student learning outcomes (Wayne, Bogo, & Raskin, 2010); (c) the requirement for a definable implicit curriculum; and (d) the distinction of field education as social work's educational signature pedagogy (Holosko, Skinner, MacCaughelty, & Stahl, 2010). All of these are important to various stakeholders in schools of social work. Regardless of how one looks at these issues, field directors are at the nexus of all roads related to field education within their respective schools of social work. This chapter makes the primary assumption that field directors require a better understanding of both leadership and management skills to fulfill their responsibilities in more-efficient ways.

The chapter presents an overview of the concept of leadership for field directors to design, implement, and guide a school's bachelor of social work (BSW)/master of social work (MSW) field education program. It begins by defining core attributes of social work leadership, interfaces these core leadership attributes with additional tasks noted in the literature, and then exemplifies how they can be used by field directors. Finally, the chapter describes how both leadership and management skills can be used for building a school's organizational capacity to set the climate for field directors to effect various organizational changes that may emerge in the school. The authors acknowledge that: (1) these are daunting tasks for field directors to undertake, but they are not impossible; (2) transforming, modifying, or reconfiguring any organizational change initiative in a school is a process that takes time; and (3) a lack of administrative support delimits the capacity of the school to move forward in general, and the capacity of the field director to make any successful organizational change.

## Social Work Leadership

Even though leadership was a core concern of the CSWE as indicated in its Strategic Plan 2010 to 2020, and the National Association of Social Workers (NASW) sponsored the Leadership Academy from 1994 to 1997 and conducted an annual leadership meeting on leadership development, Brilliant (1986) referred to leadership as essentially a missing ingredient in social work education and training. After reviewing its sporadic attention in the professional literature, she concluded it was essentially a nontheme in social work training and education. Stoesz (1997), similarly, lamented that social work professionals are often forced to rise to positions of leadership within the profession with little or no mentoring.

Rank and Hutchinson (2000) studied individuals (N=75) who held leadership positions within the CSWE and the NASW. They concluded that education and training in social work fell short of both the demands for leadership in the field and the curricula's ability to adequately teach and educate students about the concept. Their comprehensive analyses made a cogent case for the uniqueness of social work leadership, and they offered a number of constructive suggestions to direct social work in this regard into the twenty-first century.

Social workers often use concepts that the profession deems important, yet fail to define them or their importance. "Leadership" is certainly a topical buzzword used routinely in the profession, along with "evidence-based practice," "diversity," "social and economic justice," "cultural competence," and "global social work practice" (Holosko, 2009). For this chapter, the authors conducted a word search for the word "leadership" in the 2008 EPAS of the ten core competencies (CSWE, 2008). Leadership was mentioned only one time in this important educational document. A word search was also conducted of the mission statements of social work's top fifty ranked schools (U.S. News & World Report, 2012). The word "leadership" was stated twenty-six times across all of these mission statements. "Social work has a rather storied history of not defining core concepts which either direct and inform its practitioners or educate and train their students" (Holosko, 2009, p. 448).

### Core Leadership Attributes

Leadership is a synergistic, transformational, and interactive process anchored in the so-called three P's—person, position, and process (Hartley & Allison, 2002). "Person" refers to the traits or personal characteristics of an individual; "position" involves the use of authority, governance, and guidance to influence individuals; and "process" involves how leaders shape events, motivate and influence people, and achieve outcomes (Taylor, 2007). Holosko (2009) conducted one of the few empirical studies identifying core attributes of leadership in the social work literature. A content-analysis of seventy disciplinary journals published in the social and behavioral sciences was conducted to sift out leadership's main attributes. These are illustrated in figure 14.1.

**Figure 14.1.  Five Core Leadership Attributes**

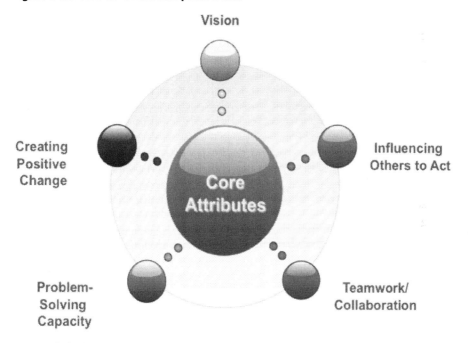

*Source*: Holosko (2009).

These five rank ordered attributes are further defined:

1. Vision

  a. Having one—To have a description of a desired condition at some point in the future

  b. Implementing one—To plan and put in place strategic steps to enact the vision

2. Influencing others to act—To inspire and enable others to take initiative, have a belief in a cause, and perform duties and responsibilities

3. Teamwork/collaboration—To work collectively and in partnership with others toward achieving a goal

4. Problem-solving capacity—To anticipate problems and to act decisively on them when they occur

5. Creating positive change—Moving people in organizations to a better place than where they once were

Having these attributes is certainly important, but being able to use them in settings to influence change is the real litmus test.

### Additional Roles of the Field Director Interfacing with Core Leadership Attributes

Field directors are assuming increasing responsibilities and roles (Buck, Bradley, Robb, & Kirzner, 2012). It is no surprise that 48 percent of field directors turn over their positions in schools of social work in less than five years (Morrow & Fogel, 2002). In an effort to understand the nuances and role complexities of the field director position in today's climate, the authors conducted a literature search (N=32) of recent field director job descriptions in *The Chronicle of Higher Education*, job postings on the Web site of the CSWE, Web sites of schools of social work, and their respective field manuals in both Canada and the United States. In addition to those roles described in chapter 2 and those also described by Pierce (2008), further roles and tasks were discovered in the literature search and in the examination of selected job descriptions of field directors. Those additional roles and tasks included (1) collaborating synergistically with, and leading, external and internal constituents to advance field education; (2) data inputting, management, and analysis; (3) developing partnerships between the university and community beyond school and field placement sites; (4) specialized staff training and development; and (5) maximizing resources. Each of these additional roles will be interfaced with the five core leadership attributes presented in figure 14.1 and highlighted below.

**Collaborating Synergistically → Vision.** The field director embodies the mission of field education and must inspire, direct, and advance that mission and its core values. Teaching and training toward the practice of social work is the common denominator for all stakeholder constituents, and serves as the rallying banner under which the field director articulates and implements a vision. The director uses a panoramic lens to unite colleagues, field instructors, and students into a curriculum of competency-based field education (Wayne et al., 2010). She or he serves as the nexus among these constituents and employs relational and administrative skills to align, and/or realign disparate dynamics into a productive pathway toward the mission.

**Data Inputting, Management, and Analysis → Problem-Solving Capacity.** Field directors must have the capacity to direct, collect, and analyze field data in order to assess required program competencies and the mastery of practice behaviors among student cohorts. Field directors provide information essential to curriculum decision-making processes. They must be able to build data-monitoring systems that can be utilized longitudinally to assess the strengths and weaknesses in field education curriculum, student learning, and field instructor and agency effectiveness. This responsibility is exemplified by the core leadership attribute of using a focused problem-solving capacity.

**Developing Partnerships → Creating Positive Change.** Field education serves as the primary interface among the school, its faculty, field site, field advisory board, and community—all of which have vested interests. Social work programs regard and utilize the field director as an ambassador of social work practice and goodwill in the community, which extends beyond agencies and field advisory boards. Schools aspire to give back to the community, and help make positive changes and contributions to the welfare of the practice and nonpractice community. The director often serves as the conduit between the community and the school's resources. In their close proximity to the community, field directors often broker outreach services and resources from the school and advocate for community partners.

**Specialized Staff Training and Development → Influencing Others to Act.** Providing specialized training to faculty field liaisons and integrative seminar instructors is an essential task for field directors (Dalton, Stevens, & Maas-Brady, 2011). Field directors must develop specialized training and materials for liaisons to effect and advance their role performance. As schools begin to offer more in-depth specializations in practice (e.g., military social work, forensic social work, spiritual social work, international social work), field directors need to train liaisons to facilitate learning in such specialized field placements. Directors should work in concert with the school's vision, mission, curriculum, and faculty to provide leadership in those practice approaches, and train field instructors who will support, guide, and supervise the program curriculum. This facilitation role reflects the core leadership attribute of influencing others to act.

**Maximizing Resources → Collaboration and Teamwork.** It appears that the importance of field education relative to the classroom is facing resource constraints in the profession (Reisch & Jarman-Rhode, 2000). Current economic conditions require that a field director adapt, make the most of limited resources, be proactive and creative, and advocate for more field program financial support. In field agencies, this could mean asking instructors to take on additional students. The authors wish to avoid an alarmist, misunderstood, reactive position to this reality that affects many schools. It is necessary for field directors to employ the final core social work leadership attributes of collaboration and teamwork in order for programs to get the most out of limited resources.

### Braiding Leadership Attributes and Management Skills: Building the Field Program's Culture within the School

Insights into how field directors can use both leadership and management skills to shape the culture of the school to recognize issues and concerns in field programs with a strengths-based perspective are described. Both leadership and management skills are needed by the director to move this agenda forward, but first it is important to offer definitional delineation.

The subject of much debate, the terms "leadership" and "management" are often used erroneously as interchangeable concepts. These are consensual definitions of each: (1) leadership is a process whereby an individual influences a group of persons to achieve a common goal, and (2) management is the exercise of executive, administrative, and supervisory direction of a group or organization (Ricketts, 2009). Management requires setting goals, objectives, and targets and focusing on consistently producing results through planning, budgeting, organizing, staffing, controlling, and problem solving (Kotter, 1990). Similar to the previously noted rhetoric about the importance of the term leadership in social work (Holosko, 2009), the term "management" is used infrequently in our education materials, unless it is a suffix to the term "case." A word search of the 2008 EPAS and ten core competencies revealed it was not mentioned once (CSWE, 2008). A similar examination of the frequency of its use in macro practice standards noted it only twice (Gamble, 2010).

It appears that the profession has had better success in taking the concept forward when it responded to the management needs expressed by their clients and practicing professionals. For example, the National Network for Social Work Managers (NNSWM), developed a curriculum focused on core competencies needed to run well-functioning, high-quality agencies/organizations. The NNSWM established the Academy of Certified Social Work Managers that grants the credential of Certified Social Work Managers (CSWM) to those social workers who minimally meet the following criteria: education, training, experience, demonstrated competency in thirteen core areas, and approval by the members of the Academy (Wimpfheimer, 2004).

These competencies include (1) act professionally; (2) manage stakeholders effectively; (3) facilitate innovative processes; (4) demonstrate effective interpersonal and communication skills; (5) involve stakeholders in decision making; (6) reaffirm the vision, mission, values, and philosophy of the school and university; (7) plan, promote, and model life-long learning practices; (8) manage human resources; (9) manage finances; (10) establish and maintain control for organizational resources; (11) use available technologies; (12) design and develop programs; and (13) design and implement strategic planning (Hassan & Wimpfheimer, 2012).

Inevitably, field directors will confront many issues of organizational change during their job tenure. Some of these will require timely episodic responses, and others will require strategic responses that are more long term. All will require that field directors use both leadership and management skills to plan for proactive change and assist the school's culture in understanding that the field program serves as an important vehicle for such change processes. Figure 14.2 offers a list of various initiatives that field directors could address in their positions. Some of these have built-in administrative tension, faculty and student tension, resource issues, and accreditation implications, while others are more day-to-day responsibilities to move the agenda forward in each school's evolving culture. Offered in Figure 14.2 are examples of issues that require various leadership and management skills of the field director to help shape the culture of the school.

**Figure 14.2.  Selected Examples of Organizational Issues Requiring Field Directors to Effect Change in Their Schools**

1. Channeling resources to field education.
2. Changing the field model.
3. Focusing field integrative seminars on competencies and practice behaviors.
4. Empowering the field advisory committee to take more leadership in the school.
5. Introducing new technologies for field education including field instructor training.
6. Developing international placements.
7. Influencing faculty liaisons and field instructors to collaborate with students.
8. Enabling students to influence implicit and explicit curriculum related to the realities of practice.
9. Leading the school in the development of field education as the signature pedagogy.

Field directors will be required to use different combinations of leadership and management skills in order to deal with organizational issues successfully. One leadership or management skill cannot be used all of the time to effect change. For effective change to occur, field directors need to be mindful of the following: (1) field directors should seek administrative support prior to implementing any change process; (2) the process of effecting change in the school culture is often as important as the outcome of such change; (3) stakeholder voice is essential for any change initiative [those voices must include students and field instructors]; and (4) field directors needs to develop a plan and planning process strategically prior to initiating change with any of the organizational examples in figure 14.2. The leadership attributes and management skills presented in figure 14.3 may be used as strategies to effect change.

As indicated in figure 14.3, field directors need to think across a matrix of leadership skills, management skills, and strategies for any given change issue (such as those cited in figure 14.2). They may use more than one leadership attribute, and/or more than one management attribute, to implement any of the issues. For example, if one organizational issue from figure 14.2 is selected (focusing field integrative seminars on competencies and practice behaviors) and dovetail it with the figure 14.3 matrix (i.e., reading across from leadership attributes to management skills), it may illustrate the use of this matrix more clearly. It would appear that vision implementation, influencing others to act, and teamwork/collaboration would be the main leadership attributes used to effect this overall change in the school. The corresponding primary management skills potentially used in this

**Figure 14.3. Leadership Attributes and Management Skills for Field Directors to Effect Change in the School**

| Leadership Attributes | Management Skills[1] |
|---|---|
| 1. Vision: Having one | 1. Act professionally. |
| 2. Vision: Implementing it | 2. Manage stakeholders. |
| 3. Influencing others to act | 3. Facilitate processes. |
| 4. Teamwork/collaboration | 4. Utilize effective communication skills. |
| 5. Problem solving | 5. Involve stakeholders. |
| 6. Creating positive change | 6. Reaffirm vision, mission, and philosophy of school. |
| | 7. Model life-long learning. |
| | 8. Manage human resources. |
| | 9. Manage finances. |
| | 10. Control resources. |
| | 11. Develop programs. |
| | 12. Orchestrate strategic planning. |

*Note:* 1. Source for this column is Hassan & Wimpfheimer (2012).

process would be managing stakeholders, facilitating processes, communicating, involving stakeholders, and reaffirming vision, mission, and school philosophy. As different challenges and organizational issues arise in the school, field directors would use different sets of leadership attributes and management skills to deal effectively with the issue.

Recommended strategies that underpin both the leadership and management skills appear in figure 14.3. These may serve as the stories behind these strategies. These are certainly not all of the strategies needed to result in successful management and leadership in the school, but they are deemed to be essential and are well noted in the literature (Flannes & Levin, 2005; Kalargyrou, Pescosolido, & Kalargiros, 2012; Smith, 2011).

**Manage Time Effectively and Delegate Responsibility.** Field directors need to stay well connected with students, faculty, administrators, field instructors, community partners, and other constituents in field education. They also need to make effective use of time by working on short-term and long-term goals and moving quickly between tasks. Teach or empower others to perform to the best of their ability, and be accountable to stakeholders and learn to delegate responsibilities whenever possible.

**Acknowledge and Use Strengths-Based Perspectives.** Positive reinforcement promotes growth and development for all and creates an energy field greater than the sum of its parts. Think of a positively charged environment as equivalent to having ten very competent people who want to get things done well. Try to reframe issues into win-win scenarios for various stakeholders, and acknowledge and thank people for their contributions.

**Use Relationship Skills Effectively.** Field directors are social workers who value the worth and dignity of human relationships and are trained in the art of communication. Working with teams and influencing individuals to work effectively toward common goals will put those relationship skills to the test. Continuous verbal and written communication that is clear and concise will facilitate collaboration and cooperation toward the goal of quality field education.

**Role Model Leadership.** Being a field director is to embody the social work profession with all of its standards, ethics, and even the expectations set forth to students in field education. The position resides in a veritable fish bowl where one is expected to "walk the talk." Use organizational power afforded to the privilege of the position to create vibrant supporting and equally demanding environments in field education. Be mindful of the power in the field director position and use that power in a thoughtful and deliberate manner. Field directors try to exhibit the values and actions they want to see in others.

**Be Creative.** Creativity is important because the field director confronts a constantly changing environment. Be positive and try to have fun with the work to promote an environment that promotes energy and hopefulness. Brainstorm ideas with multiple constituencies, reframe a problem from different perspectives, draw mind maps, or try other forms of artistic expression to shake up the thought process and find new solutions. Model the constructive input desired from staff, faculty, field liaisons, students, and field instructors.

**Seek Training and Mentorship.** Realize that the field position is often tied up in having a favorable reputation and the confidence of others. Be prepared to exercise judgment and make decisions under difficult circumstances, which can have career- and program-altering consequences on students. Critically and continually evaluate decisions, plans, and actions for quality improvement. By seeking out a mentor, enrolling in leadership and management training, and joining a local field consortium, a field director can boost his or her capacity to function in their role.

**Distinguish the Plan from the Planning Process.** There are no shortcuts to achieving the various complex and sometimes competing goals in field education. Delivering the curriculum of field education is guided by policies, resources, procedures, expectations, and assignments. Keep in mind that students grow and develop in a process mode of experiential and self-reflective learning. It is not always linear learning in field because the process is often the content. Focus simultaneously on both the process steps to achieve goals and the outcome of these goals. There is a need to clearly distinguish any plan for change from the planning process itself.

**Be Prepared for Barriers to Emerge in Any Change Process.** Be prepared to experience major, minor, known, and unforeseen barriers and obstacles so as to not be caught off balance. For example, some students may complain about their assignment to a certain field agency. Be creative in solving problems and avoid polarizing others and groups. Stay focused on the goals of field education; identify and negotiate barriers as they inevitably arise in any change process.

**Strive to Be Flexible/Adaptive.** The unexpected usually happens and it is the response to such events, not the event itself, that determines the outcome. Remember to not react to situations, but rather take the time to develop an appropriate professional response, especially when difficulties arise. For example, a field instructor may leave an agency in the middle of the semester, leaving one searching for adequate supervision or a new placement for the student. Persevere in the face of challenges, setbacks, and criticism. Utilize trusted others in approaching and solving problems and be willing to compromise and work in a collegial manner.

## Conclusion

This chapter provides information and insights about topics that have received minimal attention in the social work literature, namely leadership and management. The authors posit that the likelihood of elevating field education, in general, and the field director position, specifically, will require more attention in these two areas. Given that EPAS (CSWE, 2008) has positioned field education to hold a more prominent role in future social work curricula, a matrix was presented showing how leadership attributes, management skills, and strategies could be used together to promote the school's organizational culture from the field program outward to the school. The chapter illustrates how important and timely issues arising in the field require the braiding of these leadership and management skills.

## Essential Readings

Hassan, A., & Wimpfheimer, S. (2012). Human services management competencies. The Network of Social Work Management. Retrieved from https://socialworkmanager.org/wordpress/wp-content/uploads/14–NSWM-Human-Services-Management-Competencies-2012.pdf.

Holosko, M. (2009). Social work leadership: Identifying core attributes. *Journal of Human Behavior in the Social Environment, 19*(4), 448–459.

## References

Brilliant, E. (1986). Social work leadership: A missing ingredient? *Social Work, 31*(5), 325–331.

Buck, P. W., Bradley, J., Robb, L., & Kirzner, R. S. (2012). Complex and competing demands in field education: A qualitative study of field directors' experiences. *Field Scholar, 2*(2). Retrieved from http://fieldeducator.simmons.edu/article/complex-and-competing-demands-in-field-education/#more-1094.

Council on Social Work Education (CSWE). (2008). *Educational policy and accreditation standards* (rev. March 27, 2010/updated August 2012). Alexandria, VA: Author. Retrieved from http://www.cswe.org/Accreditation/41865.aspx.

Dalton, B., Stevens, L., & Maas-Brady, J. (2011). "How do you do it?": MSW field director survey. *Advances in Social Work, 12*(2), 276–288.

Flannes, S. W., & Levin, G. (2005). *Essential people skills for project managers.* Vienna, VA: Management Concepts.

Gamble, D. N. (2010). EPAS matrix for core macro practice competencies [template]. Retrieved from http://www.acosa.org/CO_ACOSA_EPAS_Core_Comps.pdf.

Hartley, J., & Allison, M. (2002). The role of leadership on the modernization and improvement in public services. In J. Reynolds, I. Henderson, J. Sedan, J. Charlesworth, & A. Bullman (Eds.), *The managing care reader* (pp. 296–305). Buckingham, UK: Open University Press.

Hassan, A., & Wimpfheimer, S. (2012). Human services management competencies. The Network of Social Work Management. Retrieved from https://socialworkmanager.org/wordpress/wp-content/uploads/ 14–NSWM-Human-Services-Management-Competencies-2012.pdf.

Holosko, M. (2009). Social work leadership: Identifying core attributes. *Journal of Human Behavior in the Social Environment, 19*(4), 448–459.

Holosko, M., Skinner, J., MacCaughelty, C., & Stahl, K. M. (2010). Building the implicit BSW curriculum at a large southern state university. *Journal of Social Work Education, 46*(3), 411–423.

Kalargyrou, V., Pescosolido, A. T., & Kalargiros, E. A. (2012). Leadership skills in management education. *Academy of Educational Leadership Journal, 16*(4), 39–63.

Kotter, J. P. (1990). *A force for change: How leadership differs from management.* New York: Free Press.

Morrow, D. F., & Fogel, S. J. (2002). Staffing patterns for field director positions in social work education. *Arete, 25*(2), 78–86.

Pierce, D. (2008). *Field education in the 2008 EPAS: Implications for the field director's role.* Retrieved from http://www.cswe.org/File.aspx?id=31580.

Rank, M., & Hutchinson, W. S. (2000). An analysis of leadership with the social work profession. *Journal of Social Work Education, 36*(3), 487–502.

Reisch, M., & Jarman-Rhode, L. (2000). The future of social work education in the United States: Implications for field education. *Journal of Social Work Education, 36*(2), 201–214.

Ricketts, K. G. (2009). Leadership vs. management. University of Kentucky College of Agriculture Cooperative Extension Service, Community and Leadership Development. Retrieved from http://www.ca.uky.edu/agc/pubs/ elk1/elk1103/elk1103.pdf.

Smith, J. (2011, February 9). How to be a good manager: 8 quick tips. Workawesome. Retrieved from http://workawesome.com/management/how-to-be-a-good-manager-8-quick-tips/.

Stoesz, D. (1997). The end of social work. In M. Reisch & E. Gambrill (Eds.), *Social Work in the 21st Century* (pp. 368–375). Thousand Oaks, CA: Sage.

Taylor, V. (2007). Leadership for service improvement. *Nursing Management–UK, 13*(9), 30–34.

Wayne, J., Bogo, M., & Raskin, M. (2010). Field education as the signature pedagogy of social work education. *Journal of Social Work Education, 46*(3), 327–339.

Wimpfheimer, S. (2004). Leadership and management competencies defined by practicing social work managers: An overview of standards developed by the National Network for Social Work Managers. *Administration in Social Work, 28*(1), 45–56.

U.S. News & World Report. (2012). Education grad schools: Social work. Retrieved from http://grad-schools.usnews.rankingsandreviews.com/best-graduate-schools/top-health-schools/social-work-rankings.

# About the Authors

**Marion Bogo**, MSW, Adv. Dip. SW, is professor, former dean, and formerly field practicum coordinator at the Factor-Inwentash Faculty of Social Work, University of Toronto. Her research focuses on field education and the development and testing of innovative approaches to assessment of student competence. She has published more than one hundred journal articles and book chapters on field education and social work practice. Her recent book *Achieving Competence in Social Work through Field Education* (2010) further develops field education principles presented in the seminal text *The Practice of Field Instruction in Social Work* (1998, 2nd ed., coauthor). The paper on field education as the signature pedagogy, written with coauthors Julianne Wayne and Miriam Raskin, received the *Journal of Social Work Education* best conceptual article award in 2010. The paper on field instructors' view of student competencies in macro practice, written with coauthors Cheryl Regehr, Kirsten Donovan, Susan Anstice, and April Lim, received the *Journal of Social Work Education* best empirical article (qualitative) award in 2013. In 2013 the Council on Social Work Education awarded Bogo the Significant Lifetime Achievement in Social Work Education award in recognition of her contributions to social work education and to improving assessment of professional competence in social work. She has lectured and consulted to schools of social work in Canada, the United States, Asia, Israel, and the United Kingdom.

**Janet Bradley**, MSS, MLSP, is the director of field education for the undergraduate Social Work Department of West Chester University. She is a member of the Baccalaureate Program Directors Field Committee and a former member of the Council on Field Education of the Council on Social Work Education. Her scholarship focuses on field education; she recently coauthored an article with Page Walker Buck, Lydia Robb, and Rachel Shapiro Kirzner on the complex and competing demands in field education.

**Page Walker Buck** is assistant professor and chair of the Graduate Social Work Department of West Chester University. She is former chair of the field practicum curriculum. With a background in community work, she teaches courses on foundation-level practice, groups, organizations, communities and diversity, and also serves as a field liaison. Her scholarship focuses on both field education and the silent epidemic of mild traumatic brain injury.

**Sheila R. Dennis** is currently serving as the interim director of field education at Indiana University School of Social Work, overseeing BSW and MSW field education for six campuses and an online MSW program. Possessing a BSW and an MSW, and pursuing a PhD in social work, Dennis' educational focus has been anchored in the social work profession. Since 2004 she has taught social work courses and facilitated field education at Indiana University, Anderson University, and Royal Holloway University of London, where she also received a postgraduate certificate in teaching and learning. Dennis has presented on field assessment approaches at the annual Baccalaureate Program Directors conference and the Council on Social Work Education Annual Program Meeting 2010 to 2012. She is a member of the Baccalaureate Program Directors Field Committee. Her current research interests and publications include issues of diversity and the epistemology of social work assessment.

**Martha L. Ellison**, MSW, PhD, has been a field director for twenty-two of her twenty-four years as a social work educator. She was a field director at three institutions: Winthrop University, Missouri Western State University, and Union College (current institution). She has published eleven articles in peer-reviewed journals, such as *The Clinical Supervisor*, the *Journal of Social Work Education*, and the *Journal of Baccalaureate Social Work*, with most of those publications concentrating on field education. Her dissertation focused on identifying the effective and ineffective behavior of field instructors in their work with field students from the students' perspective. She is a member of the Baccalaureate Program Directors Field Committee.

**Michael J. Holosko**, PhD, University of Pittsburgh; and MSW, University of Toronto, holds the endowed chair as Pauline M. Berger Professor of Family and Child Welfare at The University of Georgia School of Social Work. He has taught across the undergraduate and graduate curriculum in schools of social work (primarily), nursing, public administration, and applied social science in Australia, Canada, Hong Kong, Sweden, the United States, and the U.S. Virgin Islands. For the past thirty-five years, he has been a consultant to a variety of large and small health and human service organizations in the areas of program evaluation, outcomes, accreditation, organizational development, communication, leadership, visioning, organizational alignment, and stress management. He has published numerous monographs, chapters, articles, and texts in the areas of evaluation, health care, social work practice, gerontology, family and child welfare, social policy, administration, research, music intervention, and spirituality. His recent texts published in

2013 were *Distinguishing Clinical from Upper Level Management* (2013) (Taylor & Francis, Routledge), and *Social Work Practice with Individuals and Families* (2013) (J. Wiley & Sons). He serves on the editorial boards of Research on Social Work Practice, Social Work in Public Health, the *Journal of Human Behavior and Social Environment*, the *Hong Kong Journal of Social Work*, the *Journal of Social Service Research*, and the *Journal of Evidence-Based Social Work Practice*.

**Cindy A. Hunter**, MSW, LSW, is associate professor and the director of field placement in the Department of Social Work at James Madison University in Harrisonburg, Virginia. She teaches an integrative field seminar and serves as a field liaison. She is cochair of the Baccalaureate Program Directors Field Committee and has trained new field directors since 2009. She is a member of the Mid-Atlantic Field Consortium and leads a Virginia satellite branch of that consortium. She has recently been appointed to the Council on Field Education of the Council on Social Work Education. Publications and presentations focus on field education, field seminars, and generalist practice. Her MSW is from Howard University.

**Lynn Kaersvang**, MSW, is professor of social work at Metropolitan State University of Denver, where she directed the field education program for eighteen years. Professor Kaersvang has served as a member of the Council on Field Education of the Council on Social Work Education and the Baccalaureate Program Directors Field Committee. She has written or coauthored training manuals on case management in child abuse, joint child abuse investigations by law enforcement and child protection, and interagency work with youth. She has trained professionals in Colorado and nationally on supervision and management issues in social services and child abuse investigations. Her current teaching and research focus includes field education, ethics, practice, women's issues, and supervision.

**Carolyn Knight**, PhD, MSW, is professor of social work in the School of Social Work, University of Maryland–Baltimore County. She teaches the social work methods courses in the undergraduate program and has served as a faculty field liaison for many years. She is a licensed social worker with thirty years of experience—most of it pro bono—working individually and in groups with adult survivors of childhood trauma, particularly sexual abuse. She is the author of two books and numerous articles and book chapters on working with survivors of childhood trauma in group and individual treatment. She also has written extensively on topics ranging from classroom and field education in social work, group work education and practice, and the use of self-disclosure in clinical practice.

**Denice Goodrich Liley** has an MSW, MS in gerontology, and a PhD in social work. She is associate professor of social work at Boise State University School of Social Work in Boise, Idaho. She teaches courses primarily in social work practice, aging, and end of life. She is licensed in clinical social work practice and holds National Association of Social Workers' (NASW) licenses of Academy of Certified Social Workers (ACSW), diplomate, and clinical practice in gerontology. She serves nationally on the Council on Field Education of the Council on Social Work Education and is associate editor for field education for the journal *Reflections: Narratives of Professional Helping*. She has published numerous articles in the areas of student development in field practicum and aging and is a regular contributor to *The New Social Worker Magazine*.

**Sharon C. Lyter** is associate professor at Kutztown University, teaching BSW- and MSW-level courses. She earned the master of social work degree at Temple University and the PhD at Rutgers University (social work with minor in abnormal psychology). She served as director of field education, southern region, for Rutgers University, and served two terms with the Council on Field Education of the Council on Social Work Education. She is the author or coauthor of scholarship in behavioral health (three book chapters, five journal articles, and developed three international workshops). On field education, she has authored or coauthored seven journal articles, including one on home visit safety, and has conducted numerous national and regional workshops aimed at reducing risks to social workers. Her most recent publication is a Field Note in the *Journal of Social Work Education* (2012), titled "Potential of Field Education as Signature Pedagogy: The Field Director Role."

**Julia K. Moen**, MSW, LICSW, is associate professor of undergraduate social work education at Bethel University in Saint Paul, Minnesota. For twenty-three years she served as the field director and taught social work practice, field seminar, and policy. She also maintains a clinical practice in the University Counseling Center. She has been in leadership roles for the Minnesota Chapter of the National Association of Social Workers and the Minnesota Conference on Social Work Education. She cochairs the national Baccalaureate Program Directors Field Committee and has trained new field directors at the annual conference since 2005. Her conference papers and presentations focus on field education, international partnerships, and antiracism. She has two publications. Her MSW degree is from the University of Minnesota–Twin Cities.

**Dean Pierce** is director emeritus of the Office of Social Work Accreditation for the Council on Social Work Education (CSWE). He holds an MSW from West Virginia University and a PhD from the University of California–Berkeley. Early in his career he served as field education director for four programs. He served as the CSWE staff person for its field education committee. He has published two text-books. He has also published several articles on lesbian and gay issues. He was the 2009 recipient of the Field Is the Heart of Social Work Education award from North American Network of Field Educators and Directors.

**Nancy Trantham Poe** is associate professor of social work and family studies at James Madison University in Harrisonburg, Virginia. Nancy holds a BA in sociology from Roanoke College, an MSW with a concentration in child and family welfare from Virginia Commonwealth University, and a PhD in human development specializing in family studies with a graduate certificate in gerontology from Virginia Tech. She has served as field liaison in social work programs at James Madison University, University of Maryland–Baltimore County, Radford University (Virginia), and Mansfield University of Pennsylvania, where she also served as director of field for the BSW program. She has written on social work pedagogy including the field seminar and field students' experience of client death.

**Sandra Posada**, LCSW, ACSW, is the field coordinator for the U.S. Army–Fayetteville State University Master of Social Work Program, Fort Sam Houston, Texas. Her MSW is from the University of Houston with a bachelor's degree from St. Mary's University of San Antonio. Her social work academic affiliations have been with University of Houston, Our Lady of the Lake University, Texas State University, and University of Texas at San Antonio, with just under twenty years of experience with field education. She has had numerous leadership positions at the state and national levels. She served in the Individual Ready Reserve as an Army Medical Social Work Officer for seven years with a call to active duty in support of Desert Storm. She served as the Chair of the Council on Field Education of the Council on Social Work Education from 2008 to 2012.

**Miriam Raskin**, EdD, MSW, ACSW, is professor emerita and served on the faculty of George Mason University, Department of Social Work for more than thirty-five years. She served as the field director for seventeen years and as department chair for fourteen years. She is a founding member of the Baccalaureate Program Directors Field Committee and the Mid-Atlantic field consortium. She has chaired accreditation site teams for the Council on Social Work Education (CSWE) and published numerous articles on field education in top-tier refereed journals. She has edited a book on field education, *Empirical Studies in Field Instruction*, and presented at major state, national, and international conferences. She also serves as a manuscript reviewer for three social work journals. She was selected as the CSWE's first senior scholar, where she researched the entire archives of the CSWE in order to trace the development and rationale for field standards from the beginning of the CSWE (1950) until the EPAS of 2001. The editorial board of the *Journal on Social Work Education* recognized her and her coauthors as having written the best conceptual article in 2010. In 2012 she received the Habit of Excellence Award from the College of Health and Human Services, George Mason University.

**Ginny Terry Raymond** has a BS in Sociology, MSW from Tulane University, and PhD in Social Work from the University of Denver. She has post-MSW practice experience in mental health and school social work. She recently retired as faculty emerita after thirty-seven years with the University of Alabama School of Social Work, where she taught BSW, MSW, and PhD classes while also serving as a field liaison, field instructor (eight years), as chair of the BSW program (seven years), and as associate dean (ten years). She was elected to the board of directors of the Baccalaureate Program Directors and elected twice to the board of directors of the Council on Social Work Education (CSWE). She served as a CSWE accreditation site visitor and team chair and as a consultant to BSW programs. She has published numerous articles, primarily in social work education journals, and two book chapters.

**Lisa Richardson**, MSS, LICSW, is director of MSW field education and assistant professor in the School of Social Work at St. Catherine University and the University of St. Thomas. She teaches the integrative field seminar and clinical supervision courses in the master of social work program, coordinates the field placement program and provides training for field instructors. Prior to coming to the university setting, Lisa spent fifteen years in clinical social work practice, working as a therapist, case manager, mental health consultant, team leader, program director, and clinical director. She has provided professional training in local, regional, and international settings, and is a consulting editor and contributing author for *The Field Educator* journal. She is cochair of the North American Network of Field

Educators and Directors, and assistant chair of the Council on Field Education of the Council on Social Work Education.

**Jeffrey Skinner,** MDiv (Vanderbilt University), MSSW (University of Tennessee), LCSW, is a senior academic professional at the School of Social Work at The University of Georgia. At that university he coordinates the BSW field education program, teaches practice courses in the BSW program, and teaches clinical courses in the MSW program. He has coauthored book chapters and articles in the areas of human behavior, practice and theory relationships, person-centered therapy, and field education. He also has presented at Baccalaureate Program Directors and Council on Social Work Education's annual meetings on field education and BSW pedagogy. Prior to entering academia, he practiced as a clinical social worker and program manager for more than thirty years. He has practiced in public and private agencies and in private practice. His area of practice interest is adolescent individual and family therapy and post-adoption adjustment. He has managed EAP programs and directed managed care programs at a private family service agency. He was a post-master of social work fellow at the Menninger Foundation.

**Lynda R. Sowbel,** PhD, LCSW-C, associate professor of social work and director of field education at Hood College in Frederick, Maryland, is an experienced clinician, field instructor, educator, and researcher. She served on task forces for the Maryland Licensing Board on Maryland Ethics Regulations and Licensing Reciprocity. Her work on ambivalence in field education and on inflation of field performance ratings has been published in the *Journal of Social Work Education*; her gerontology articles have been published in the *Journal of Gerontological Social Work* and the *Journal of Baccalaureate Social Work*. She gave the keynote address at the University of Wisconsin's Social Work Field Conference. She has been appointed to the Council on Field Education of the Council on Social Work Education.

**Julianne Wayne,** EdD, MSW, is currently associate professor and director of field education at the University of Connecticut School of Social Work. Prior to joining the University of Connecticut faculty, she spent twenty-three years at the Boston University School of Social work as a member of the group work sequence, director of field education, and later as associate dean. In all, she has provided educational and administrative leadership in field education for nearly thirty years. She is widely published in the areas of social work education, field education, and social group work practice. She was able to integrate these academic arenas in the coauthored book (with Carol Cohen), *Group Work Education in the Field*.

**Raymie H. Wayne,** PhD, JD, MSW, is associate dean of the School of Graduate and Professional Studies, and associate professor of social work at the University of Saint Joseph in West Hartford, Connecticut. Prior to becoming associate dean, she served as department chair and baccalaureate program director for the Department of Social Work and Latino Community Practice. Much of her scholarship centers on the intersection of social work and law. Topics of study include legal issues in field education, child welfare, and therapeutic jurisprudence. She earned her PhD from the University at Albany, her JD from the University of Connecticut, and her MSW from Fordham University.

**Riva Zeff,** MSW, is the field director since 2006 in the undergraduate social work program at Seattle University. She was both a field liaison for three years and a field instructor since the 1980s. She has coauthored and presented on field instructor orientation, academic writing, and assessing core competencies and learning. She is a member of both the Baccalaureate Program Directors Field Committee and the Council on Field Education of the Council on Social Work Education, where she trains new field directors at the annual meetings. Zeff coordinates the Northwest Field Directors' Consortium.

# Index